ALREADY
FREE

ALREADY FREE

BUDDHISM MEETS PSYCHOTHERAPY
ON THE PATH OF LIBERATION

BRUCE TIFT, MA, LMFT

SOUNDS TRUE
BOULDER, COLORADO

Sounds True
Boulder, CO 80306

Cover design by Rachael Murray
Book design by Beth Skelley

Printed in the United States of America

Library of Congress Cataloging-in-Publication Data
Tift, Bruce.
Already free : Buddhism meets psychotherapy on the path of liberation / by Bruce Tift.
    pages cm
ISBN 978-1-62203-411-6
1. Psychotherapy—Religious aspects—Buddhism. I. Title.
BQ4570.P76T54 2015
294.3'3615—dc23
                                            2014042619

Ebook ISBN 978-1-62203-456-7

10 9 8 7 6 5 4 3 2 1

To my parents, Kay and Floyd
My sister, Barbara, and brother, David

To my wife, Reva
My daughters, Rachael, Ciel, and Elena

To my teacher Chögyam Trungpa, Rinpoche,
my teacher Shyalpa Tenzin, Rinpoche,
and his teacher HH Chatral, Rinpoche

With deep appreciation

CONTENTS

FOREWORD BY TAMI SIMON

ONE OF THE AREAS of inquiry that is endlessly fascinating to me, like a jewel that I could hold in my hand, turn over, and continually marvel at, is: How do the discoveries of meditation and the discoveries of psychotherapy fit together? How do we build a healthy self and discover the lack of any enduring self at the same time?

When I had the chance to sit down and talk with Bruce Tift, Boulder's most well-known Buddhist psychotherapist, I of course wanted to bring out this jewel of a question and explore. Perhaps Bruce could help me make sense of how the Buddhist path and the path of psychotherapy fit together? I knew I was benefitting greatly from the regular work I was doing with a psychotherapist (reports from other people, especially my intimate partner, were that I was becoming much more available in relationship, for example). I also knew I was benefitting tremendously from the practice of meditation, discovering how to rest and be more and more at home in the wide, open space of awareness. But these two approaches felt like separate tracks. Perhaps Bruce could help me understand and articulate a unified vision?

When I asked Bruce about this and how he worked with his psychotherapy clients and students, he said, "I alternate between a Buddhist approach and a psychotherapeutic approach *without any hope of resolution.*"

"Excuse me?" I thought. "No hope of resolution." I had been searching for some grand unified theory, and here this "expert" was explaining that he alternated between the two approaches based on what was needed in the moment, knowing that each path had different blind spots and offered different gifts.

As I considered his response to me, I suddenly felt like I was on a beach drinking a piña colada. I mentioned this to Bruce. He smiled at me, as if he were saying, "What is so bad about that?" Could I entertain a dialogue, a meeting, if you will, between the teachings of Buddhism and the practice of psychotherapy that wasn't about definitive conclusions but instead about opening my mind wide like sitting on the beach and looking out at the ocean? Could the inquiry be that spacious, enjoyable, and un-problematic?

Bruce Tift is an unusual teacher. He writes and teaches from his own experience and the perspective that our lives are not problems to be solved. He approaches the meeting between Buddhism and psychotherapy with a deep pragmatism, employing the best that each approach has to offer in a welcome embrace of contradictory energies.

His specialty, if you will, is the unwanted, the neglected, the disowned—those parts of ourselves that we would rather disavow than confront. In *Already Free,* Bruce invites us, again and again, to turn toward our disturbance, not away. Now why would this be of interest? Why might we want to turn toward our fear and anxiety and feelings of desperation? Bruce makes the very good point that if we want to be *free,* then we can't have walled-off pockets of experience that we spend our life avoiding. If we want to experience what Bruce calls being "undivided," then we need to have the capacity to be with intense (even if unwanted) experience, without cutting off and separating from the intensity.

According to Bruce Tift, "Sanity is a counter-instinctual process." And at first, it certainly feels counter-instinctual to turn toward what is painful and terrifying. Shouldn't I be running as fast as I can in the opposite direction? But the counter-instinctual move turns out to be tremendously empowering. If we can face our worst fears, then maybe they won't continue to secretly run our life. And where does real confidence come from if not from knowing that we can handle whatever experience comes our way?

So how do we engage with the difficult and unwanted? Bruce teaches his clients and students how to practice what he calls "embodied immediacy"—in whatever moment we find ourselves, in the immediacy of this moment, we experience our physical sensations without analysis or interpretation. We are with the flutter in our stomach, the heat in our hands, the pounding in our heart. And we stay with it and stay with it.

In my own life, I have found this practice of embodied immediacy to be of central importance. Often when I find myself in some type of neurotic spin, worried about this or that fictitious possibility, what is clearly needed is a return to embodied immediacy. There is something happening in my body that I am avoiding feeling through mental spin. In fact, Bruce writes, "disembodiment is a requirement of neurosis."

Bruce Tift is wise, provocative, and above all, practical. *Already Free* is not so much a theoretical book as it is an actual handbook to realize the open ground of our being. Bruce's approach to freedom is not transcendent but instead all-inclusive. The freedom Bruce describes is not a freedom from any experience but a freedom that welcomes every experience as intelligent and meaningful.

Take for example the experience of anxiety. Bruce offers the counter-instinctual advice that we can "commit to the feeling of anxiety as an approximation of an open state of mind." Instead of viewing anxiety as something that we need to get rid of, we are invited to "commit to it," to stay with the experience and discover its intelligence. There are so many books and teachers that try to "cure us" or try to "pump us up," encouraging us to achieve some future positive state. Bruce's approach is different. What if we are already free? What if even our intense anxiety is not actually a problem, but instead, as Bruce writes, "an intelligent response to the perception of groundlessness from the ego's point of view"?

Being able to commit to our disturbance when we are alone, perhaps on the meditation cushion or lying in bed, is one thing, but committing to disturbance in relationship, in my experience, is of a whole different order of magnitude. Bruce writes in *Already Free* that he thinks it is accurate to say that in his forty-year relationship (a relationship that appears to be loving and committed), he has "found himself disturbed every day." I found that statement so shocking, refreshing, and normalizing! Most spiritual teachers who write about the open ground of being never discuss disturbance in relationship, and yet in my experience, it is where so much of our personal growth lies. Fortunately, Bruce devotes two chapters to exploring our patterns in intimate relationships and how we can benefit from the teachings of both Buddhism and psychotherapy to explore what triggers us and why, how to replace blame with personal responsibility, and how to find a freedom in intimacy that honors our need for separateness as well as our need for closeness.

Bruce Tift is confrontative. He confronts us with our patterns of escape and he confronts us with our freedom. Read *Already Free* as a process of inquiry, as a way to grow in consciousness, and ultimately, as a way to discover a freedom that leaves nothing out.

INTRODUCTION

RECENTLY A YOUNG MAN in his mid-thirties—we'll call him Darren—walked into my office. He was looking for help with a recurring pattern he had noticed in his life. In brief, he had a very hard time following through on almost anything he started. He would leave relationships after they became too serious; he would find a reason to change his job or even his entire career just as he was approaching success; and while he had experimented with a variety of therapies and spiritual paths, he hadn't stuck with any of them long enough for them to prove helpful.

As he approached midlife, Darren was becoming increasingly anxious that he would never settle down in a relationship, livelihood, or spiritual path. He had done enough personal work to know that he was the common denominator in all these scenarios, but he felt hopeless about changing the pattern.

Darren is by no means alone. This kind of recurring pattern is what brings clients, both individuals and couples, into my office every day. Some find me when they're going through unfortunate life circumstances, but the majority of the people I see are suffering from more chronic issues—patterns of behavior and experience that have been with them for years. Usually, there is an intuition that this suffering is largely unnecessary and somehow self-created. Perhaps, like Darren, they have trouble maintaining successful relationships, finding enjoyment in their work, or seeing results from their spiritual practice. Perhaps they feel disengaged and uninspired by the lives they've created for themselves. Or perhaps, more simply, they have a hard time feeling happy and content, but they know that somehow a more satisfying life is possible. You might have picked up this book for very similar reasons.

Over the course of more than thirty-five years in practice, I have investigated and worked with a variety of different approaches to bringing awareness of and freedom from the deeply embedded conditioning that keeps us in these historical patterns—often these patterns have been with us for our entire lives. From my experience of what actually works most effectively, my practice has evolved into a combination of Western psychotherapy and traditional Buddhism. Used together in an ongoing dialogue, these two styles offer guidance for how we can liberate ourselves from unnecessary suffering and experience a freedom that is already present in our lives.

After many years of working in these ways myself and of offering this path to my clients, I now have the pleasure of offering it to you in this book.

FREEING OURSELVES

Clients come to see me for all sorts of reasons—relationship issues, personal issues, work issues. But underneath it all, they come to me for one reason: in some way, they are not experiencing themselves as free.

What do I mean by "free"? Freedom is by its very nature hard to define. It seems to include the qualities of freshness and spontaneity, expansiveness, contentment and well-being, completeness, openheartedness, and open awareness. Freedom is also experienced as inherently satisfying and meaningful, not as a means or condition for some greater good. By contrast, many of our more familiar goals—a good relationship, good health, money, political and social justice, and so on—are usually seen as *conditions* that will bring about a greater good. "If I just had better health, more money, etc., *then* I would be happy." With the experience of freedom, life does not become perfect, but we do have a sense that everything is workable, that nothing is missing. When we don't feel free, on the other hand, it seems like something is keeping us from experiencing joy and contentment. At times we feel this sense of completeness and presence, and we know on some level that it's available at any moment. But something about our life feels off, and we experience a sense of complaint. I almost always find this sense of basic dissatisfaction beneath the specific problems my clients present when they first sit down in my office.

Whenever we're talking about freeing ourselves, we're implying that we are already experiencing a type of imprisonment. We're saying there's something we need to resolve or remove in order to experience freedom. So a major theme in my work is to investigate the nature of any such obstacle. Do we feel imprisoned in our lives because of our life circumstances? Because of unresolved issues from our history? Or might our imprisonment be more about how we relate to our experience?

The first view is basically that of Western psychotherapy. The Western tradition says there are actual difficulties in our lives that can and should be resolved. The goal of Western therapy is to improve our sense of self and our life circumstances so that we can feel more free, more satisfied, and more engaged. The second view is the Buddhist view, which says that *how we relate to* whatever we're experiencing is even more important than the experience itself. Obviously, it makes a big difference for most of us whether we're healthy or sick, whether we're in poverty or have adequate money, and whether we have to deal with depression or have an easy sense of well-being. But from the Buddhist view, how we relate to each of these experiences is actually more impactful to our sense of freedom than the circumstances themselves. So from the Western view—which I will also refer to as the *developmental* view—we try, appropriately, to improve ourselves and our circumstances. But from the Buddhist, or *fruitional,* view, our work is not primarily to improve our experience; instead, it's to invite a shift in perspective so that we are willing and able to fully relate to any experience we might have, regardless of what it may be.

My passion for the past thirty-five years or so has been to combine what is most skillful about therapy with what is most skillful in Buddhism. Both are powerful, yet both focus on a limited range of phenomena; neither addresses everything. Some people have a tendency to appreciate therapy and be cautious about a spiritual path; others are very invested in a spiritual path and somewhat cynical about therapy. My experience is that although both are very helpful and important, they are probably impossible to fully reconcile. In my opinion, the basic assumptions of therapy and the view and practice of the spiritual journey cannot be integrated into one path. Therapy, as an expression of Western culture, takes as a given that we are independently existing selves. It makes complete sense, therefore, to protect and improve this self; the challenge is to do so in a skillful and up-to-date way. Buddhism asserts the view that our experience of being a separate self with some essential nature is mistaken. Therefore, our work is to investigate this appearance, see through it, and experience the freedom that comes from having open awareness and compassion, rather than a personal self, as our basic ground. The fundamental lack of resolvability between these two views is what I find most fertile and interesting to work with.

MY INTRODUCTION TO THE TWO VIEWS

The ideas, views, and practices discussed in this book come not only from my clinical work with clients, but also, most fundamentally, from my own personal experience. I have never felt comfortable taking other people's ideas without testing them myself. And both Western psychology and Buddhism have been central to my own personal journey, starting when I was in my twenties.

After college, I started a PhD program in clinical psychology, but I dropped out after one year. More accurately, I ran out screaming. There seemed to be an assumption built into the program that anyone studying psychology was, by definition, sane, and anyone in the client chair was, by definition, neurotic (or worse). I was so disturbed by this unexamined assumption that I left the program and, soon thereafter, the country. I spent two very formative years abroad, traveling by motorcycle through Europe, North Africa, and West Asia. In India and Nepal, I encountered the Tibetan community in exile and became very interested in Tibetan Buddhism. When I returned, I met my teacher, Chögyam Trungpa Rinpoche, a Tibetan lama who had moved to the United States and had begun offering the Buddhist teachings to a lay audience.

In this tradition, I found a sophisticated and deep understanding of the nature of mind, practical ways to work with one's most difficult experiencing, and a view based on our greatest potential rather than on pathology. When Trungpa Rinpoche began the Naropa Institute, he encouraged the establishment of a master's program in psychology, which I soon enrolled in. At that time, in the 1970s, no one was really articulating a way to join therapy and Buddhism, so our classes alternated between work with very skilled Western psychotherapists and lessons in Buddhist practice and theory. In hindsight, this was a fortunate experience: we were forced to hold these two approaches with no theories offered about how they might be integrated. (Trungpa Rinpoche himself had no apparent problems with contradictory energies. At one moment, he would be encouraging of our training, and in another, he would describe therapists as "cosmic vultures," living off the experience of others.)

Over time, I have become more and more passionate about this work. I think about it every day. Every day, with some exceptions, of course, I ask myself how I can be helpful with whomever I may be relating to. When working as a therapist, I am continually experimenting with how I might support the person who has courageously placed his or her vulnerability in my hands. How can this person find some relief from any actually unnecessary suffering and experience more freedom in daily life? Freedom that may *not* require that person to be in therapy every week for ten years. Even though I am a therapist and working with clients pays my bills, like all ethical therapists, I am not interested in keeping people dependent on therapy. I would rather offer them tools that might actually make a significant difference, teach them how to use these tools, and then support the integration of this work into their daily life.

For me, something shifted a number of years ago. I think of it as a change in my psychic center of gravity. Before this shift, my baseline—what I returned to, spontaneously, off and on, every moment—was feeling, to some extent, like a problematic person. I was always trying to improve, trying to wake up, trying to feel completely at peace. From that ground of dissatisfaction, moments of clarity, peace, and freedom would arise. But those moments were temporary, and I would always return to a more fundamental sense of problem.

Then this shift happened, over some time and with no apparent cause; it was certainly supported by my Buddhist meditation practices, my many years of personal therapy, and the good fortune of relating to some very wakeful and kind teachers. My personal opinion is that waking up is not caused *by anything*. Not meditation, not prayer, not devotion. How can we cause something that's already present? But it does seem accurate that we can invite this experience, make it more likely that what's already true may arise into our awareness. As American Zen teacher Baker Roshi once said: "Enlightenment is an accident—but meditation makes us accident-prone."

Since this shift, my baseline has been an experience of open awareness, freedom, and well-being. Coming from this new basic ground, it makes sense to be kind to oneself, to everyone. I no longer have to approach this as a practice; it simply takes place spontaneously. I still get captured by historically conditioned issues at times and disturbing emotions continue to arise, but they happen less and less frequently and are difficult to take too seriously. This shift has been so powerful for me that, especially as a therapist, I'm endlessly interested in how I might invite others to experience a similar change. How can we investigate our experience in a way that ends our constant postponement of experiencing freedom? How can we cut to the chase and see what's true, right now, in the present moment? How can we discover whether there's actually a problem in our self or in life?

My experience is that waking up seems to happen along a continuum. It's usually not some sudden, black-and-white change. I have found that my own conditioned history hasn't stopped displaying itself. I still have my personality style, my core vulnerabilities that I don't like to feel. But I don't seem to be adding the *drama* anymore. I don't really mind that I still have to work with my familiar patterns, my confusion, and my messiness as a human being. In fact, it's actually very interesting.

In the environment of freedom, it turns out that there's no problem with being fully human. There is no goal of transcendence or of invulnerability in the fruitional view. We're not trying to rise above our humanness. In fact, in this environment, it's completely the opposite. The intention is to go so deeply into our confusion, our panic, our joy, our rage, our boredom, and our fear that we find out for ourselves that there's no essential nature to any of these experiences, as vivid as they may be. This discovery not only strengthens our confidence in the workability of being another confused human, but it also gives rise to a spontaneous sense of compassion for, and interest in, others. We see that others not only have real pain in their lives, but that they, too, are creating unnecessary suffering on top of it. We realize we're all in the same boat. We begin to ask how we can help ourselves in order to better help others. Are we ready to stop pretending to not be fully present and engaged at every moment? To stop waiting for some future enlightenment, or for our past wounds to heal, before we're fully committed to, and available to, life? We find that pain is a valid part of life, but that it's completely workable. It is difficult to have pain, but it's not a problem.

My training in the Western, or developmental, view was, of course, congruent with Western culture. As I mentioned earlier, in the West, we believe that a better quality of life comes from improving our sense of self and our life circumstances. Obviously, much of this approach is very accurate; it's true that better health, financial security, political freedoms, and positive feelings about ourselves are all wonderful qualities. In our culture, we associate many of these positive experiences with a state of freedom. Yet this means that our experience of freedom depends on a combination of external circumstances and how we feel—neither of which we have full control over. Because of this, there's a certain tentative quality to any freedom we might achieve using this approach. At any moment, our circumstances, both inner and outer, could change for the worse, and our sense of freedom could be diminished or lost once again.

In a less familiar way, the Buddhist, or fruitional, view asserts that freedom lies in how we *relate* to our experience—whatever that experience is, whether we like it or don't like it. So it's not about whether we feel depressed or happy; rather, it's about our willingness and ability to participate fully in any and all of our feelings. The experience of freedom arises not from acquiring our preferred lifestyle and our preferred state of mind but from a willingness to stay with ourselves—to be completely committed to experiencing our lives—regardless of circumstance.

As different as these two views are, together they offer a powerful path to move from a sense of suffering to a sense of freedom. We want to be free. We want to feel whole. We want to feel at peace. The dialogue between Western therapy and the Buddhist view asks, "In what way is our experience of freedom dependent on our life circumstances and how we feel? And in what way is our experience of freedom arising from our unconditional commitment to the truth of our experience, whatever it may be?" Throughout this book, we'll go back and forth between these two views. Both have their value. Both have their limitations. The purpose of this book is to welcome a dialogue between them, making use of the gifts both have to offer as we begin to experience ourselves as being more wakeful, more free.

ABOUT THIS BOOK

The book is divided into eight chapters. Chapter 1 offers an overview of the core of Western psychology, which I call the *developmental view*. This view is the idea that we can improve our life circumstances and our sense of self by changing our historically conditioned behavioral patterns or strategies. It is called the "developmental" view because it postulates that what we experience as young children has a profound impact on the way we engage with life and take care of ourselves as adults. Chapter 2 covers the *fruitional view,* which arises from the Buddhist idea that our basic nature—freedom—is available right here, right now. If we can shift our perspective on whatever is happening, we'll find that all the qualities of our own basic nature are already present. Chapter 3 explores the dialogue between the developmental view and the fruitional view from the perspective of my own clinical practice. For example, we can more effectively challenge patterns of experiencing that no longer serve us when we understand the healthy function they played when we were young. And finding that it's completely workable to show up in each moment, without relying on a familiar drama, gives us an alternative to that drama—a ground from which to challenge our historic patterns.

In chapter 4, we turn our attention to the experience of anxiety and struggle. Although anxiety is a very disturbing experience, it's actually a natural part of being human. It's also central to how we generate unnecessary suffering for ourselves and others. Anxiety is explored as a physical and an emotional experience, as well as a signal of how intensely open our minds and our lives actually are. Chapter 5 is about embodied awareness. Most of us tend to take our thoughts and ideas as actual descriptions of reality, which is not accurate and is rarely helpful. Embodied awareness provides direct access to the unique and inherently workable nature of our noninterpretive experiencing. As we train ourselves to stay in our immediate experience, it's helpful to have an ongoing dialogue between our *ideas* and our immediate, embodied *experiencing.*

Chapters 6 and 7 are about relationships. I find relationships incredibly provocative. It's extremely difficult to pretend that we have our lives together when we're in an intimate relationship. In chapter 6, we discuss how all of our normal experiencing is relational and how this guarantees an irresolvable tension. This discussion will be the basis for examining what are called codependent dynamics. In chapter 7, we explore a view of four evolving stages of relationship, each of which is an expression of our increasing tolerance of open mind and of intimacy. Chapter 8 discusses what it means to have a good state of mind that is independent of our history, of current circumstances, and of how we feel at any moment. Increasing our conscious participation in our always-present open awareness is seen as central to this capacity. By increasing this participation, we discover an unconditional confidence and freedom, which become the ground from which we engage with ourselves, with others, and with life.

Chapters 1–3 are about what's called *view*. Before we take on any practices, it's important to clarify just what our intentions are and to consider how we might most effectively move toward our goals. The views explored in this book arise from the intention to understand our incredibly complex human experience in ways that relieve unnecessary suffering and that invite more freedom. These discussions are sometimes abstract and may at points feel difficult to fully grasp. But the more practical considerations that follow would be hard to understand without first exploring these views; the fruitional approach, in particular, is not familiar in our culture. When we are introduced to any new theory, we usually begin with an intellectual understanding, which can then gradually become a view that is integrated with our experiencing.

Chapters 4–7 are about practices. A *practice* involves a conscious participation in some activity, usually with an intention to improve our experience in some way. When a practice is difficult, we often think of it as a discipline. A discipline is hard to sustain without a view, which helps us understand how it might be to our benefit to make such an effort. In these chapters, we explore how the two basic views being presented in this book might be applied to real-life issues, especially several very basic themes continually dealt with in therapy.

Chapter 8 is about the potential *results* of these practices. When we commit to certain practices, it's important to see whether the results we hope for arise. If so, then we will be motivated to continue our efforts. If not, then we should reexamine our views and our practices. What might we expect our experience to be if we were to commit to experimenting with the ideas and disciplines presented in chapters 1–7?

In all of these discussions, I invite you to consider a fundamental assumption: this book is about how we understand and relate to our *experience* of reality. It is not about the *nature* of reality. As an example, the experience of awareness is said to be impossible to really define. Approximations are sometimes used—we talk about awareness as being "unborn," "unending," and "without limitation." Without examination, we might assume that awareness has an objective existence with these somehow infinite qualities. I find it more useful, however, to take these descriptions as being about our *experience* of awareness—"it feels like this," "it seems like this," "this is a way to talk about this experience." Similarly, we could think of the First Noble Truth in Buddhism—the truth of suffering—as if it were a description of reality: that is, reality *is* suffering. But I think it's more helpful to understand this idea as being about our *experiencing*: we experience life as suffering because of how we relate to reality, not because reality itself is inherently a problem. There is a similar possibility in therapy. We might think that we're relating to our *actual* history, rather than relating to our current *experience* or *recollection* of our history. And so, in all of the discussions to follow, any talk about basic nature, awareness, and so on will be best understood as being about our *experience*, rather than as making any claim about *reality.*

It's said that the Buddha was asked about what happens when we die, whether other beings exist in other realms, and questions about the nature of reality. The Buddha responded:

> If a man has been shot with an arrow and the doctor
> is called, does that doctor ask him who shot the arrow,
> what his motives were, what he was wearing, and so on?
> No. The doctor's job is to remove the arrow and help
> the patient heal. My teachings are about the relief from
> unnecessary suffering. I teach about liberation, not
> about the nature of reality.

Following this example, and as an expression of these teachings, this book is offered with the hope that it might be of some help in accessing our already-present open awareness. With greater conscious participation in awareness comes a greater ability to reduce unnecessary suffering and to increase our experience of freedom.

Throughout the book, I'll take the point of view that our experience of our basic nature is already that of freedom. I'll discuss some of the reasons we may not consciously experience this liberation and some of the ways we might invite the experience of freedom into our everyday awareness. My hope is that the chapters that follow will be useful, provocative, and practical for you—whether you happen to be a clinician working with clients or someone who's simply interested in Buddhism, therapy, or the dialogue between the two. Or perhaps you are someone who is seeking freedom in your own life, like my client Darren—whose story we'll continue in the next chapter. Whatever brings you to this book, I hope you will continually check out the ideas I'm presenting to see if they are, in fact, relevant and useful to you. Since direct experience has been so central to my own life and work, I invite you to test any theories you find in the pages that follow in the fire of your own experience.

1

THE DEVELOPMENTAL VIEW

THE DEVELOPMENTAL VIEW is central to the Western psychotherapeutic approach. It's based on the idea that the experiences we have as children, mostly in our families of origin, have a profound impact on the rest of our lives. In response to difficult experiences, we create strategies or behavioral patterns to help us deal with what we experience as threats to our emotional, and sometimes even physical, survival. What we first use for our survival, we later use as a generalized and familiar way of engaging in life. These formulas or strategies are usually very intelligent and appropriate at the time they are created and are of very real benefit to us. As a result, they tend to become habitual and to then persist long after they are needed. Because they are responses to disturbing and even dangerous realities, they're usually associated with quite a bit of anxiety. We avoid feeling this anxiety by pushing these strategies out of our awareness. They then continue to operate without our conscious participation, potentially for the rest of our lives, unless brought into awareness and challenged once we are adults.

USING OUT-OF-DATE STRATEGIES

To illustrate such strategies and their impact, let's return to Darren— the client we met in the introduction. As I mentioned, Darren came to me because he couldn't find lasting satisfaction in his work, relationships, or spiritual practice. He knew he was the common denominator in each situation, but he was beginning to feel a type of despair about his seeming inability to engage with depth and commitment in these significant parts of his life.

It didn't take long to discover that this was a life-long theme. Growing up, Darren felt like no matter what he did, it was never enough. He had painful memories of coming home with a 98 on his test and his father asking why didn't he get a 100. In sports, his parents would ask why he wasn't on the starting team, and his mother criticized the friends he chose as if they were not acceptable.

Darren was quick to explain that he felt loved by his parents and felt they had provided well for him. He believed they were on his side and wished the best for him. There was no physical abuse and no alcoholism in the family. In fact, it was extremely difficult for Darren to say anything critical about his parents. When I started to investigate the possibility that he had felt shamed or humiliated by his parents, Darren was quite defensive and did not want anything negative to be said about them.

And yet, his hope to be approved of, appreciated, and acknowledged was never met. He developed a belief that approval was not going to occur, despite his best efforts. He had done his best to be a "good boy," to please his parents, to be who they wanted him to be, but it hadn't gotten him the acknowledgment he so desired.

Like many children, it seemed that Darren ended up believing *he* was the problem—that there was something fundamentally inadequate or unworthy about him. As is often the case, he developed an *unconscious survival strategy* to cope with this continual lack of approval. Instead of being himself—which wasn't working—he tried to be positive, cooperative, dependable, and reliable all the time. While this reduced the painful and scary friction he felt with his parents, he paid a price. First, he hadn't learned how to be honest with himself or others. Second, he was not allowing himself to feel his own anger and aggression, both of which are a natural part of the human experience.

Almost all of us develop strategies like Darren's to survive and protect ourselves as children. But as we grow older, these same developmental strategies can hold us back from experiencing ourselves in an honest and spontaneous way. In this case, Darren created a strategy of never getting his hopes up, never wanting to put himself completely on the line, because he "knew" he would fail. No matter how hard he worked, his efforts would never be acknowledged as good enough by his parents. Rather than seeing his parents' expectations as unreasonable—and likely driven by their own unconscious developmental strategies—he took the blame. He agreed with them that he was not good enough. And rather than risk losing the love that he did genuinely receive from them, he kept his anger and disappointment at their impossible-to-satisfy expectations to himself—even placing these taboo feelings out of conscious awareness.

As an adult, Darren would often transfer the unconscious anger he felt toward his parents onto his intimate partners, subtly blaming them for his own lack of commitment. Often a partner would try to support him in his struggles around work, becoming invested in his success. When he did not follow through—when he bailed from the job or lost interest in the project—he would subtly communicate that his partner had not been adequately supportive. Or he would make relationship agreements that he would not keep, and his partner would end up feeling unsupported or abandoned—like she couldn't count on Darren. Either way, Darren's drama that relationships must involve a lack of support would be perpetuated. As a result, the relationship would end, and Darren would once again be left wondering what had happened. The repetition of this pattern of relating—which Darren was cocreating, but which was still out of his awareness—provided him with continuing evidence that his young strategy—of never getting his hopes up and never expecting his needs to be met—was still necessary and justified.

Often in developmental work, the first step is to help clients see that the recurring patterns they're experiencing are not caused by, or really *about,* current life circumstances or current relationships. Moreover, these strategies do not arise from pathology or bad intentions. Instead, they represent our young efforts to take the very best care of ourselves possible. Usually the issue with these strategies is that they are several decades out of date. Darren, like most of us, was still trying to take care of himself in the only ways he knew how—ways that were appropriate when he was a dependent child in his family. He was still trying to never disappoint others by being a "good boy," avoiding conflict, and ineffectively asserting his own needs. But his repressed anger at never receiving the love and approval he wanted was expressed in passive-aggressive and self-sabotaging behaviors. Of course, such strategies were no longer necessary or appropriate as an adult—in fact, they had become obstacles, keeping him from experiencing a conscious choice about how much effort to give any endeavor he undertook.

The ways in which our necessary childhood strategies become our unnecessary adult neuroses is a basic theme in Western developmental work. These strategies were usually worth the price tag when we were young, dependent, immature children in our families of origin. But as adults, the benefits we get are no longer worth the price we pay.

Darren never really tried; he never put himself on the line. In exchange he got the benefit of never having to acknowledge feeling like a failure and a disappointment, because he didn't stay with anything long enough to fully invest himself. But the price tag was a chronic withholding from life and a corresponding tendency to withhold his full participation in his relationships. Ironically, by avoiding immediate intense feelings of failure and disappointment, Darren lived in a subtler but pervasive atmosphere that perpetuated those same feelings.

Darren and I continued to discuss the possibility that, in addition to his parents being genuinely loving and supportive, they may also have had their own unresolved, unconscious issues that led Darren to never feeling fully validated or successful. He began to see that he had learned to never give anything his full effort—expecting to be told that he was a disappointment, inadequate, or not enough. Over time, Darren began to tolerate a more complex understanding of his parents; he began to realize that his parents were complicated human beings, just like he was. Not only sane, not only neurotic, but like all of us having their own strengths and limitations.

As Darren began to realize that he was still paying the price for his parents' limitations, he began to experience more anger about that history. His childhood strategy of keeping his anger to himself was coming undone. At first this was uncomfortable for him; he worried it meant he was supposed to have confrontations with his parents about his past. But we worked with the view that Darren's anger was his own responsibility to work with now. It was not about his parents, even if their unconscious issues had deeply influenced his survival strategies. To blame them or anybody else would actually perpetuate the young, victimlike position.

At this stage of our work we entered territory common in Western therapy: the process of recovering one's right and ability to embody aspects of oneself that had been disowned as a child. For Darren, it was especially important to explore his anger, his power, and his healthy aggressive energy. We explored his experience of having boundaries, keeping his integrity in relationships, and having constructive conflict with others. In this process, he felt an increasing willingness to work from the position of personal responsibility. He understood, more and more, that for him to feel satisfied in his adult life, he would need to take responsibility for the full range of his emotions. It was helpful for Darren to understand the history that had given rise to his childhood strategies. He realized that these were long-term issues that he brought into his current life and that they were not problems caused by his current life circumstances.

On one hand, that meant not looking for his worth in pleasing others, and on the other hand, it meant not blaming anyone else for his feelings. Darren experimented with feeling his difficult feelings and with being completely responsible for working with them. As he did this work, he reported feeling more powerful in his relationships, less anxious about what other people thought of him, and more able to assert his needs. As Darren set more effective boundaries, he acted in less passive-aggressive ways, and he reported both better feedback from others and having a greater tolerance of feeling fundamentally alone. At this point we ended our work together. It was too soon to know or predict whether Darren's pattern of not following through was going to be significantly changed. Perhaps this repetition would be enacted in his therapeutic work as well. But he already reported being aware of his impulses to escape from relationship and work, and he had begun experiencing some choice about whether to act on those impulses.

From the developmental view, Darren was entering emotional adulthood, which includes the ability to discriminate between feelings and behavior. He recognized that his history would likely give rise to familiar, difficult emotions and that he did not have to allow these emotions to run his behavior or control his life. He began to live a life that was engaged with current realities and to use his current adult capacities, rather than reenact past realities.

IT'S NOT ACTUALLY ABOUT THE PAST

While Western therapy is sometimes seen as overly focused on the past, it's actually about the present. It's about how most of us are, in a variety of ways, living as if the present *were* the past. We're operating as if we're still young children in our families of origin, especially in the realm of relationships. It's as if we were given a role in a play, and we got such a good response (and we've played the part for so long now) that we've actually forgotten we're playing a role. In truth, there is a *larger* sense of self—a larger life—that we could be living, if only we were able to drop our unconscious identification with this character and become curious about who we might be right now.

Western psychotherapy has a variety of techniques, theories, and approaches that can help improve the story we've been telling about ourselves. While growing up, Darren learned to tell himself that he was apparently never going to be good enough to get the love he wanted and needed. He believed that he would always be a disappointment to others and to himself, so best to cue off of others' realities, avoid conflict, and resign himself—resentfully—to a life of emotional poverty. He also believed that all of this was, somehow, his fault. In therapy, Darren took the risk of rewriting this story. He learned to think of himself as a more emotionally complex person, as one who could reveal his differences to another and still survive. He learned to discriminate between his current responsibility to work with his feelings and the fact that, as a child, he was not responsible for his parents' issues. Like most of us, Darren was still identified with a sense of self. But, as long as we're telling a story about who we are, it's better to have a good story than a bad story.

There is a potential problem with looking to the past as a way of better understanding the present: we may start to think that an improved present is dependent on clearing up the past. Out of this belief, many of us try to rework the past. But you can't rework your past—it's gone. Any memories about the past are speculative, incomplete, and partial. Our version of our childhood is probably different now than it was ten years ago and will probably be different ten years from now. If we start to believe that the past is *causing* our present circumstances, then we've positioned ourselves as powerless victims. We can't actually change the past, but we can subtly create the drama of trying to change what can't be changed. Talking about the past, without realizing that we're only talking about our current way of relating to our past, can actually function as an avoidance of being fully present. This unexamined project of freeing oneself from the past can result in an endless self-improvement project—as well as endless therapy.

Many people in therapy find it interesting and helpful to explore their emotional history. However, many others do not. When I'm working with clients, I'm curious about their past—I want to know something about their family of origin dynamics, their parents and siblings, their various life experiences—but I don't really worry if they don't want to go into the details. Why? Because in therapy we are looking for patterns of experiencing that are out of date, out of synch with current reality. It can be helpful to understand the past origins of these patterns, but it's not necessary. If someone feels abandoned when their partner doesn't immediately return a text, that can be identified and worked with in the present, without needing to know about a history of parents divorcing, an absent father, many moves to new homes and schools, and so forth. All of us are only living in the present moment. That's the only moment in which we can intervene. So history can be helpful in therapy, but it's not necessary.

THE METABOLISM OF EXPERIENCE

One way to look at Darren's experience is that he felt deeply divided against himself. He wasn't willing to feel his genuine feelings of anger, and he wasn't diving into the life he wanted because he was convinced that he would have to feel like a failure. These "parts"—recurring patterns of experience—were repressed, but they did not go away. Instead, they were operating unconsciously, causing him to feel dissatisfied and unhappy and to behave symptomatically, like being passive-aggressive and not following through. One way of understanding this sense of internal division is to see it as the result of "poor metabolism." Metabolism is the body's process of extracting energy from the food we eat. We have to be able to make use of what we eat; otherwise, we won't have the energy to grow and survive. Metabolism is the process of digesting this food and converting it to energy.

Using metabolism as an analogy can be useful in the realm of experience. In a certain way, we're always "eating" our experience. We're taking it in, processing it, and digesting it. As Aldous Huxley once wrote, "Experience is not what happens to a man; it is what a man does with what happens to him." How we process our experience deeply influences how we make use of it. As infants and young children—beginning at conception—we rely on our parents to digest our experience for us. Just as a mother bird digests a worm and then spits it back up for her babies, our parents have to digest our experience and feed it back to us. The realities of life would be too much otherwise. You would not give a one-month-old infant solid food to eat. It's not that solid food is unhealthy; it's that the baby can't digest it. In the same way, parents need to buffer their children from too much emotional intensity. They must interpret intense experience in order to protect the child, to hold the child—both literally and figuratively—to help the child feel unconditionally loved and safe. A parent doesn't tell a child every day that anyone in the family might die unexpectedly. Even though that's the truth, a child cannot handle this reality yet. Life *is not* unconditionally loving and safe, but there seems to be a very important developmental need for a child to *experience* a certain safety as a foundation from which to deal with the actual complexity of life.

All of us need to develop appropriate ego functions, or capacities that allow us to deal with the challenges of life—both internal and external. These functions include defending ourselves, discriminating between fantasy and reality, delaying gratification, having a coherent sense of self, and so on. Of course, as infants we've developed almost none of these abilities. Our parents' job is to provide "external ego functions" for us. Much of our developmental work is the gradual internalization of these initially external capacities. Parents provide the child with an adequate experience of safety, engagement, and nurturance. They allow the child to feel loved, to feel as if the child has a place in the world. Of course, all parents—myself included—are limited. We do the best we can, but the ability to give our children these experiences is limited by our own capacity, life experiences, and psychological issues. So all children have to deal with a certain amount of experience that is just too intense; that cannot be properly digested because of their immaturity as little beings.

If, on the whole, parents are able to protect their child and if the intensity of the child's experience is not too much, then the child learns to handle reality quite adequately. Some Western therapists would say such a child had an adequate holding environment. When we are adequately held by our lives—by our parents, by our world—we are able to rest in being a mystery to ourselves. Every moment, we can show up, not having to know who we are or how we're going to handle the next moment. Such a childhood environment is an ideal experience in which to grow. If we can show up without needing to constantly control, plan, or protect ourselves against what might be coming, then every moment is fresh, every moment is a new experiment. Our way of engaging with life can stay current. As we change, as our life circumstances change, our strategies of engagement can change.

Most of us, however, did not grow up in such a fortunate environment. Instead, we found ourselves facing overwhelming experiences—experiences like grief, fear, rage, panic, physical discomfort, and powerlessness. Because of the intensity of such experiences, we learned to show up in each moment with some amount of defensiveness already in place. We devised our own formulas to protect, process, and defend against the natural experience of being a young human, which is, at times, just too much.

One of the fundamental ways in which we protect ourselves as infants and children is to do our best to not have to consciously participate in what is most terrifying or overwhelming. We learn to train our attention to ignore what we don't know how to handle. Out of sight, out of mind. So we divide ourselves into parts that are "safe" to experience and those that are "unsafe." This defense mechanism is the beginning of what we term *neurotic organization,* or neurosis.

THE BIRTH OF NEUROSIS

The developmental view suggests that, by the ages of four, five, or six years old, we have hopefully achieved what's called a *neurotic level of organization*. What this really means is that we have the capacity for a stabilized repression of particular feelings. We can push out of our own awareness those feelings that are too disturbing to handle, digest, or make use of, while retaining awareness of those feelings that we can adequately work with.

My own parents valued independence and were somewhat phobic around the energy of dependency. So it was very smart for me to learn to not feel dependent. If I felt dependent, I would have acted dependently. If I had acted dependently, in a family where dependency was not embraced, bad things would have happened. Perhaps I would have been pushed away, love would have been withheld, or my parents would have been anxious. I can't remember the specifics, so it's somewhat speculative, but I imagine it was very healthy and functional not to feel or behave like a dependent person in my household. Independence, on the other hand, would have allowed me to receive approval and love and to fit into our family. And, of course, independence had its own benefits out in the world as well. The challenge, however, was that I had to find a way to never feel dependent. Dependent feelings would have been associated with a type of survival-level panic.

As children, we don't yet have the ability to effectively discriminate between feelings and behavior. We tend to control our behavior by disconnecting from the feelings that might "cause" the behaviors, which could get us in trouble. When we are not able to disconnect from these feelings or when life triggers them, we almost always feel anxiety or even panic. In my experience as a therapist, I find that almost all of us have a sense of annihilatory panic associated with our core vulnerabilities. This is an intense sense of threat, impossible to really put into words—"If I have to feel this feeling, I will cease to exist." This makes sense since, as children, our actual emotional survival—and sometimes even our physical safety—was often at stake. So what an incredible achievement! Even as a young child, we somehow figured out how to not feel overwhelmed by intense feelings. We protected ourselves from emotions we didn't know how to handle, and our environment was not handling for us. Such a strategy is not pathological; it's actually very healthy. It's entirely appropriate, even wonderful, to have that capacity. It allows us to first adapt ourselves to our all-important parents, and then to go out into the world and act in a stabilized, socially approved way.

There is, of course, a price tag for this achievement. The price tag is that we have managed to push parts of who we are out of our awareness. Very disturbing parts, yes, but very important parts. And just because we repress these parts does not mean they go away. Just because I grew up learning not to *feel* dependent doesn't mean that I *wasn't* dependent. I was, of course, incredibly dependent—all children are. But I had a very strong motivation to never be aware of my own dependency.

To the extent that such childhood strategies work, we practice them over and over, and they become structural. Because these strategies are associated with survival-level anxiety, we drive them out of awareness. As unconscious structures, these formulas for engaging with life understandably persist into adulthood. As an adult, then, of course I have difficulty dealing with being a dependent person and with the energy of dependency in others. (What we find unacceptable in ourselves, we often find unacceptable in others.) The price tag for such repression can be especially high in relationships. As we'll talk about in chapter 6, it's very, very common for us to "mysteriously" end up with partners who manifest exactly those traits that we have disowned in ourselves—and vice versa.

But there's a deeper price tag I'm especially interested in working with as a therapist. When we disown parts of who we are, we end up feeling divided against ourselves. We feel there's a part of us that is problematic and even dangerous; shameful or embarrassing; unworthy of love from others. To fit into our emotional world, our unique family system, our culture, our gender, and so forth, we turn against this part of ourselves and push it out of awareness. We subconsciously feel that there's a problem with who we are and that we must never go there; we must never have a relationship with that part of ourselves.

Imagine being a little child standing out in the world and feeling threatened. You might put up a wall for protection or even hide in a little box. That would help, but it would also keep you from feeling connected with the environment. In the same way, when we put up a psychological barrier, we end up feeling disconnected from ourselves and from life. Being alienated and disconnected from life doesn't feel good, and so we suffer. What we don't understand is that we're the ones choosing—with very good reason—to put up the wall. It's not happening *to* us; we're doing it ourselves. The very success of our effort to protect ourselves leads inevitably to an experience of feeling divided against ourselves and separate from the world. We feel alienated from life. We also become distrustful of it, because of course life is unpredictable, and it may, at any moment, cause us to feel those feelings we're doing everything to avoid.

INVESTING IN OUR STRATEGIES

This leads to something I find all the time in my work, which I don't think is being discussed enough. As adults, we all seem to want to resolve our neuroses, but we don't understand that *we have an incredible investment in maintaining them.* Our young strategies were put into place for our own survival, well-being, and protection. It's not until we actually investigate—in a very immediate, embodied way—whether these protective strategies are still required that we can hope to resolve them. Until we can do that work, we're going to constantly—and unconsciously—look for evidence that proves our survival strategies are still required, necessary, and justified.

Most of us are not aware of this paradox. Consciously, we want to relieve ourselves of the suffering these patterns carry with them. But unconsciously, most of us are even more invested in making sure that those patterns stay in place, so we don't have to feel the feelings that were overwhelming to us as children. If they fail and the unwanted feelings arise, we experience panic.

For example, it would be to my *young* benefit to unconsciously look for evidence that dependency is weak and undesirable. I might notice that weak people are more likely to be victimized. That would validate my strategy of independence. I would not be as invested in looking for the downsides of independence, such as isolation and a sense of being cut off from the world. Instead, I would look for evidence all around me that weakness is a bad thing, and I would likely find it. So I would continue to deepen my investment in independence, perhaps adopting a relationship style of giving rather than receiving. After all, in order to receive, you have to acknowledge dependency; you have to acknowledge that you have needs, that you want something. To give, on the other hand, requires no neediness. Subconsciously, I've adopted exactly this type of strategy, placing myself in life circumstances that require I be strong, take risks, and be competent and self-sufficient. The role I play in my life thus serves as evidence, proving over and over every day, "See, it's necessary to be independent. Independent is the right way to be. Dependency is unwise and maybe even dangerous." It wasn't until my forties that I started to see that I am, shockingly, an incredibly dependent person. At first I felt an annihilatory panic at this discovery. But once I became used to the panic itself, there was incredible relief and relaxation in owning the dependent part of myself, in feeling less divided and more whole.

Many times in my therapeutic sessions, this exact same process takes place. Clients claim that they want to change their habitual patterns, but when we actually start to investigate what would be required—which is to feel exactly the feelings they have dedicated their life to avoiding—a lot of very mixed feelings come up. And that becomes exactly our work: to acknowledge and be kind toward the feelings they've been running away from since childhood, as well as toward not wanting to feel those feelings. I encourage my clients to value having mixed feelings about changing their habitual patterns. It's natural, because changing those patterns requires quite a bit of discomfort. To persevere, clients must be willing to tolerate a fair amount of panic, at least for a while. My opinion is that it's worth the effort, but most people are not going to intentionally invite horrible feelings into their lives. Generally, those who persist are either suffering greatly from the consequences of their out-of-date formulas, like Darren was, or are emotionally resilient, mature, and curious enough to be willing to risk having those feelings for a period of time.

When we examine these neurotic avoidance strategies, we often find they involve strong self-aggression. For example, whenever the experience of dependency might arise in me, I would tend to have an inner dialogue in which I'd call myself bad names for feeling weak. I would bring out the "shoulds," predict bad consequences if I didn't get it together, and so on. Once we see what we're doing, we often don't understand why we're doing it. Why in the world would I attack myself, sometimes viciously, sometimes almost obsessively? But imagine yourself as a young child, maybe one or two years old. And imagine that your parents come into the room and give you a choice—either they hit you, or you hit yourself. Which would you choose? Almost all of my clients say they would choose to hit themselves. Of course, if we hit ourselves we can pull the punch, know when it's coming, and have a little control in a difficult situation. But I believe the major benefit is that by hitting ourselves—or in this case, by aggressively shutting down our own emotions rather than having them shut down by a parent—we can continue the fantasy that our parents are only kind, protective, and loving. They're not hitting us. We already have the unconscious clarity that our parents are limited, sometimes severely so. But as a little child, we can't afford to consciously see that. We don't yet know that in fifteen or so years, we're going to grow up and be able to leave our family. When young, we're living in a type of eternal time. If we acknowledge our parents' limitations—that they are sometimes cruel, uncaring, and unloving—then we're going to be in big trouble, forever.

So most of us actually have an investment in making *ourselves* the problem. "If I'm the problem, then that explains why my parents are not loving me as I need to be loved. If I just fix what's wrong with me, they'll show up. They will be there for me." But, of course, we have to make sure we never solve the problem of what's wrong with us, because if we do, it will become clear that it *isn't* us, that we are, in fact, dealing with very limited parents, siblings, and life circumstances (poverty, discrimination, violence, and so on). And trying to do so as powerless, dependent, immature little beings.

By the time we're adults, there's a lot of momentum in place. We've had a lifelong investment in *not* solving the problem of our neurotic suffering. If we were to solve it, to see our lives clearly, we would be at risk of having to deal in a direct way with the truth—which is not always pretty. We might have to acknowledge that we don't really know who we are or what the meaning of life is; that there's no evidence we will ever have a life free of pain and disappointment; that we and everyone we love will die; and so on. As little kids, we relied on our parents and the world to metabolize and digest our experience for us. If they didn't do their part, we had to come up with some very solid survival strategies. Naturally, it's going to take a lot of courage and tolerance of anxiety to bring ourselves up to date. We will need to weather a period of intensity in order to know whether we have the capacity to handle our own experience now, in a direct and unmediated way—to see if we can, in fact, take adequate care of ourselves and become the confident and kind person we want to be.

PRACTICE INVESTIGATING OUR STRATEGIES

Perhaps we all want to resolve the suffering our young survival strategies create, but equally, we do not want to experience the disturbance and panic required to do so. Rather than ignoring our contradictory feelings, the kindest thing to do—for ourselves and for others—is to bring awareness to those feelings. We can keep ourselves company as we check out our more vulnerable experience, reassuring ourselves that we are safe by going back into what might be called neurotic experience *whenever we choose—taking little risks, then retreating into safety, and then going back again. If you care to try this out, continue with this meditation.*

Find a few minutes when you won't feel distracted. Sit somewhere comfortable. Take a few deep breaths, if that might help bring your attention to the present moment.

Bring to mind a core vulnerability in your life—something you've developed strategies around *not* feeling. You may have some clarity about what your vulnerabilities are, or you may not. If not, just bring to mind some fear you're aware of.

For example, if you're *afraid* of feeling something, that experience must already be there; it must already be a part of your life. First comes a feeling you can't handle, then come your strategies for not feeling it. Imagine acknowledging that fear from as great a distance as you choose, and just let it be there. No need to understand, heal, process, or make it go away. Just experience being in relationship with that fear. How is it to hold that fear in your awareness? What do you feel in your body? Does it feel familiar or unfamiliar?

Now, give yourself permission to ignore that fear. Participate in that experience as well. Where does your mind go? Is it easy or difficult to move away from that fear?

Once again, step back into relation with that fear. Feel what that's like. What do you notice? Is it easier to be with the fear? Harder? Do the same sensations arise in your body this time?

You might go back and forth like this several times, doing your best to stay present and embodied while you do so. There is no agenda to resolve anything—just an invitation to be more aware of what's already true. ◾

NEUROSIS AS A SUBSTITUTE FOR EXPERIENTIAL INTENSITY

Carl Jung once said, "Neurosis is always a substitute for legitimate suffering." I agree with him, though I would say neurosis is always a substitute for *experiential intensity*. I say that because we tend to contract away from not only pain but also aliveness, sexuality, joy, open awareness, and a number of other intense experiences. One of the things I like about Jung's understanding is that it characterizes neurosis as an activity of intelligence (which is not synonymous with wisdom). It's not pathological; it's not some pattern that blindly got put into place. Neurosis is not something that happened *to* us. It's an unconscious choice we make, moment after moment. It's what happens when we say, "I would actually prefer not to feel this incredibly difficult, vulnerable, disturbing experience right now, so I'm going to try to go around it. I will distract myself. I'll be self-aggressive. I'll get very activated. I'll get involved with parenting, or with work. I'll learn to meditate and be calm. I'll exercise." We might try to get out of our immediate experience of intensity through any number of ways, and basically, they all work in the short term. It's like taking a drink. If you're disturbed and you have some alcohol, there's a good chance you'll feel a bit calmer after that drink. Other people may use meditation to escape from their disturbance. But these, like all neurotic habits, are temporary solutions, giving us temporary relief. The pain and intensity we're experiencing is probably going to come and go all of our lives. As children, this choice was often the best we could do. As adults, it's an expression of a basic lack of trust in ourselves.

In the long run, neurotic habits have a counterproductive effect. Why? Because we are not dealing with the truth of our lives. Avoiding our difficult experience doesn't make it go away. We are not training ourselves in how to work skillfully with it. We perpetuate a sense that there's something about us that's not workable. And our avoidant strategies have their own price tags, because they're based not on reality but on fantasy. Engaging with our current life based on out-of-date avoidant strategies becomes increasingly unskillful and unsatisfying, as more and more time goes by. Our sense that something is off becomes harder and harder to ignore, even while we are unable or unwilling to really challenge ourselves.

I often see clients in their late thirties or forties who have spent decades avoiding their disturbance and anxiety through neurotic strategies. They often describe having a very thick, complicated state of mind. It feels heavy and dissatisfying. Something is off, not working. They can't actually explain it based on any current life circumstances, as everything might be going okay. Yet they still feel heavy and confused. From my perspective, this heaviness is often the result of a cumulative avoidance of the truth of their experience. If we are constantly putting up a smoke screen to hold disturbing experience at bay, it's natural that we'll lose clarity in other parts of our lives. If we've felt at war with ourselves for decades, we're probably beginning to feel a deep exhaustion.

In addressing neurotic or unnecessary suffering, the approach of traditional Western psychology is to address specific life issues, one after another, trying to find the source of the dissatisfaction in repetitive, historically conditioned patterns. Is there a problem in our marriage? With our boss? Are we too invested in our kids' success? If so, Western psychology seeks to find the reenactment that's beneath these current problems and then resolve it. My preference, however, is to clarify the reenactment and then investigate how we might be invested in maintaining it. The function that is served by this investment turns out to be the same, regardless of the symptom: the avoidance of experiential intensity. Addressing specific issues one after another will hopefully improve our circumstances—we might learn how to have better boundaries, better conflict skills, or an improved self-image. It's a very valid approach. In my experience, however, it doesn't get to the heart of things. Perhaps it will be more direct to increase our willingness to consciously participate in any form of experiential intensity. Central to this effort is learning to recognize and challenge our life-long aggression toward our vulnerabilities and instead learn to practice kindness toward them. When we approach neurosis not as "wrong" but as *our best out-of-date effort to take care of ourselves,* then our neuroses actually become more available to work with. If we're in a conflict with another person and that person treats us in a kind way, it's easier to work with that person skillfully. If, on the other hand, we treat each other like enemies, it's very difficult to find common ground. So rather than attacking each life issue as if it were a problem, my intention is to invite awareness, presence, and kindness to all of our experiencing, without exception. Why not work with the foundation of all neurotic experiencing, which is aggression toward and denial of the incredibly intense and open nature of every moment of our experiencing? Why even be aggressive toward our aggression? Isn't that more of the same? Why not be kind to our aggression, and then look for what's beneath it?

I see the nature of neurosis as arising not out of pathology, but instead out of our clarity and vulnerability. Each neurotic pattern represents our best effort to take the very best possible care of ourselves. If we can appreciate neurosis from that point of view, we can work with it rather than attacking it. However, when we feel anxiety and fear—which are right at the heart of our evolutionary hardwiring—we usually make an automatic effort to get away from our disturbance or conquer it in some way. The next section discusses how this aggression manifests in our emotional life and how we can work with it more effectively.

THREE TYPES OF FUNDAMENTAL AGGRESSION

Although we're working with the developmental, or Western psychotherapeutic, view in this chapter, one of the most accurate and helpful frameworks I know to help us understand our fundamental aggression toward ourselves comes from Buddhism. In the Buddhist tradition, the neurotic aggression we maintain toward the parts of ourselves we've disowned—our core vulnerabilities—is said to have three forms: positive, negative, and neutral.

In our culture, we usually think of aggression as synonymous with anger or negativity. But there are so many ways in which we are aggressive toward the truth of our own experience, and they often don't look like anger. From a developmental point of view, we're talking about aggression toward the truth of our experience—toward the aspects of ourselves that we have found unworkable and have tried to reject. These aspects become our emotional vulnerabilities. For example, Darren was not able to tolerate feelings of being a disappointment or failure, so these experiences became what he was least able and willing to work with. Unfortunately and necessarily, they were therefore the parts of himself that received the *least* amount of self-compassion. I find that when people open to the possibility that they are being aggressive toward themselves, it invites curiosity and, perhaps down the road, maybe even a little more gentleness. That gentleness allows us to begin to unwind the childhood strategies that are no longer serving us. We can become curious about what feelings or experiences those strategies are keeping at bay. "What is it I don't want to feel? Is it actually serving me to repress those feelings? What if it's no longer necessary to do so?"

All of us are in the same boat; all of us aggressively disown aspects of our experiencing. Perhaps we are drawn to some spiritual path in the hopes of living a life of harmony and peace, transcending any anger and conflict: positive aggression. Maybe we place ourselves in a competitive and stressful job that seems to require that we always push ourselves and never indulge in feeling weak: negative aggression. We could create a lifestyle that feels too overwhelming to deal with and may feel that the only response is to collapse and space out: neutral aggression. Understanding that there are three different styles of aggression may help us develop some empathy for others; some understanding that all of us are pretty freaked out about dealing with life; that we all have difficulties and we're all being very aggressive—it just takes on different forms.

In Buddhist language, the "positive" form of aggression is often called *passion* or *attachment*. In Western psychological language, we might call it the *neurotic feminine*, because it is an out-of-balance expression of the attributes generally associated with the feminine side of the connecting–separate spectrum. Note that "feminine" is not interchangeable with "female." Although it's perhaps more common for women to show up with neurotic feminine strategies, men display them as well. All life forms must have both connecting and separate energies. The point of any style of aggression is to get out of an experience of disturbance as quickly as possible. The passion, or positive, form of aggression uses the strategy of trying to keep our engagement with life always positive. To maintain this hope, we tend to locate any problems within ourselves, privately, where they won't disturb our relationships with others. People displaying neurotic feminine aggression become very accommodating when faced with a threat. It's as if they are trying to erase themselves, so as to erase the tension that comes with any conflict.

Darren is a good example of neurotic feminine aggression: He had effectively erased his anger by repressing it and withheld his full authenticity in his work and relationships out of fear of failing or disappointing others. He tried to be a good boy who would always behave positively. People with this style will tend not to assert needs, not to have boundaries, to always be accommodating, to avoid conflict, and to put others first. With this style, we end up feeling like victims because we're not taking care of ourselves; passive-aggressive behavior often results.

I recall a time, twenty years ago or more, when I saw a powerful neurotic feminine response in my own life. I had just seen a client who was the husband of a therapist in town. He'd come to me because he and his wife were having difficulties. He felt like she belittled and patronized him, while she felt like he was passive-aggressive and mean. This is territory I work in regularly, so I figured I would be able to help. Yet throughout our first session, he dismissed and refused pretty much every suggestion I offered. No matter what I said, he would reply with "yes, but . . ." He'd say, "Yeah, I've heard that before, Bruce, and it hasn't been helpful to me." Or, "I think I read that somewhere, but it's not really relevant here. Do you have any other ideas?" After an hour of this, as we were getting ready to part, I asked him if he wanted to set another appointment. Not surprisingly, he said, "I'll think about it. I'm not sure if I found this very helpful."

The rest of the day I was sitting with an intense feeling of failure. "Geez," I thought. "I'm a poor excuse for a therapist. Why am I even doing this work? It's obvious I'm not helping anybody. I need to find a new career." The torturous, self-aggressive thoughts continued all that day and into the next. I remember being in the shower the next morning, when it finally occurred to me that I might take some of the advice I give my clients every day.

"What if I just accept all these feelings I'm having?" I thought. "I'm going to let myself feel like a failure. I'll let myself feel like maybe this *is* the end of my work as a therapist and that it's time to find a different career." This wasn't easy. It felt like voluntarily dropping into a deep well of despair.

Almost immediately, the whole inner dialogue dropped away. To my surprise, I started to have some speculations about what was really going on with that client, which were probably more accurate than the likelihood that I was a failure as a therapist. In fact, it dawned on me that this guy had probably been doing to me—another therapist—the same thing he did to his wife. She probably put him down, and he probably responded by being passive-aggressive in a way that made her feel incompetent and powerless. I'd experienced the very dynamic that had brought him into my office. I saw that I now had the potential to actually be of some benefit if we were to meet again. I realized I might be able to bring some awareness to their relationship dynamics based on our own interaction. On the other side of my willingness to feel all of my feelings—even the awful ones—I'd received helpful insight.

Prior to feeling my feelings, on the other hand, I had been too self-absorbed to sense what had been going on with him. I hadn't wanted to feel the horrible feelings of shame and failure, so it was extremely difficult to use my mind for anything but my own self-aggressive commentary. Unwilling to stay embodied with these vulnerabilities, I'd had no choice but to dissociate—and my method of dissociation, in true neurotic feminine style, was to beat myself up.

The more familiar form of aggression is called *anger* in the Buddhist view or, in Western psychology, the *neurotic masculine*. This style—which happens to be my primary pattern—is to experience anything that feels threatening as coming from outside ourselves, from others, and then to annihilate that threat. In this case, we attack whatever is causing our disturbance, keeping alive the hope that all disturbance comes from others. If we can keep enough distance and not allow others to disturb us, then everything will be okay.

Over the course of my work as a therapist, I've become aware of one of my many biases: I tend to feel less tolerance and kindness when someone presents as a whiny victim than as an arrogant control freak. Obviously, both persons are doing their best to work with their fear/grief/powerlessness. But, because of my own conditioned history, I am less tolerant of the neurotic feminine style than the neurotic masculine style. In other words, I'm less tolerant of feeling *myself* as a victim than I am as a perpetrator. (I'm discussing feelings, here, of course—not behavior.) This lack of tolerance within myself is experienced, in the neurotic masculine style, as if it were a problem in the other person. I find I have the impulse to tell "victim" clients to face reality, be responsible, take better care of themselves, and so on. Obviously, this is what I grew up telling myself, and it may be neither helpful nor kind to the person I'm working with. As with all blind spots, I've had to make an effort to be aware of this conditioned impulse, to investigate what vulnerabilities lie beneath it, and to act consciously for the other's benefit, regardless of my own history.

By externalizing the apparent location of disturbance, the neurotic masculine leads us to blame others when our vulnerabilities surface, thinking they're the source of our discomfort. We might not want to be bothered by people in general, so we may become fiercely self-sufficient and independent. For those of us who hold this style, as Jean-Paul Sartre said, "Hell is other people."

When we are strongly out of balance in this way, we can potentially behave toward others as a perpetrator. Because we're not actually feeling connected or empathic with others—and, in fact, others are seen as the cause of our disturbance—we may feel justified in being outwardly aggressive toward them. This can manifest as a private superiority, relating to others with criticism and judgment, behaving in controlling and intimidating ways, and so on.

The third form of fundamental aggression is *neurotic neutrality*, which in Buddhist terms is called *ignorance* or *ignoring*. In this style, we're trying to get out of our disturbance by spacing out and not being fully present. We unconsciously generate the experience of feeling confused, stuck, or paralyzed. We don't keep agreements and have a hard time making decisions. We might even withdraw from the world, spending our time meditating or doing other spiritual practice, with the unexamined goal of rising above our messy human life—being always calm and accommodating everything. People with this style will often have a floaty type of presence and may let others—or life itself—make their decisions for them. While they may appear to be the opposite of aggressive, there is, in fact, a very self-absorbed quality to their fogginess and an unconscious demand that others take care of the life details that they refuse to be aware of. If they were to gain clarity, they would have to feel disturbances and take responsibilities that they fear they can't handle. So unconsciously, they will do everything they can to remain apparently confused or disengaged.

Neurotic neutrality, or ignoring, is the most difficult of the three forms of fundamental aggression to spontaneously wake up from. There is little drama; everything is sort of okay, even if flat. There's not much contrast. When I work with clients who lead with this style, I tend to become very concrete: What are you feeling in your body right now? When are you going to pay that bill? Is that a yes or no to my question? In doing so, I'm inviting a contrast with their neurotic strategy. The more these clients are willing to feel embodied, to engage in life circumstances, or to talk to their partner, the more they can see their strategy of subtly claiming that they are not really here.

We all experience all three forms of aggression, though each of us tends to lead with one preferred style. In my experience, this aggression is always serving a function. The developmental view helps us see that our self-aggression is not just a relic from the past; it's something we choose to reinvest in, over and over, every moment. We actually maintain a practice, with great effort, of being aggressive toward who we find ourselves to be. If we can become curious about the function this serves, if we invite greater awareness, then we might find that we can work with our issues much more skillfully and kindly. The result is an increased aliveness and satisfaction in our everyday lives and an increased ability to engage compassionately with others.

When we begin investigating our neurotic strategies, we often find that we have a very strong tendency to believe that we ourselves, and our lives, are problematic. Claiming that we are problematic means we don't have to engage with our lives fully, because we aren't "ready yet"—there's something wrong that needs to be fixed first. Before we can be truly intimate, we must heal old relationship wounds. Before we can go for our dreams, we need to resolve our self-doubts. Before we can be fully embodied, we need to lose this extra weight. Once these issues get fixed, then we will actually show up and be fully engaged. But right now, we have a good excuse to not show up. And it turns out that really showing up—being fully present, embodied, openhearted—is often a very intense experience. Having a complaint also gives us an explanation for our difficult experience—and if there's a cause, there should be a solution. "I should be able to have the life without disturbance that I deserve once this unfair problem is cleaned up." It allows us to continue our disengagement indefinitely, since there will always be some unfair problem in our lives.

When I'm working with people, I often suggest a little practice as a homework assignment. For some period of time—a month maybe—I suggest they drop any claim that there's something wrong. No more complaints, resentments, or blame for a whole month, just to see what else is there. Whenever they become aware of a complaint, I suggest they ask themselves: "What am I feeling right now that I don't want to feel?"

The usual response I get from my clients is, "You've got to be kidding! How can I handle my life without complaining? There's so much to complain about!" But when people do experiment with the practice, the results are very interesting. They start to realize that their attitude of complaint—of problem—has been serving a function. It has been allowing them to keep their life at arm's length. It's given them an excuse to postpone living their life in the moment. You could try this experiment yourself and see what happens. ∎

VIEW, PRACTICE, ACTION

So once we recognize our patterns and decide we want to work with them, what's next? How do we effect sustainable and significant change? From my experience, change can happen in many ways: in the context of relationship, individual emotional work, body work, behavioral disciplines, working with our thinking, spiritual path work, spontaneous insight, and so on. Different methods work for different people, but I always suggest approaching change as a practice. As mentioned in the introduction, "practice" can be understood as a conscious participation in what we are already experiencing or doing, usually with a considered intention to intervene in some pattern that we would like to change. By bringing our attention to our immediate experiencing, we are more able to challenge habitual patterns and experiment with new ways of thinking, feeling, and behaving. We then continue to bring conscious participation to these changes to see if they help us move toward our intentions. I find that practice is the most reliable vehicle for change and that the attitude of practice can be applied to most methodologies.

In Buddhism, there's the idea that practice is best understood within the organizing principles of *view, practice, action*. We begin with an understanding, or *view*, of how things are at present and how we would *like* them to be. This larger view usually begins as an intellectual understanding; but with continued experience and refined practices, it can slowly become an experiential view. Whatever view we have—that is, what makes sense to us—suggests the *practices* that may be helpful. For example, if I usually feel pretty resilient but have recently been feeling somewhat depressed, the way I work with this mood will be strongly influenced by my ideas of what might be causing it. If I have a view that depression is evidence of a biological problem, I might try exercise, get more sleep, try a certain diet, or experiment with meds. If my theory is that depression is a response to some underlying vulnerability I'm trying not to feel, I might investigate the possibility that there's anger, powerlessness, or some other feeling that I'm repressing. I may have the idea that I'm confronting an existential crisis in my life and must now be responsible for looking at the stark reality of my human condition. I may think it likely that a number of factors are involved and try a variety of practices. *Action* refers to the results that spontaneously arise out of our practices. We might think about our situation, study, discuss, and experiment. We try some new approach that may help bring our experience into greater alignment with our goals. We experiment with these approaches and pay attention to any results that arise in our life out of these practices. We then modify our view and our practices in a circular process of becoming more and more effective in moving toward our intentions.

In my experience, the practices that carry the greatest potential for transformative change are usually *counterinstinctual*, meaning we don't want to do them, or they go against our basic evolutionary survival responses. To work with our neurotic defense mechanisms, we need the willingness to go into exactly those vulnerabilities—the fear, the rage, the grief, the horrible feelings—that we've spent decades dedicated to not feeling. But who wants to do that? Who wants to go into feeling stupid or abandoned? No one I know wants to sit with the anxiety that they're going to turn into a monster if they let their anger out. To sit with these feelings goes against our instincts. So the *view* part of *view, practice, action* becomes a discussion, an investigation into all of the reasons it might be in our best interest (and perhaps in the interest of others) to do something so apparently stupid as to intentionally have a relationship with our pain and fear.

I invite my clients to consider this view by offering my perspectives and interpretations. Many therapists have a style that encourages the client to do most of the talking, but my style is different. I offer my opinions, and I ask a lot of questions. What is the client doing in a particular situation? Why? What's the benefit? Does the client perhaps have mixed feelings about change? My intention is not for clients to take on what I say as a belief system. But if they can really think about what's in their own personal interest, they may find it's to their benefit to do practices they don't initially want to do and, in fact, may *never* want to do.

Another word for doing practices we don't want to do is *discipline*. That's not a favorite word in our culture, but I find discipline to be essential in addressing these difficult, embedded patterns we all enter adulthood with. The results we can expect are the *action* component. We start to see why we might do these counterinstinctual practices by looking at what the results might be. Why, for example, might I do something so stupid as to practice relating to others from a dependent energy? That is truly counterinstinctual to my neurotic masculine style. Feeling dependent provokes anxiety in me. But if I look at the results—at what might arise in my life if I were willing to feel and behave more like a dependent person—the value might seem worth the effort. I may find myself less critical of others' dependency, less compulsively resentful as a caregiver, more able to receive love and support, and less at war with myself. If it brings good results to do that work, I might continue that practice. If it doesn't, I probably won't.

One way to work with the very powerful momentum of neurotic organization is to investigate our claim that something horrible will happen if our strategy falls away. Let's say you have a history of abandonment. Perhaps you had a self-absorbed, narcissistic, or absent parent. Of course, as a little child, you were incredibly dependent. Since your parent is not initiating adequate connection, you start to specialize in being the one to make the connection with your parent. You must learn to read your parent's mind, to cue off your parent's moods, and to give your parent hugs so that you, yourself, will get a hug. As you grow up, you tend to be the one trying to make your adult relationships work. Subconsciously, you believe that if you're not doing all the work, you will not get the love you want. But, of course, if your specialty were to do 90 percent of the work, your best choice of partner would be somebody who specializes in doing 10 percent of the work. The result is that you once again experience your loved one as not showing up for you. That experience reinforces your style of always being the one doing the connecting. "See? I am always being abandoned. I have to do all the work, or I won't get the connection I want." If you want to work your way out of these neurotic strategies, you must begin to participate consciously in your feelings of being abandoned. As much as you may consciously fight those feelings, the truth is that you already have the subconscious belief that you will always be left. However, if you can gradually learn to tolerate feeling abandoned—which is already how you feel; it's nothing new—you may find it's not going to kill you. It's not going to harm you. It's not giving you cancer. You're not becoming dysfunctional. It is not pleasant, of course. Perhaps it's never going to be pleasant, but it's not actually harmful.

This is an informal technique I often use in my work. I call it the *worst fear technique.* It has to do with identifying the specific feelings and experiences that we have organized our life around trying not to feel and then, intentionally, going into exactly those feelings, especially as immediate, embodied, sensation-level experience, with no interpretation at all. The purpose is to find out for ourselves whether it's true that we will be annihilated if we feel these feelings. What bad thing is going to happen? Why are we continually dropping into this sort of survival-level response, as if some really bad thing would happen to us if we were to feel these feelings? In my experience, going directly into the immediate embodied experience of our fear turns out to be a much faster, more direct way to dissolve neurotic organization than addressing the historic issues that gave rise to that organization in the first place.

STAGES OF DISSOLVING OUR INTERNAL DIVISIONS

This "worst fear" practice is part of a larger view of how to gradually—at a pace that is provocative but not overwhelming—move in the direction of dissolving our neurotic strategies. There seems to be a series of stages we go through as we dissolve these patterns and, by extension, dissolve the feeling of being divided from ourselves and from life. We can also understand these stages as representing our increasing capacity to be unconditionally kind to ourselves.

The **first stage** could be understood as *awareness* or *recognition*. We wake up out of our familiar trance states, in which we have been unconsciously taking whatever we experience as if it's the whole story—whatever's happening, that's the way things are. We become aware that very powerful habitual patterns run a large part of our lives. We begin to see that we've unconsciously maintained these strategies in order to avoid our worst fears—feeling difficult emotions, not being who we think we should be—and we see the price we've been paying for pushing these aspects of ourselves away. So we might say the first stage is awakening out of taking our experience at face value and seeing what's really been going on. Seeing these already-existing patterns can sometimes happen from reading a book or going to a talk, but usually it takes some type of difficult life experience or crisis to force us to look beneath what we have taken for granted.

The **second stage** could be understood as learning to *tolerate* our worst fears. We begin to trust that feeling our fears isn't killing us. We hate the experience and want to get out of it, but as a practice, we hang in there longer and longer. This discipline begins to increase our tolerance for the feelings that our neurotic strategies have allowed us to avoid all this time. Our tolerance for those feelings is generally low, because we don't like the experience of having them. We can strengthen our motivation at this stage by having a better understanding of how our unnecessary suffering is actually being perpetuated. We ask, "What is it that's driving my habitual patterns? What am I trying to not feel?" What we usually find is that our habitual patterns are being maintained and driven by the attempt to not feel our core vulnerabilities—to not experience our worst fears. We see more and more clearly that neurotic strategies are avoidant strategies. Less neurotic suffering requires less avoidance of difficult experiencing. We don't like the experience of feeling abandoned, not feeling good enough, or feeling angry. But these core vulnerabilities are already there. No matter what we do, they are a part of our experience. We're already living with them. We are already acting like an abandoned person or an angry person or a worthless person, because that's how we feel. But because we don't want to acknowledge these feelings, these behaviors are expressed unconsciously and indirectly. We have a choice: do we work with the truth of these vulnerabilities, or do we continue to ignore them? Either way, they're still there. An important distinction: it's not our fears that are perpetuating our avoidant strategies but our efforts to not be aware of these fears. If my *grief* is the problem, then I have to somehow get rid of my grief. If it's my *avoidance* of my grief, however, then the grief can remain, and my work is to train myself to have a relationship with that grief.

Almost all of us begin this investigation with the sense that our difficult feelings are being done *to* us; that they're happening *to* us. "You're making me feel like an abandoned person because you're not paying any attention to me." Or we believe that these feelings are a part of us that's alien, bad, shameful, and to be fixed or gotten rid of. So the first step is realizing that feeling abandoned—or whatever our particular core issue is—is a vulnerability that we've been experiencing for a long time. The second step is to investigate and begin to increase our tolerance for this disturbance.

The **third stage** could be understood as *acceptance*. Here, we're beginning to feel a little less panicky when the core vulnerability comes up. In my case, this stage came when I was finally willing to say, "Yes, I guess I am a dependent person! I can't say it's my favorite experience to feel dependent, but after sitting with it over and over, I can admit that it hasn't killed me." Once I realized I was out of danger, it was easier to practice acceptance of the truth of my experience—which sometimes included feeling dependent.

The choice is whether we're going to approach ourselves with fundamental aggression or with fundamental kindness. If it's the latter, we are able to say *yes*. "I'm going to say yes to this experience of feeling abandoned. I don't like it. It's one of my worst fears. I wish it were gone, but what can I say? If it's there, it's there. I'm going to say yes to it." As we start to say yes to the truth of our experience, at some point we recognize that we're not just saying yes to our fears and vulnerabilities—we're actually saying yes to *ourselves*.

At this point, an energetic or experiential center of gravity begins to shift. Up until now, we've only reluctantly been willing to acknowledge the core vulnerabilities that have been there all along. But at this point, we enter the **fourth stage**, practicing *being kind* to our fears. We move toward our disturbance. As we move with kindness toward what's difficult, the disturbance—which up until this point has felt bigger than us—starts to feel more manageable. When we start going toward our fears, we begin to have the experience that now we are larger than they are. We each have to find our own unique way of bringing this sense of warm engagement to our difficult feelings. It may be a sense of an open heart or of literal warmth or a shift in how we talk with ourselves—whatever works for us. This is a very important shift. We increasingly feel more relaxed, more confident, and more willing to be present with whatever may arise in our experiencing. In developmental language, this is where we can begin to really relate to our difficult experience from our adult capacities, rather than reenact the position of being a child.

After we have stabilized the capacity to be kind toward our disturbance, we practice actually *welcoming* our disturbance. At this **fifth stage**, we say, "I *want* to feel this feeling. I *want* to feel abandoned. I *want* to feel dependent. I *want* to feel my rage." We don't want to feel it because we *like* it; we're never going to *like* these feelings. But we want to feel these feelings because they're *us*. We're starting to get some clarity that all of our experience is us. We are not actually divided against ourselves. We are not problematic persons just because we have aspects of ourselves that are difficult to work with. At this stage, we may find that we actually begin to look for feelings that we don't want to experience. And any avoidant behavior can be an opportunity to look deeper, to reclaim some disowned part of ourselves.

The **sixth stage** is one of *committing completely* to the truth of our experience. We may find that we have still been operating on the subtle hope that if only we do this work—if only we are kind to our disturbance and so forth—our disturbance will go away. Now we invite the feeling that this pain or fear is a completely valid part of our life, of us, and we commit to living with it until we die. To be clear, all of these practices are about relating to our experiencing, not claims about reality or about the future. We can't know what our future experience will be. So these are practices that help us relate to our immediate experience with no withholding, "as if" we will feel them forever. The practice of giving up our fantasy of a life without disturbance—actually committing to a life with disturbance—invites an even deeper level of relaxation and confidence. We are finding less and less to protect and defend. We are addressing our continuing tendency to withhold our full engagement from life until life will conform to our wants and demands.

The **seventh stage**—which is very powerful but very difficult, especially at first—is to practice actually *loving* our worst fears. Loving our vulnerability. I mean "loving" experientially, not intellectually. This is more of a heart practice than an awareness practice. If my client is a parent, I can remind him of what it felt like to bring unconditional love to his young infant. Maybe his infant was smelly and crying, and he couldn't soothe this little being. But he was still practicing unconditional love for that little infant. He held that child; he wasn't throwing the baby away until it felt better. This is how we begin to relate to our own core fears and vulnerabilities.

As we're able and willing to practice unconditional love toward our worst fears, we very quickly start to dissolve the fantasy of any division inside of ourselves. We can love all of us, rather than just the parts that feel "good." This is actually the point where we can stop doing to ourselves what was perhaps done to us. We stop avoiding our fears, because every time we do—every time we dissociate from our immediate embodied experience because it's too disturbing, every time we go into our interpretations, drama, story, or defenses—we abandon ourselves. We abandon our own vulnerability, just as we were perhaps abandoned when our young, intense experiences were too much for our parents to handle. When we love all of ourselves, we stop attacking ourselves, because we now understand that we're attacking our own vulnerability. Perhaps our parents attacked us when they felt overwhelmed and powerless, but we don't need to continue doing this to ourselves now.

The self-abandonment and self-aggression are very painful and perpetuate our history. If, on the other hand, we stay with our vulnerabilities, hold them in love, and feel the embodied sensations that arise, we are training ourselves to be present with whatever arises in our immediate experience.

We can practice these seven stages with the understanding that at each stage, we're actually doing the same practice: we're doing our best to bring unconditional kindness into our familiar, conditioned experiencing. The different stages reflect the degree of resistance we encounter in our efforts to be kind to ourselves. At first, we usually practice being kind to specific difficult feelings or thoughts. But as our discipline becomes established, we find our practice gradually becomes one of waiting, with an already present attitude of kindness, for whatever may arise. The content of our experience comes and goes—our feelings, thoughts, sensations, fantasies—but the attitude of kindness is always there. At this point, we may experience a significant shift in our sense of self: we may realize that what's always there is the activity of kindness. Regardless of whether we like or dislike what arises in our experience, we have *become* most reliably the *activity of kindness*. When we experience this shift, there's almost always an increased sense of relaxation, trust in oneself, openheartedness, and presence. We realize how exhausted we have been, feeling divided against ourselves, struggling for self-improvement or enlightenment. What a relief to be unconditionally kind to the messy, confused human that we are.

Each of these steps further dissolves the claim that we are not workable people. We can no longer maintain that there is something wrong; that there's something dangerous about who we are. As a result, we begin to feel more confident, more embodied, more openhearted, more present, and more engaged. It doesn't mean our issues go away, and we don't suddenly just feel happy all the time. But that's not the point. The point is that we have made significant progress toward dissolving our neurotic avoidant patterns. While these developmental strategies served us well for several decades, now that we're adults, they have begun to have significant diminishing returns. The price tag is no longer worth whatever benefit we were once getting.

As our attention becomes more relaxed and expansive—as we stop being so absorbed with our claim of being problematic—then a very interesting question may arise: what is it that has been aware of this whole process I've been going through? This is the focus of the next chapter—the fruitional view.

2

THE FRUITIONAL VIEW

ANA ARRIVES AT MY OFFICE complaining of a type of low-grade despair. From the outside, her life looks charmed. She's married to a man she loves, and they have been living in relative harmony for nearly twenty-five years. She has three kids—two sons who have left for college and a daughter who's a junior in high school. Her husband is a successful software developer, and they've never wanted for money. They've traveled to Europe many times as a family, and she and her husband just returned from a vacation by themselves in the South Pacific. Ana herself has engaged in quite a variety of spiritual pursuits—meditation retreats and yoga, most prominently. Yet even with all of this bounty, she has a feeling that something vital is missing from her life. She believes there's some aliveness, some depth of experiencing, some openhearted or passionate connection with the world that is not available to her. She's had glimpses of all of these things, so she knows they're possible, but her daily life feels routine and "almost dead."

Lately, as she's been helping her youngest look at colleges, she's begun feeling a deep sense of dread that she might feel this deadness for the rest of her life; that she's destined to live out her days in this same state of feeling sort of okay but not fully alive. At the same time, some somatic symptoms have started showing up that she thinks might be related: trouble sleeping and intense moments of anxiety that she thinks might be mild panic attacks. At first she thought it might be hormonal changes, but she's been to the doctor, who found no medical problems.

At this point, I could start in one of two places. I could begin with a more developmental approach—asking her to tell me about her childhood, for example. For many of us, this Western psychotherapeutic approach, as discussed in the previous chapter, is effective in improving the quality of our lives. Once we recognize the survival strategies we created as children, we can begin to dismantle them and get into a more current and realistic engagement with ourselves and with life. Yet although the developmental view helps us see the patterns we've been perpetuating, to identify and to feel our vulnerabilities, it does not generally offer tools for how to find a sense of freedom in our lives, just as they are, right now. Another approach—the view of Buddhism—offers tools for how to be with *whatever* experiences we're having, regardless of our preferences for or against them. I've found that this unconditional approach, which I call "fruitional," can very quickly invite a sense of freedom and, by extension, a resilient and satisfying state of mind that's not dependent upon fluctuating circumstances.

So rather than looking at her past, I ask Ana to tell me about something that's happening right now. Specifically, I ask her about her objections to feeling dead. Perhaps not surprisingly, she doesn't like that question. Isn't the answer obvious? And why are we talking about the problem, when what she's looking for is a solution? But I gently keep the question alive. What exactly is her objection to participating in the truth of her experience? Like it or not, the reality is that she feels dead. So I invite her to try a variation of the worst fear technique that I mentioned in the last chapter. I suggest she try saying out loud, "I give myself permission to feel dead, off and on, for the rest of my life," and then see what feelings arise. What are the actual sensations in her body when she gives herself permission to feel dead? After a moment of resistance, Ana is able to repeat the sentence and reports feeling a contraction in her gut, some mild nausea, a little panic in her chest, and some constriction in her throat.

So I ask her if, in fact, any of that experience is harming her. Is it damaging? Is it killing her? Is it a problem for her to have this energy in her body, right now? She reports that while it *feels* like it's harmful, she's pretty clear that no actual harm is happening in the moment. I then invite her to consider giving herself permission to just feel these sensations, without inter-preting them or telling a story about them. These sensations *are* her present reality—they're already a part of her life. And in this immediate moment, she's told me that they aren't a problem.

Part of this fruitional approach is to keep inviting the client to drop any interpretation at all of the immediate embodied experi-ence. No interpretation, no attribution of cause, no explanation. We're just investigating what, in fact, is most true in the present moment. Is it true that there is a problem with feeling dead? Or is it more true that the feeling of deadness is a disturbance that does not, upon investigation, prove to be problematic?

In a matter of one or two sessions, Ana begins to report a mixture of deep disappointment that her despair and deadness may prove to be a valid part of her life—as well as a surprising amount of lightness. Like many of my clients, she says it feels like a relief to acknowledge what she's already experiencing. Her feeling of deadness was already true, and she had been fighting it. In fact, she hadn't realized until she stepped into an acceptance practice how much energy she'd spent trying to have something true be *not* true. In a way, it can appear paradoxical. The effect of this fruitional approach—of Ana's accepting her feelings of deadness without trying to change them—is that she feels lighter and more alive already! Without any changes to her external circumstances, she has begun to feel more free.

A BASIC BUDDHIST VIEW

This fruitional view comes out of a tradition that, for 2,500 years, has actively investigated fundamental questions about our basic human experiencing. Buddhism, like other great wisdom traditions, is incredibly complex, with many differing theories and approaches within it. Basic to all Buddhist views, though, is an assertion that our sense of being an independently existing—and therefore alienated—self is the central source of unnecessary suffering and confusion. Common to most Buddhist schools is the idea that we are only living in the present moment. The past profoundly shapes what arises in this moment, and how we engage in this moment profoundly influences what arises in the future. But our *experiencing* is only found in each present moment. And in this view, our *experience* of our current reality is seen as having a more powerful impact on our state of mind than *what* we are experiencing, important as that may be. By training ourselves to bring first our attention and then our awareness to immediate embodied experiencing, we can most accurately and productively discover for ourselves what is most true. As we become able to consciously participate in increasingly deep, moment-by-moment experiencing, we may find less and less evidence of a continuing significant "self." The varieties of techniques we use for this investigation are collectively known as *meditation*. For those interested in a deeper understanding of this tradition, there are now many good books and resources available. ▪

GROUND, PATH, FRUITION

The discussion of a Buddhist psychotherapeutic view is not easy, because it refers to experiences that are difficult to describe with language. The term *fruition* itself is hard to define. Broadly, it refers to the goal or outcome of a particular endeavor—in this case, developing a good state of mind that's independent of external and internal conditions. The fruitional or Buddhist view asserts that the state of mind we're seeking is already present, right now, regardless of circumstance. By contrast to the developmental or Western view, which focuses on releasing old strategies in order to achieve the freedom we seek at some point in the future, the fruitional view takes the position that we're *already* free. Nothing needs to change for us to feel complete and at peace except our own perception of reality.

The term *fruitional*, as I'm using it, comes from the view that a spiritual journey can be described as having ground, path, and fruition. This *ground, path, fruition* model is useful in helping us explore the hypothesis that everything we need in order to have a good state of mind is already present, right now. When we talk about *ground,* we're talking about the place we're starting from. What are we experiencing right now? What's the truth of our experience in this moment? Fruition is where we want to be—our goal, the direction we want to go in, how we would like things to be. The term *path* refers to how we get from here to there. What are the things we might do to head in the direction of the fruition we seek?

Paradoxically, Tibetan Buddhism considers the *ground* and the *fruition* to be essentially the same. What we're going to find out, after walking the path, is that our immediate experience was the whole point—right from the beginning! The whole journey is—and always was—about being present with reality. But something must differentiate the ground, or starting place, from the fruition. When we begin, the ground—our day-to-day reality—is experienced as if it were the whole story. We believe it to be completely real. Not only that, but we embellish it with a running commentary in our mind—"content" that keeps us from noticing the "context" in which our experience is arising. During the *path* phase, we gradually shift our perception so that we no longer focus solely on the content of our experience—our thoughts, feelings, sensations, and ideas. Instead, we begin to recognize the *context* within which these experiences arise—a context that can never be captured and understood conceptually. We call this context "awareness." We still experience the content, but we are simultaneously aware that it's not the whole story; it does not completely represent reality.

So you might say that the *ground* is our present-moment experience *without* awareness. The *fruition* is that very same experience *with* awareness. The *path* creates the conditions for this shift of perception to arise. We meditate, we do different spiritual and psychological practices, we study, and we think about things. And in the process, something shifts in our perception. It's as if we're walking down the street past a house with a big picture window, and the sun is shining directly on the glass. It appears opaque; we can't see into the house. All we see is the sun shining back at us. Yet if we walk another ten feet, the angle of the light changes. The glass becomes transparent, and all of a sudden we can see into the house. The glass hasn't changed. The sun hasn't changed. *We* haven't changed. It's only our *perspective* that has shifted. In that same way, this whole approach is not about improving the content of our experience. Instead, it's about creating a shift in how we relate to the experiences we are having at any moment.

PRACTICING AWARENESS

The title of this section is actually misleading. You can't use awareness as a practice, because awareness is always already there. We are simply out of conscious participation with it most of the time. So any so-called awareness practice—including Buddhist meditation—is actually a practice of inviting more conscious participation in the awareness that already exists. When we look back from the fruitional perspective, we see that these practices were never going to "cause" anything to happen. The fruition—awareness—was already there, all the time. These practices weren't really necessary. Yet at the same time, we understand why we do them. They somehow create an environment in which a shift of perception, an increasing capacity to be *aware of awareness,* is more likely to arise.

Most spiritual path work involves practices that are intended to do exactly this: to invite more conscious participation with what is already true. The simplest and perhaps most popular of those practices is basic breathing meditation.

Here's a simple version of a meditation practice. If you like, you may set a timer so you know how long you will be practicing. I suggest starting with five minutes if you are a beginner. Over time, you may want to increase your practice to fifteen, twenty, or thirty minutes.

Find a quiet place with minimal distraction.

Sit down in whatever posture feels upright, awake, and comfortable enough to not call attention to any bodily tension or pain.

Begin by paying attention to your breathing, without commentary. Once you feel settled, attend to any experiencing that arises. Maintain a sense of open curiosity and awareness.

If you become fascinated with some drama or dialogue, return to your breathing as a way to return to embodied immediacy.

Practice with a sense of nothing to accomplish, only appreciating your irresolvable and unending stream of experiencing. ▪

The metaphor of the sun shining on the window can help us understand the shift from ground to fruition. At first, our perception of reality has an opaqueness or solidity to it. We have a sense that the world is reflecting back something about our "self." We unconsciously relate to almost everything in terms of how it might affect us—as positive, negative, or neutral. This constant self-referral feeds an ongoing drama about how we're doing, whether we'll get what we want, whether we're safe, and so on. This chronic self-absorption supports the sense of being a significant self, the center of the universe, a self we must protect. From the fruitional perspective, however, our perspective has changed. Now we see through the apparent solidity; we're aware of a larger context. Our attention goes out, but it doesn't bounce back to us. In this way, fruition is the same experience as ground, but within the environment of and as the expression of awareness. We may investigate just what this mysterious "reality" is for the rest of our lives, but we can do so without the imposition of a subtle layer of self-referential interpretation.

THE NATURE OF AWARENESS

The experience of awareness cannot be completely captured or defined, so it is usually talked about in metaphor. One common simile is that awareness is like space. It's not space, but it's *like* space. More precisely, our *experience* of awareness is like our *experience* of space. Space accommodates everything. Its nature is openness without conditions. Space can accommodate an airplane, a butterfly, pollution, clouds, the earth, anything. That said, we can never actually get a hold of space itself. Another common image would be that awareness is like the sun. It's constant, and it shines on everything without bias. The sun's energy shines on a little baby or on a murderer. It goes out into empty space without any agenda. Similarly, awareness is said to be *without bias*. We're just as aware of feeling happy as we are of feeling sad; we're just as aware of being healthy as we are of dying. Awareness doesn't have preferences. It's always there, regardless.

Awareness could also be considered to be like light. We're never going to experience light directly; we only experience it as it interacts with matter. Imagine a stained glass window, for example. The light shining through the window animates and enlivens the display. The display itself is visible—we can see all the colors—but we cannot define or capture the light. In the same way, awareness enlivens the display of the self. We can try everything to protect that self or give it the best possible quality of life, but we are still talking about the display of our experience, not awareness itself. Gravity is the same way. We'll never be able to get a hold of it; we can only know it through the experience of it pulling us downward. Likewise, we'll never experience our breath directly. We experience our breath through changes in temperature, the sensation of our chest expanding, the rush of something against our skin. But we can never hold onto the breath itself. A lot of meditation practices talk about following your breath, but in truth we can only follow the interaction of this ungraspable experience as it interacts with our senses. Similarly, the only way we can really *talk* about awareness is by referring to how we are experiencing it through our sensations, feelings, thoughts.

From a Buddhist view, awareness is always present, even if we can't grasp it completely. It's nothing we achieve or create or attain—it's always there. Awareness is said to be what is most fundamental to our experiencing, a nonconceptual knowing. We will never find anything more basic, more intimate, in every moment of our engagement with life. If we were to ask ourselves off and on throughout the day, "What am I aware of experiencing right now?" we would find an ever-changing display of sensations, feelings, thoughts, and fantasies. But what will always be present is our awareness of this display. Moreover, the only thing that turns out to be aware of awareness is *awareness itself.* Awareness is "self-aware," though we usually approach this understanding by first trying to make awareness an object to be grasped. That sounds a little abstract, but it may be that there's nothing definitive that can be said about it. Still, those who begin to experience their lives within the context of awareness report an increasing sense of relaxation, confidence, clarity, humor, and openheartedness. There seems to be a very consistent report about the effect of experiencing our thoughts, feelings, sensations, and so forth in the larger environment of awareness, even if we can never get a hold of that experience. It can be experienced; it just can't be captured or adequately described.

So in approaching the fruitional view, a paradox arises. We have the experience that we're "doing something"—we're beginning to practice living in the greater context of awareness. But more and more, we start to understand that what we are "doing" is only happening in the present moment. It's not designed to create anything in the future. We're not trying to "achieve" enlightenment or wakefulness; it's already here. Our work, then, becomes holding the intention to relax, over and over again, into what is already present. This experience can be talked about, but it's difficult to truly convey.

So how does awareness relate to the freedom we're discussing in this book? From the fruitional perspective, every experience—however depressed or however joyful—arises in a larger environment of awareness. When viewed from the perspective of awareness, our preferences fall away. We no longer have a bias toward joy and away from depression. Regardless of circumstances, our experience is one of freedom. Resting in awareness is resting in a freedom that is not dependent on any conditions. We begin to see that, in the present moment, nothing is incomplete. There's no deficit; there's nothing missing. Everything is just what it is, with no comparisons possible until we introduce interpretations. Whatever the moment brings is workable, because our state of mind is always workable. As Trungpa Rinpoche said, "There's no such thing as an underdeveloped moment."

WHAT IS FREEDOM?

In the West, we tend to think of freedom as an absence of limitations. In our culture, we may feel limited by our circumstances—our job, relationship, health, or financial situation. So we feel free when we get some time off from work and can go on a vacation or when we have plenty of money. When we feel healthy and our relationship doesn't feel like a burden, we feel free. When we can have as ideal a life as possible, one that is perfectly free of limitations, when we can do whatever we want whenever we want, then—we think—we'll be free.

Upon further examination, however, we find that this absence of limitations can only go so far. As embodied beings, we are always living a life of limitations. We have our bodies and their relative levels of health. We have our physical needs to sleep and eat. We are all aging and heading toward death. We have to deal with our physical and social environments. We have to deal with other people. For every capacity we have, there are thousands of things we can't do. We're never going to be without limitations.

Strangely enough, the Buddhist idea of freedom is completely the opposite—a more profound experience of freedom arises from an unconditional commitment to the truth of our experience, and our relative experience is basically a collection of limitations. So, rather than arranging our lives to have as few limitations as possible, we unconditionally commit to being embodied with, and being kind toward, whatever it is we experience. We intentionally explore the claustrophobia of our profoundly limited human lives. As we discover that this is not a problem, we start to relax our struggle with reality. We stop complaining about reality and even commit to it unconditionally, without reservations. We agree to stay present with whatever is happening—good, bad, or otherwise—to make space for all of it without bias.

We may begin to feel more relaxed, present, and confident, and we may gradually start to dissolve our self-absorption. When we're struggling with life, trying to accomplish and avoid things in order to feel free, our attention tends to become very self-referential. When we feel that our survival is threatened, our awareness tends to contract. It's a biological response. It's very difficult to look at the flowers when we're running from a bear. But as we become less and less preoccupied with resisting our limitations, less self-absorbed, our awareness relaxes and spontaneously becomes more expansive. Eventually it may even occur to us to ask, "*What* is aware of all this that I'm experiencing?"

THE LARGER CONTEXT OF AWARENESS

The fruitional approach is about realizing, over and over again, that everything arising in our experience is inseparable from awareness. Over and over, we experience the simultaneity of awareness with that which we think, feel, and sense. Awareness, as I've mentioned, has no bias. It's simply open to whatever happens. As it stands, however, most of us are trying to put our thoughts, feelings, and experiences into a context of positivity. Of course, that's very intelligent, as most of us prefer positive feelings and experiences to negative ones. But it's not sustainable, given the way life works. What's more, we begin to draw meaning from whether we can keep our life in a positive context. If I feel attractive, rich, and secure, I start to think, "I must be doing something right. I'm a good person. I'm okay. My life is going well." Of course, the converse could also be true: "Oh, I'm feeling depressed. I just got a divorce. I'm not feeling very healthy. There must be something wrong with me."

This bias toward positive emotions, feelings, and experiences is pervasive in Western culture, perhaps especially in America.

Many people come to therapy or spiritual work with the unexamined goal of having a life free of disturbance—a "happy" life. Western therapy, as a historical, developmental view, tends to work with the idea that we have wounds or traumas that need to be healed before our lives can be positive. We've inherited issues from our parents and the experiences of our childhood that have to be cleared up before we can be free of negative feelings. Because we are identified with these circumstances, we believe that we need to improve them. Thus, we look for unconscious patterns that seem to be causing negative emotions and experiences, and we investigate them until they begin to loosen up. And we do, in fact, start to feel better, because some of the outdated limitations we've been living with have been removed. The "display" of our life is improved.

But from the Buddhist point of view, self-improvement is never going to give rise to freedom. It's only going to give rise to an improved display of our experiencing. Improvement can, in itself, be very valuable. (In chapter 3, we talk about how this is helpful, even from a fruitional point of view.) Given the choice between satisfaction and dissatisfaction, good relationships and difficult ones, health and illness, most of us would certainly choose the more positive experiences. But a positive display cannot be continually sustained, since life is incredibly complex, always changing, and not under our control. The content of our lives will sometimes be positive, sometimes negative. From the Buddhist point of view, freedom arises from a profound disidentification with any content—good or bad. When our circumstances and experiences are held in the context of open awareness, we are not captured or identified with them. We are no longer "inside" the content; rather, we are "witnessing" it within the context of awareness. With that shift in perception, we begin to have a choice about how to relate to our experience.

The current display is revealed not to be the whole story; in fact, it's not even "about us." We talk about this shift as a move toward placing all of our experience in the larger context of awareness.

From the developmental view, the larger context in which our "unworkable" experiencing is placed is called our *unconscious*—what we have repressed or disowned. Even though we do our best to have a positive sense of self, that project is happening within the larger context or environment of what we're *trying not to feel*. As discussed previously, our very efforts to not feel certain difficult feelings unfortunately create the sense that these feelings are not workable and somehow larger than us. Most of us experience a basic split between conscious content and unconscious content, and the work of the developmental approach is to bring that which is unconscious into consciousness.

From the fruitional view, on the other hand, it doesn't really matter whether the content of our experience is conscious or unconscious. Again, there is an attitude of nonbias. We're not trying to bring everything that has been repressed into consciousness. We accept that we will always be a mystery to ourselves. All of our experiencing—our thoughts, feeling, fears—is held in the context of awareness, regardless of whether it's conscious or unconscious. The work, from a fruitional point of view, is to gradually dissolve the apparent split between the content of our experience and the environment of awareness, whereas the work of the developmental view is to gradually dissolve the apparent split between the conscious and the unconscious.

Think about going to the movies. The whole setup encourages us to be captured immediately. Within seconds, we're captured by the display on the screen. If it's a happy movie, we laugh; if it's a sad movie, we cry. If that's all that we're aware of, we don't really have much choice. However, if we were to take that same movie and project it on a screen in the middle of an open field in broad daylight, we would be much less likely to get captured. If there's a big explosion or a love scene, perhaps we'll pay attention for a little bit, but then our attention will get drawn elsewhere. We see dogs playing, we feel the grass beneath our feet, we hear a plane going overhead. Everything in the environment is so much more real, vast, and vivid than what's on the movie screen that we don't get so fascinated by it as easily. The movie is still there, but we're not bound by it. Our attention is free to roam beyond the film's storyline, because the context has become so much bigger than the dark theater. From this point of view, we can consider that freedom may not actually come from improving the story that's playing on the screen. In fact, it might come from placing whatever that story is, in all of its complexity, in a larger environment of awareness. Perhaps we don't have to improve the story we tell about ourselves, about life, in order to experience freedom.

IMMEDIACY AND THE CONTINUITY OF SELF

Another way to approach this somewhat abstract language of awareness or freedom is to talk about the practice of immediacy. Most of us generate a state of mind that appears to be continuous. This state of mind seems to be about us, and it seems really significant. We create this continuous state of mind by linking moments of experience together as if they were related to one another. For example, perhaps I am having a conversation with a colleague, and she asks me a question. I answer it, but my answer comes out awkwardly. The next moment, I feel some embarrassment arise. The next moment, I'm linking the experience of embarrassment to having said something awkward. The next moment, I am judging myself for having done that, and the moment after that, I think, "Well, maybe *she* was to blame for having asked that question in the first place." This linkage of experience after experience, moment after moment, hundreds or thousands of times a day, every day for decades, generates a sense of continuity. We add a constant self-referential commentary to the linkage, and soon we actually think that there is an "us."

To use a silly analogy, let's say we have a doughnut. We think we actually see a hole. There's no hole, really; there's just space. But because it's surrounded by all this doughnut, we actually *experience* a hole. In a similar way, if we point toward our self over and over again, sooner or later we just take for granted that there is a self there. How many of us believed in Santa Claus when we were young? There were stories and pictures, we wrote letters and sang songs about Santa, we saw Santa's helpers in the stores. All of these references to Santa Claus created a vivid experience, which, of course, we took to be true. Santa wasn't a theory. He seemed to be a real person with whom we had an emotional relationship. But at some point, perhaps with some disappointment, we discovered that a vivid appearance does not mean that something actually exists. Maybe our belief in our *self* will turn out to be just as reliable as our belief in Santa. Maybe this "obviously real" self is actually maintained through linking our continual self-referential commentaries and is supported by our pervasive social agreements about the reality and significance of this *self.* We pay attention to aspects of our experience that seem to be relevant to our self. We engage the world with all sorts of dramas about our self. We have issues with our self-worth or lack thereof, and we spend time trying to heal those issues. We take all of this effort as a type of self-evident proof of having a solid, significant, continuing self. From a Buddhist point of view, however, this is fantasy. There's the appearance of a self, but the fantasy that it's an objectively existing, solid, and therefore alienated self gives rise to unnecessary suffering and confusion in our lives.

From the fruitional point of view, one powerful practice we can explore is that of immediacy. The practice is simple: Whenever it occurs to us, we bring our attention into our immediate experience. We notice what is actually going on right now—what's most fundamentally true in this moment. One of the first things we encounter in this practice is that we're very rarely experiencing reality in a simple and direct way. Instead, we're constantly making interpretations about what we are experiencing; we're thinking about it. So we might be saying, "I'm stressed out." But what does that really mean? A complaint like "stressed out" is an umbrella interpretation that we give to a series of different feelings. We might be feeling overwhelmed, afraid of failure, or anxious. As we investigate our moment-by-moment experience, however, what we discover is that underneath our interpretations are feelings. Even one step deeper than our feelings, we find our sensations—what we're actually feeling in our bodies. We become aware that we are feeling warm or cool, relaxed or contracted, heavy or bubbly, and so on. And if we want to go a layer deeper still, we might find that underneath our sensations is an experience of intense energy or aliveness that is actually very difficult to stay with.

When we practice immediacy, we start to challenge and dissolve the apparent link between each moment of our experience. In other words, we see how our mind works—how we have an experience, immediately interpret it, and then create a story about ourselves based on that interpretation. The practice of immediacy allows our experience to simply arise, without interpretation. We create an environment of space or openness—no commentary, no discussion. The result is that it becomes harder and harder for us to maintain a continuous story about who we are.

When I'm discussing this idea in the classroom, I sometimes demonstrate it using a set of dominoes. I set up a row of dominoes on the floor and then have a student tip over the first one. The rest of the dominoes follow suit, and the display starts to look like one continuous event—a wave passing across the floor. Of course, the visual effect is misleading. There are fifty or a hundred individual events happening when a row of dominoes goes over. But they are happening so close to one another, in such rapid succession, that to the eye, it appears as one continuous event.

This is how the mind works as well. We have a single experience, then another, then another—but they happen so fast, we start to believe that each of these moments is connected to the next. Like the dominoes, our thoughts actually do resemble a single, unified cascade. It appears that each moment of experience is necessarily connected to the next.

I then take the dominoes and set them up again—in the same pattern, same organization—but I place them several inches apart. When I knock over the first domino, it just falls on the floor; it doesn't reach the next domino. It happens in space. At that moment, it's clear that what appeared to be a linkage or causation between the dominoes was actually just a lack of space. The dominoes were simply close enough together that they touched one another.

In a similar way, we all understand that when watching a movie, we're really just seeing a rapid succession of images, not something that's actually alive and in motion. But given the way the brain works, and given our unexamined wish to be captured by the appearance, we experience this display as if it were reality. If we slow the movie down, however, we just see frame followed by frame, which is not so entertaining.

Upon investigation, the same is true of our thoughts. The apparent continuity of our experience arises from too close a connection between one moment and the next. The connection is made mostly through our interpretations and emotional reactions, most of which are based on sensations we feel in our bodies. When we have sensations that we associate with feeling very vulnerable or disturbed, we feel threatened and usually dissociate from our embodied experience within a fraction of a moment. Without even thinking about it, we abandon our own immediate experience and jump into interpretations. In our Western culture, at least, interpretation is the preferred escape from immediacy. But what's waiting for us in our interpretations is our conditioned history. So we interpret our immediate experience based on our historic conditioning, which once again provides endless opportunities to link a story together.

For example, say there's a moment in which I drop a glass on the kitchen floor. That experience is entirely unique and complete in itself, with a series of occurrences taking place in rapid succession. Glass in hand, glass out of hand, gasp of surprise, sound of glass shattering—something like that. If I were in the practice of immediacy, I might then experience myself feeling upset, walking carefully to the broom closet, reaching for the broom, and sweeping up the broken glass. But that's pretty rarely what happens. More likely I'll hear the glass breaking, and in the next moment, I'll have some emotional reaction: some shock, some fear, some anger toward myself or—given my style—toward my wife for choosing such slippery glasses. (Emotional reactivity is rarely reasonable.) I could, of course, let that emotional response be complete in itself, without linking it to the previous moment or the next moment. Most of us, however, will interpret the disturbance as if it were about our having dropped the glass. We'll start telling a story: "Oh, I'm a clumsy person." Or, "Gosh, why did she buy these new glasses? They're very hard to hold onto." We could go on and on, endlessly linking our immediate experiences with familiar stories.

The problem with this "domino effect" of our thought process is that when we are making these interpretations, we necessarily dissociate from the immediacy of the present. We take the immediate experience we're having, and we flip through our memory file to find a similar experience from the past. Then we project our past experience onto the present moment, using it to solidify a story. In order to carry a concept across time and link it to a previous experience in this way, we have to make it very generic. If we see a tree, and we want to relate it to another tree, both trees must be reduced to their most generic elements. We see trunk, branches, and leaves—then we can link this particular living organism to previous organisms we've seen that have those same elements. But we lose the nuance of this particular tree, the one outside our window right now. The particular color and shape of the leaves, the way the sun is shining through the branches and hitting the grass below. No moment can be truly unique if we're constantly linking it to previous moments.

The same goes for the sense of self. If "me" is a representation that we carry over time, all of us have to create a generic "me." The self must be a very generalized, down-to-the-lowest-common-denominator sense of self, in order to carry it over time. We may be feeling a sense of heaviness in our chest, a sense of loss or longing. Tears may be welling up in our eyes. Suddenly we take this set of experiences and make an interpretation: "I am sad." Now we've created a story that makes sense of the heaviness, the sense of loss, and the tears. We can point toward past moments when these elements were in place and we interpreted them as sadness; so, we make a generic connection. We don't question its validity; it appears so logical, we don't even have to think about it. Yet what's lost is unique awareness of this moment—*these* tears, *this* sense of heaviness. When we automatically connect this moment to a past moment, we miss out on the unique experience of the present.

If, on the other hand, we experience a moment in its rich uniqueness, it's very difficult to link that moment to the next moment in a familiar way. One of the effects of meditation practice is to start to place moments of experience in an environment of greater space and awareness. When we do, we find that it is harder and harder to completely believe in the stories we have about our experience. For example, it will be hard for Ana to continue her story of despair if she discovers that, moment by moment, in the immediate now, she feels alive instead of dead. So if we really want to challenge our story about ourselves—part of which may be rooted in the historic conditioning we've uncovered through developmental psychotherapeutic work—we practice immediacy. We bring our attention into every moment of experience, without telling ourselves what it's about. We simply experience it for what it is, without interpretation.

IMMEDIACY AND PREFERENCE

The practice of immediacy invites an investigation into the nature of awareness. It clears away some of the confusion caused by our stories and helps us tolerate the possibility that our experience is not "about us." Sometimes when I'm working with people, I suggest that perhaps even their emotions are not about them.

Consider the possibility that our emotions are sort of like the weather. The weather happens. We have to deal with it, because it affects us, but it's not *about* us. For example, say you walk outside and the sun is shining and the sky is blue and there is a pleasant breeze. You might say, "Oh, it's a beautiful day!" But that doesn't mean that the day has an inherent quality of beauty.

Just because it reflects our preferences doesn't mean that there is a fundamental beauty to the scene. Someone who enjoys skiing, for example, might think it's disappointing that the sky is not cloudy and snow is not falling. Our announcement that the day is beautiful does not mean that it is so; it just means we like the weather that day. Yet in our own minds, we've made the weather about us—about our preferences. In the same way, our emotions are something we have to deal with, because they affect us, but perhaps they are not *about* us, either.

Yet we're always projecting our preferences onto our experience and assuming our interpretations are a reliable measure of what's really going on. "What a great meal!" "What a lousy driver!" We're confusing external reality with our internal reactions, and we're behaving as if our experience actually has something to do with *us*. We're always trying to have more experiences that we like and to get rid of experiences that we don't like, which in classic Buddhist philosophy is a primary cause of unnecessary suffering.

As we start to practice embodiment and kindness toward everything that arises—as we practice immediacy—we find less and less and less evidence that any of our experience is *about* us. That begins to help us with practicing an attitude of nonbias. We are willing to feel happy. We are willing to feel sad. We are willing to be healthy. We are willing to be dying, if that's what's happening.

We start to boycott, or go beneath, the automatic unconscious addition of preferences to our experience. It doesn't make our experience suddenly happy. It just means that we are less confused. From the fruitional practice viewpoint, it's also the first step toward the experience of freedom. It paves the way for us to ask, "If I don't have a solid sense of self, then what is it that's aware of this display? What's the nature of awareness?" This is an experiential investigation more than an intellectual one. As we train ourselves to stay more and more in our immediate experience, without interpretations, without trying to hang on or push away, we actually become more capable of investigating our experience. Our perception seems to be less loaded with the survival-level dramas that began when we were in childhood. If our experience is about us and our preferences, then we always need to be vigilant. If the quality of our life, even our survival, is dependent upon always-changing life circumstances, then it's smart to always be on guard, always alternating between hope and fear. If, on the other hand, we relate to the display of our experiencing as having its own life, it becomes safer to investigate it with a sense of objective curiosity. When we investigate our experience from the position of immediacy—without interpretations—we find something interesting. Our experience continues to be very vivid in its appearance, but we find *no essential nature, no independent existence,* to that appearance.

This is a difficult concept to understand; when I'm offering this material to clients, I try to suggest some analogies. Imagine swinging a sparkler at night. We see a continuous ring of light, yes? It would be silly to say we don't see a ring of light, because we do. Because of retinal retention and the way our minds organize experience, the display appears to be a continuous ring of light. Upon investigation, however, we're not going to find a ring of light at all. Instead, we find a single point of light in constant repetitive motion. So there's a vivid appearance, but we can find no essential nature to that ring. The same goes for a rainbow. If we see a rainbow, it would be silly to say we don't see a rainbow. Upon investigation, however, we aren't going to *find* a rainbow. The display is all relational. There's no rainbow existing by itself up in the sky; rather, its appearance has to do with the way the sun's rays bounce around inside raindrops and with the angle of the observer. If we look at this rainbow and then face the other way, there isn't a rainbow still up in the sky waiting for us. If we spin a color wheel, we're going to see white. If it slows down, however, we're not going to see white anywhere on that wheel—we're going to see the primary colors. If we look at a photograph, we're going to see a coherent image; but upon investigation, we're just going to find pixels. It's the way they're arranged on the paper and the way our eyes and brains work that give us the perception that there is an image.

To take it another step, say there's a table sitting right in front of you. You might look at it and say, "Well, *that* seems pretty real. That's not a rainbow or a ring of light. It's a table. It's solid wood." But unfortunately for the human sense of pride, it turns out that our capacity for sensory experience is not the gold standard for the universe. It's not the only criteria for reality! Imagine if you were an aware photon, flying through space. Such an aware photon would not find a table in front of it; it would only find a slightly more dense cloud of energy.

I offer these analogies to help with an intellectual understanding of a very basic Buddhist concept—the simultaneity of appearance and emptiness. This view asserts that we are always going to experience vivid appearances, but upon investigation, we will never find an essential nature to any of those appearances. So what about the *observer* of all of this experience? Well, it's the same thing. There's a vivid appearance of self, a sense of agency. There's an identification with "me" and an experience of that "me" being located within a separate and solid physical body. It would be silly to try to get rid of this sense of self. And yet upon investigation, we may never find any solid, continual entity we can call a self. Instead, we appreciate and work with the appearance of self, while we gradually stop taking this appearance as if it were evidence of an actually existing self. Just as we gradually learn to appreciate the rainbow without trying to possess it or protect it from fading away, we might learn to appreciate this experience of self without needing to protect and improve it.

AWARENESS AND PERSONAL IDENTITY

The more we allow experience to be just as it is, the more we find that all experience tends to arise (from no one knows where—it's really sort of mysterious), remain for a period of time, and then dissolve. Appearance arises and then falls apart, moment by moment. This cycle is always happening, and there is no need to control or manage it. This brings up another Buddhist concept, which is that experience is self-liberating. That is to say, we don't have to *do* anything about our experience; it will take care of itself. This does not mean that we shouldn't work to improve our experience, but that we might first pause and see if we *must* improve it. When we discover the confidence that whatever we are experiencing is workable, as it is, we engage from *choice*. When we feel we must first improve our experience in order for it to be acceptable, however, we engage from *compulsivity*. Often, when we intervene and try to manage our experience—interpreting it, suppressing or hanging on to aspects of it, creating stories about it—that experience seems to then appear frozen. As the slogan goes, "What we resist, persists." The result is that we then seem to have an ongoing chronic condition to work with.

We saw this process in the achievement of neurotic organization as young children. Realistically, we could not tolerate and work with certain intense feelings. So we learned to manage our disturbance by continually driving these experiences out of our conscious awareness. In support of this repressive function, we usually then added dramas about why these particular feelings are bad, shameful, dangerous. While this is a necessary and healthy developmental accomplishment, it results in a chronic sense of being divided against oneself, of being a problematic person. Most of us seem to have an intuition that moving in the direction of increasing awareness is going to be disturbing. It turns out that awareness, in its unconditionally open nature, provides absolutely no support for personal identity. So, as we move toward immediacy—toward considering that all of our experience will take care of itself, that we don't have to make ourselves a project, that nothing is missing, that we might as well commit to working with things as we experience them—we find less and less material to support our familiar dramas. These familiar dramas, like those we talked about in the previous chapter, are very understandable, given our history. They had origins in our childhood, and in many cases, they served our health and our survival. But as adults, they reinforce the idea that there is some type of problem or issue with who we are or with our immediate circumstances. Many of my clients, like Darren and Ana, become aware that these familiar dramas—these chronic reactions—are causing more harm than good. At this point, I suggest that they investigate developing a commitment to their immediate experience rather than to their interpretations of their immediate experience.

From the fruitional view, the question is not how our history has shaped our identity dramas, but how we manage to perpetuate patterns of experiencing that used to be relevant but now are no longer necessary or useful. Because we are only living in each present moment, we must re-create these patterns over and over, even as our current adult experience provides little evidence that they are valid. To do so takes incredible effort and creativity. As we've discussed, most of us are unconsciously and continually looking for evidence that will justify these out-of-date survival strategies. The evidence we create and selectively attend to is used to prove that certain feelings will harm us if consciously acknowledged. We don't realize that it's our refusal to experience these difficult feelings that gives them the appearance of threat and unworkability.

As with Ana, I invite my clients to investigate whether there's actually any sort of problem in being who they already are. I have them turn their attention toward their experience at the level of sensation, beneath the interpretations. You may remember that I suggested Ana give herself permission, out loud, to feel dead—on and off for the rest of her life—while noticing what came up in her body. Then I suggested she ask herself whether those sensations were truly a problem. Was she really going to die from them? The answer, of course, was no. Slowly, over time, this practice of investigating our experience—and discovering that there is no problem in the present moment—helps dissolve (or at least begin to unwind) the neurotic patterns that we carry from childhood.

I will be honest: this process is usually anxiety provoking. We find that we have very contradictory feelings about dissolving our chronic patterns, even if we believe they are causing us suffering. Most people, it turns out, are actually heavily invested in their problems. From the developmental point of view, we understood this investment as arising from our best efforts to protect and take care of ourselves—efforts that are now out of date. From a fruitional point of view, on the other hand, we start to consider our "problems" as a form of entertainment. A lot of people don't like that idea, of course! It contradicts their belief that their problems are solid, significant, real, and involuntary (which unconsciously supports the sense of being a solid, significant, real victim of one's problems). They may also find it insulting to suggest that they are fascinated—entertained—by negativity and drama. Yet let's face it, that's exactly why we go to the movies. Who's going to pay ten dollars to watch two hours of peace and well-being? It's boring; most of us would walk out of the theater. What we pay money for are problems: romantic problems, financial problems, problems only James Bond can solve. *That's* what entertains us. It captures us, and we want to get captured. But most people don't consider the possibility that their own dramas—their stories of abandonment, of dependency, of the quest for spiritual enlightenment—are, in a way, pure entertainment. In truth, we have a fascination with getting captured by a story, and the best way to get captured is to claim that our survival is at risk. That's what is *most* capturing, actually. So in my work, I'm always—and I mean, many times a day—hearing people talk about their experience in a way that implies, "If I had to feel this or that feeling or if this happened in my life, I would die. Something horrible would happen! This is a survival-level issue. This is really, really important. I have to fix this issue. I have to get clear about it!" We really don't like the idea that maybe we're entertaining ourselves with the claim that there's a problem. But right now, in the immediate moment, where is this supposed problem?

Of course, this doesn't mean that we shouldn't address our real-life circumstances intelligently. We should pay our bills, be kind to our kids and our partners, and so on. Our life will work better if we do. These are practical issues. But in the immediate moment, where's the threat to our survival, the evidence about our worth as a person? Where's anything that's missing? But if there's no problem, then there's no entertainment. In fact, the loss of entertainment is one of the effects of meditation. Trungpa Rinpoche said that often after some initial period of very dramatic, intense, disturbing experience, meditators hit a stage where they actually become bored with drama. It's so repetitive! When we hit this stage, we start to see that the same movie has been playing over and over inside our heads for years. Maybe it's a good, exciting movie, but we've seen it so many times! It's been playing over and over forever, but it wasn't until we sat down to meditate that we became aware of it.

Trungpa said this phase of meditation could be called "hot boredom," when we no longer have a lot of drama arise, but we're sort of antsy. We want to get out of there. We want the bell to ring and the meditation session to end. If we hang in there, though, we might enter an experience of "cool boredom." In that phase, we're not so antsy. Meditation is sort of boring—it's not that interesting—but we can do it. We've committed to the practice, but it feels flat and not so engaging. If we can hang in there still longer, it's possible that we may start to experience every moment as inherently interesting. We start to realize that each moment is full of aliveness. Life is not interesting because it's about us; rather, it's interesting precisely because it's *not* about us. It's just interesting of its own accord. As we're able to allow every moment to arise fresh, out of mystery, it's impossible to feel bored.

This process may sound good, but it's quite threatening to our status quo. To use the movie example again, if we're watching a movie and it becomes very, very boring, we're in danger of waking up out of the trance state we just paid money to be put into. If a movie has boring aspects, it might be considered an "art" movie, rather than an "entertainment" movie. Some people like those movies, but most of us don't want to feel bored as entertainment. We want problems, we want drama, we want challenges, we want risks. If we extrapolate this to our everyday lives, we can see how much of a threat it might be to allow boredom to enter. If we get bored enough, we just might wake up to the truth of our experience—which is that there is no solid sense of self, that there is nothing to hold onto.

Another analogy I like is to imagine that in our natural state, we are all being swept along in the river of life, a stream of experiencing, moment by moment. We feel as if we're not in control, which is true. We can't really determine the pace or the direction of our experience. This causes a certain level of anxiety, which naturally we want to get away from. So we imagine that we can dam up the river. We invest in life circumstances and interpretations of our experience that help us avoid the reality of uncertainty and change. We're in a little calm pool now. But as we gradually take our sense of safety for granted, we start to feel like there's a lack of aliveness. We feel stagnant. So what do we do? We start a drama to shake things up. One such drama I see frequently is, "Should I have more aliveness in my life, or should I have more security in my life?" We forget that the safe harbor we created is, itself, hallucinatory. We're actually still in the river, floating downstream. We're still fully alive in every fresh moment, making it up as we go. But we've got ourselves in a hallucinatory sort of trance state, where we're pretending that we're in this dilemma between aliveness and security.

Meanwhile, we're still in the river, and we're not even consciously present. At any moment, we could bang our head on a rock. We could actually get in trouble, because we're not committed to just being present. So even though there is an entertaining quality to taking all of our experience very seriously—as if it were about us, as if there were always some vague but important survival-level drama at stake—we will probably deal with our lives more accurately by remaining connected to what's true. We can choose to practice staying present, training ourselves not to continually add self-referential commentary. This practice of immediacy gives rise to a more skillful engagement with our life, which usually means that our life will work better.

UNCONDITIONAL PRACTICES

Considering this view of immediacy, you might say, "Well, now what? It *sounds* okay, but I can't just suddenly walk around in the environment of awareness." But that's where practice comes in. It's rare that you can suddenly achieve a goal. But you can always commit to a practice that you hope will move you in that direction. You can experiment with various practices that may invite this type of experience. And generally, if you practice something, you will get better at it. If you don't practice, you probably won't get better at it. My suggestion is that if you have this interest, then consider what I would call *unconditional* practices. Three such practices that I have found very helpful are those of unconditional immediacy, unconditional embodiment, and unconditional kindness. For me, these practices have a deep energetic resonance with the nature of awareness. It's almost like tuning forks: if you take two forks tuned to the same frequency and you hit one of them, the other starts to vibrate. It's a process of resonance. I've heard that on a sitar, when you pluck one line of strings, another line of identically tuned strings that you never touch will resonate. Playing the first set of strings produces resonance in the second set. The result is this very rich overtone. So my preference is to invite people to practice in ways that have the greatest resonance with the fruitional view. Doing so might invite more and more frequent and conscious participation in what is already always there—which is our open and unconditional awareness.

Other practices are, of course, very valid and useful. We can practice by going to therapy and learning to set boundaries, working with our self-image, and understanding our history. In spiritual work, we can practice returning to our breath and living a decent and respectful lifestyle. But all of these practices tend to be based on a sense that our immediate experience is somehow problematic and needs to be fixed, managed, or improved upon. We're not quite getting what we want right now; what we want is in the future. In this way, people can actually become addicted to the path. Addicted to therapy, addicted to spiritual practices that can give us the gratifying drama of trying to reach some goal in the future. But from my experience, it's more direct to commit to immediacy, embodiment, and unconditional kindness—as if there were nothing missing and nothing problematic about any moment. Such a practice won't *create* awareness, but it can create conditions that seem to *invite* awareness.

We've already talked about the practice of **unconditional immediacy.** It has to do with going deeper and deeper, more and more precisely into an investigation of what is most true in this moment. I must confess that the instructions here are an approximation. I don't actually think there's any such thing as "a moment." But this instruction points us in the direction of immediacy, and the more immediate we can be, the fewer problems we find, the fewer references to a self we find. We don't find evidence of anything missing. We don't find evidence of our worth, either positive or negative, as a person. We find no evidence of anything being permanent. What we do find is an endless stream of fresh, unique moments, which we find to be inherently interesting and workable.

When working with Ana, one of the first things we addressed was how she was unconsciously elaborating difficult momentary feelings of deadness into a generalized story about her life. By attending to immediate experience, Ana began to see for herself that she was actually aware of an endless display of many different feelings. This made it more difficult to completely believe her drama. By attending to her immediate experience of deadness, she found that rather than an absence of aliveness, there was a very disturbing vulnerability, which she was defending against by first deadening herself and then relating to this deadening as a problem. Often when Ana was telling her story, I would interrupt and ask what she was experiencing in that moment. This technique doesn't solve one's story, but it can introduce a type of experiential dialogue between the interpretation of one's experience and one's immediate experience. We can then examine which is actually more accurate.

The practice of **unconditional embodiment** is a very big topic. So big, in fact, that I devote all of chapter 5 to it! At this point, however, I simply say that the more we can bring our attention to immediate, sensation-level experience, the more difficult it is to be captured by our interpretations. When we stay in our immediate embodied experience—noticing our sensations but not tying them to any past experiences—it's very difficult to link any stories together. Our experience is seen to be very unique. It's always in motion. Our feelings arise, dwell for a period of time, and then fall away. There's no such thing as a permanent sensation. We can't find anything self-referential in sensation, either—I have never found any sensation of shame, guilt, abandonment, jealousy, and so on. These are not sensations; rather, they are interpretations of our sensations. *Unconditional embodiment* means a commitment to all of our bodily experiencing, without exception. We're not looking for aliveness or joy or well-being; instead, we are bringing an open curiosity to whatever we find. Feelings of deadness, as with Ana, are just as valid as feelings of aliveness.

We've talked a bit about **unconditional kindness** already. *Unconditional* actually means *unconditional.* We practice kindness toward everything that arises in our awareness—good, bad, or otherwise. Whether we like it, don't like it, or feel neutral about it, we still approach it with kindness and even love. In our culture, I've observed that many people doing spiritual work tend to choose practices that focus on the mental experience of clarity more than on cultivating an open heart. An example would be a meditation practice in which you put your attention on your breath, while noticing and letting go of the thoughts that enter your mind, one by one. But in my opinion, for many of us, the practice of unconditional kindness is much more powerful than clarity. It requires us to cultivate an active, heart-opening attitude toward our experience. We begin to feel a sense of YES toward everything. We don't just *say* YES; we actually *feel* it. It's frankly far less disturbing to be aware of horrible feelings—as in a clarity practice—than to actually feel a YES to these feelings.

If clients want to go even deeper with unconditional kindness, I suggest they practice feeling a sense of sweet love toward everything, including things they don't like. In this practice, it's as if we're actually holding what we don't want to feel inside with a sense of sweetness. Recently I was preparing to record the audio companion to this book. Being recorded in a studio is new to me and was quite anxiety provoking. But luckily it occurred to me that I could do one of these practices. I thought, "Oh! I can practice holding my sense of panic with a sense of sweet love." It didn't make the panic go away, but something very significant shifted for me. Suddenly it was okay if I felt the panic, because I was ready at any second to practice loving it. I was ready to recognize that it's me—it's not something that's happening *to* me.

As you may remember from the beginning of this chapter, Ana had not found any harm or actual threat when she felt the sensations of deadness in her body. Since she was able to acknowledge that she was not in any mortal danger, I invited her to experiment with being kind to these sensations. At first she didn't like this suggestion! She didn't like those sensations, she told me, so why should she be kind to them? And what does it mean to be kind to a sensation, anyway? While we each must find out for ourselves just how kindness-with-all-that-arises is experienced, in this work, it often involves opening one's heart to the experience—bringing a sense of warm engagement and staying with it. I suggested to Ana that the willingness to stay embodied with her sensations was, in itself, an act of kindness toward them. Rather than pushing them away and saying no to the feelings—which are our own vulnerabilities—we learn we can welcome them and hold them with love.

As discussed in chapter 1, if a client is a parent, like Ana was, I often use the analogy of these unwanted feelings being like a small child. I had Ana imagine back to when one of her children was six months old and inconsolably upset. I asked her whether she could remember what it was like to hold her child in that state and what she might have tried to do to soothe him. She responded that she would try getting him to breastfeed first; then she would try rocking him, taking him outside for a walk, and jiggling her car keys, which he really liked. I asked her to continue imagining that the child was still not soothed, that he was still crying. Then what would she do? Well, Ana said, she would just keep trying.

Like most parents, Ana seemed to have an instinct for something I might call "unconditional love." Her inner dialogue might have run like this, "I'm not going to abandon my child, even though I can't make him feel better. It's tearing my heart open to have my poor little baby so upset and not be able to help, but I'm not going anywhere." I use this example to remind my clients of the visceral sense of what it feels like to stay in relationship with inconsolable disturbance or pain. They remember that it's possible to be that kind. I then suggest they try being as kind to themselves as they were to their children. What would it be like for Ana to be unconditionally kind, even loving, to her own sense of deadness? Many times this inquiry opens a little door to a new, more loving way of approaching our own pain.

What all of these practices have in common is that they support us in releasing our fascination with the drama of who we are. As we let go of this drama, a more spacious awareness arises. In that more expansive awareness, if we want to, we can continue to investigate these very interesting questions at the heart of the fruitional view: "Well, what exactly is it that's aware? Has awareness always been there? What's the nature of awareness?"

My hope is that this discussion of the fruitional view—which admittedly tends to be abstract and difficult—might at least suggest a direction of inquiry for you. I encourage you to make an experiential investigation into how you can honor your conditioned history (the developmental view), while also learning how to access an alternative to these familiar dramas in your immediate experiencing (the fruitional view). Anyone reading this book has the capacity to challenge, right now—as practice, if not sudden achievement—our habit of taking our experience as if it were about us, as if it were about our worth as a person or the viability of our life. We then may actually find a sense of appreciation—and even enjoyment and humor—in what we would call our "neuroses."

With this in mind, the next chapter investigates the dialogue between the developmental and fruitional views. It looks at how I use both views to work with clients, and how you can use them in your personal life. Together, these two views create a rich friction that's never resolvable; rather, each approach helps address some of the blind spots of the other.

3

A DIALOGUE BETWEEN
THE DEVELOPMENTAL
AND FRUITIONAL VIEWS

I REMEMBER THE MOMENT I first felt the power of psychology. I was in ninth grade, standing by the car in front of my childhood home, and I was having an argument with my mother. I don't remember the details, but I recall at one moment having the clarity that she was avoiding a point I was making. Moreover, I had the words and the understanding that this was about her, not me—she was being defensive. There was something she didn't want to feel. Instead of feeling misunderstood, I understood something about *her*. My mother is intelligent and articulate, so my feelings of clarity probably passed quickly, but obviously this was an important experience for me. Ever since, I've been curious about what's going on for people beneath the surface, underneath the outward display. I like to pay attention to larger issues and unconscious dynamics. It's no surprise that sooner or later I would find my way to working as a therapist.

As I said earlier, after college I began a very traditional doctoral program in clinical psychology—and left very quickly. I was only able to return to therapy after I'd discovered that I could take a different approach by incorporating what I was learning from my Buddhist practice and study. In Buddhism, I'd found a view that helped me engage with psychotherapy from a sense of mutual dignity, curiosity, humor, and a confidence that all experience, without exception, is workable. It gave me hope for a type of therapy that would go beyond, as Freud said, transforming "hysterical misery into common unhappiness." The resulting dialogue—between the therapeutic view and the Buddhist view—has been very alive and very life giving to me for many years. What's more, I've found it valuable for many of the people I work with. No style or approach works for everyone, of course, but this never-resolvable interplay offers a type of open investigation that seems to be helpful for many people.

So first, a short recap of these two views. The developmental view looks at how, as children, we all create strategies to survive and function well in our families of origin. These survival strategies necessitate a type of aggression toward—a disowning of—the parts of ourselves that are not welcomed by our world. This self-aggression allows us to function and to get the greatest amount of support, love, and approval possible. This is not the activity of pathology; rather, it represents our best efforts to take care of ourselves. But there is a price tag attached, which is a basic sense of being divided against ourselves. This division becomes stabilized over the course of many years; by the time we're adults, it results in the unconscious maintenance of a chronic sense of self-absorption. Self-absorption arises out of a type of hypervigilance. We are continually alert to anything that might bring into awareness those feelings that we have organized our life around never feeling. As adults, these avoidant strategies result in the experience of neurotic, or unnecessary, suffering. And while most of us claim we want to resolve these patterns of unnecessary suffering, on an unconscious level, we are actually invested in making sure they are never solved. If solved, they would no longer serve their protective, distracting function.

When unchallenged, this price tag of a basic split within ourselves usually persists for the rest of our lives. A defense against threatening feelings will not be very effective if we know that we're trying to not feel something; so a good avoidant strategy must operate out of awareness. As a result, these patterns of neurotic suffering seem to have lives of their own, and we often claim to be mystified by their persistence. A major intention of developmental psychotherapy, then, is to address this split between our conscious and unconscious experiencing. There are many theories and techniques for inviting more conscious participation in exactly those aspects of ourselves that we had to disown and repress while growing up.

The fruitional approach takes the view that this split does not actually exist. It says that any experience of being divided against ourselves—or divided against life—is created and maintained through a lot of effort, moment by moment. This hallucinatory experience of being an essentially divided separate self, a small self in a vast universe, is seen as the fundamental source of unnecessary suffering. While improving our quality of life is certainly valuable, it is even more valuable to investigate this appearance of alienation. So rather than trying to create an improved experience or an improved sense of self, the fruitional approach encourages us to relax into our human experience as it already is, investigating experientially whether there's actually any problem. As we gradually find less and less evidence of being a problematic person, our need for hypervigilance and self-absorption gradually dissolves. Our awareness naturally relaxes and becomes more expansive, and we increasingly trust our ability to engage spontaneously, without formulas, with our own experience and with life. At some point, we may become curious about the nature of awareness itself and begin to have increasingly frequent moments when we are aware of awareness.

This chapter discusses how we might hold both of these views in therapeutic work. We might understand the "dialogue" between the two views in several ways. Simplistically, we might assume there is just one truth, and the dialogue is a way to test our theories in order to discover which is true. Or we might assume that most theories are useful approximations of what's true in some ways but that they have their own limitations in other ways; so the point of the dialogue is to come up with a synthesis or integration that combines the best of both. Perhaps an even more interesting use of dialogue is to investigate our experience of standing in the middle, with no fantasy of resolution. What is it like to have no ground to stand on, no theory to identify with? To use theories for practical purposes rather than as positions to take?

The developmental view is especially useful in articulating and working with patterns that exist over time, in recognizing how powerfully our conditioned history shapes the ways in which we relate to our immediate experience. The fruitional view is very helpful in training ourselves to participate consciously in each immediate moment, which is the only moment in which we will ever find ourselves, and to discover if what used to be true is what's true now.

Many of us understand the view that our experience of reality is inevitably a reconstructed one, one step removed from whatever is "really there." All of our experiencing is through our senses, perceptions, emotions, thoughts, and it is profoundly conditioned by our personal history, our culture, and our environment. Psychotherapy is mostly focused on the quality of our constructed experience, especially in the realms of emotion and meaning—how can we bring our out-of-date versions of reality into more current and accurate versions of reality? Buddhism investigates the ways in which we construct any version of reality, moment by moment. The focus is more on the *process of constructing* than on *what is constructed*.

Both of these views are so important to our human experiencing. Can we learn how to value both without taking sides? Can we live consciously in each moment while we also are informed by the past and plan for the future? It's the meeting—the interplay—of these modes of engagement that gives rise to the simultaneity of both conceptual clarity and open aliveness. And in this meeting, which is happening every moment, we find the experience of mystery, creativity, and freshness.

So, instead of hoping for some synthesis or integration, this chapter discusses these two ways of working with our experience in the same way I work with clients in my office—by opening a dialogue between the two views, alternating between them, and seeing what happens. What I've learned, after years of working with these differing approaches, is that they offer no guarantees; there is no formula. Both views have a common intention to relieve unnecessary suffering, and both agree that the experience of split or division is at the heart of that suffering. So there is an overlap between them. But there are also significant differences. The developmental approach helps clients develop a range of skillful means and insights they can use to improve their life and experiences. The sense of division addressed is the one between the conscious and the unconscious. The fruitional approach has more to do with returning, over and over and over, to whatever we are experiencing in the immediate moment and asking ourselves whether it's really a problem at all. The sense of division addressed is that between our fascination with the drama of our "self" and the always-present environment of open awareness, which provides no support for a "self."

FROM THE DEVELOPMENTAL VIEW

We could say that the intention of developmental work is to increase one's tolerance of experiential intensity through a variety of means—greater understanding, helpful techniques, a corrective relationship experience with one's therapist, and so on. As mentioned, Carl Jung believed that neurosis is always a substitute for legitimate suffering, and I would say that neurosis is always a substitute for *experiential intensity*. I find that we tend to avoid intense experiences of vulnerability, intimacy, power, and openness, as well as avoiding negative experiences. If this is indeed the case, then as we increase our tolerance for experiential intensity, we decrease the need for neurosis. We decrease the impulse to escape from the immediate truth of our experience, however intense. We begin to actually dissolve neurotic organization itself, rather than just working with specific neurotic issues.

I have a client, we'll call her Marcie, who came to me complaining that whenever her partner raised his voice, it caused her to shut down. Within a few minutes, I established that her partner wasn't apparently abusive or inappropriately angry; she herself acknowledged that he often had a legitimate reason to be upset, that he didn't yell or threaten her in any way. But she'd asked him to stop raising his voice, and he didn't seem able to do so when he was worked up. She told me that he couldn't "manage his anger enough" for her to stay engaged during conflict, and so she didn't think she could stay in the relationship.

It was immediately clear to me that Marcie, like so many of my clients, was pointing a finger in the wrong direction. She was making her partner's aggression the issue, when in fact his raised voice was triggering her own defensive habit of shutting down. Our partners are almost guaranteed to trigger our core issues, but they are rarely the cause of this vulnerability. Marcie couldn't be in conflict without having a very intense, reactive, and physical response. In my experience, such responses generally are evidence of an issue that has been with that person all of his or her life. Usually such vulnerabilities have their origins in childhood and perhaps will be with that person until death. These core vulnerabilities are deeply embedded; they don't just go away.

I asked Marcie whether this response to conflict was something unique to her situation with this partner or whether it felt familiar from other areas of her life and in her history. Not surprisingly, Marcie reported the response was very familiar. She remembered shutting down in the face of aggression as early as elementary school. When a teacher would reprimand her, she would make herself "as small as possible." She also remembered shutting down in conflicts with her parents and, to some degree, with coworkers over the years.

So with Marcie, I started with a developmental approach, calling attention to the possibility that shutting down and trying to escape was a pattern of hers. She had it before she got into this particular relationship, and it would probably remain, even if she were to leave the relationship. Given that her partner's behavior appeared to be in the normal range of conflict and that, in other ways, the relationship was relatively healthy and satisfying, I suggested it might be helpful for her to work with her experience of aggressive energy before deciding to end the relationship. She might give herself some time, a few months perhaps, to see if her personal work might result in experiencing the relationship as workable. She agreed.

As soon as we are willing to look at how we relate to our core vulnerabilities, we've already taken a big step forward. We begin to no longer feel like a victim of circumstance, of our past, or of another person's behavior. I helped Marcie see that her partner's aggression—which was triggering a preexisting vulnerability—was just that, a *trigger*. Since her partner wasn't the cause, breaking up with him would not provide a real solution. Instead, I suggested that it might be to Marcie's benefit to investigate how she could increase her tolerance of her own very intense response. In therapy, there's always both personal work—how we relate to our own experience and vulnerabilities—and interpersonal work—or how we relate to others and to the world. For Marcie, her *personal* work was to first learn how to work with her intense, reactive, physical experience of fear and panic. I find the fruitional approach most helpful for this, with a focus on immediacy and embodiment. Her *interpersonal* work began with finding ways to reduce the frequency with which the trigger occurred. I find the developmental approach most helpful for this, offering a variety of skillful means, including an understanding of her history, so that she didn't believe she had to engage with her partner to work through this issue; communication skills to help negotiate boundaries and behavioral agreements; and so on.

REGULATING INTENSITY—A FIRST STEP

One of the possibilities I offer my clients is that they may not be required to participate in experiences that trigger their core vulnerabilities. Perhaps we have the right, and maybe even the responsibility, to *not* take part in activating situations in which we do not yet have the capacity to retain our adult abilities. By becoming more and more familiar with our triggers, we may be able to notice them before they gain too much momentum. At that point, we can remove ourselves from the interaction for a time to avoid getting more deeply drawn into our reactivity. Of course, sometimes there is no choice—if you're a single parent, for example, you legitimately may not be able to remove yourself from a child who is pushing all of your buttons. Other skills are called for there. But in many other circumstances, we have a choice. For example, when her partner gets aggressive, Marcie could say—in her own words—"I notice I'm getting triggered, and I'm about to shut down. I love you and want to stay engaged, but I need to take a few minutes for myself. I will come find you in about half an hour, once I feel able to reengage."

As we become more familiar with what the triggering experience feels like in the body and find that intense feelings are perhaps never harmful in themselves, gradually we can learn to stay more engaged. By becoming more able to be intimate with ourselves, we are able to be more intimate with our partners, our children, and our world. We are actually always fully intimate with life. But because life is disturbing, we usually pretend to be disconnected in various ways as an unconscious strategy for regulating intensity. Part of our work in therapy is to learn how to give ourselves permission to regulate our intensity in conscious adult ways, rather than to do so using unconscious, out-of-date strategies. By taking responsibility for regulating our own levels of intensity, it becomes safer to explore that intensity. And, as we gradually increase our tolerance of experiential intensity, we will be able to stay more consciously connected to life itself and everything it brings. ◼

FROM THE FRUITIONAL VIEW

Rather than looking for ways to improve our relationship with our circumstances—such as learning techniques for a more adult relationship with our neurotic strategies—the fruitional view is about coming back to what's happening in the immediate moment. We become curious about our real-time experience, asking ourselves if there's any evidence that there's actually a threat we must escape from.

Marcie told me she felt like she was "going to be annihilated" when her partner yelled at her, and clearly it actually felt that way to her. Taking the fruitional approach, I invited her to recall a time when her partner had raised his voice and she had felt this panic. I encouraged her not to go into any story about the experience—about why it was so unfair of him since she never yelled and about how she is so reasonable and he's not. Instead, I suggested that she stay in the immediacy of her own experience and use her intuitive intelligence to investigate whether there was really a problem. Is there any damage? Is it killing her to feel this panic? Is she becoming dysfunctional? Does she think it's actually making her sick? These are all legitimate questions, and there's no right answer. But I find that when we are willing to stay embodied in our immediate experience of intensity, most of us discover that no harm is actually happening to us.

This technique works even if someone is having a dissociative response. For example, Marcie at first reported resistance to feeling her vulnerability. At that point, I invited her to stay embodied with her experience of resistance. That was her immediate experience; there was no requirement for her to break through and feel her vulnerability. Sometimes clients can't get out of their thoughts, and that's fine too. I have them just experience what that's like, without getting too fascinated by the content of those thoughts. I ask, "What does it feel like to be caught in your head that way? Is that a problem?"

In other words, from the fruitional approach, we're always returning to immediacy. We're always checking out our experience and contrasting it with our familiar claim that there's something problematic about that immediate experience—and, in a larger sense, about us.

THE SPIRAL STAIRCASE

The developmental approach could be understood as a gradual approach, while the fruitional approach could be seen as a sudden approach. Within Buddhism, these two approaches actually represent two different traditions. Some schools advocate for a gradual approach to enlightenment, and others focus on a more sudden experience of enlightenment. Perhaps these are different ways to view the same process. It's like an apple growing on a tree. At some point, the apple is going to fall—a sudden occurrence. But of course it has been ripening there for months, so it could be thought of as a gradual approach as well.

We could also use the language of being and becoming to describe these views. The developmental approach is about becoming: we're always looking for ways to improve our experience. How can we live to our full potential? The fruitional approach is about being—accepting and relaxing into being at peace with the immediate moment. Living to our full potential in this moment means participating fully right now, regardless of what's happening. Both approaches are, of course, legitimate, but they don't work without each other. If, on the one hand, we're always "becoming," without learning how to *be,* then we're always postponing our commitment to experiencing the present. We tell ourselves that we'll fully participate once we've acquired our preferred conditions. But such conditions, of course, are a moving target. We're never going to feel like we've "arrived," that there's nothing left that needs improvement. In our culture, this is a pervasive source of confusion and suffering. It seems like all of us are trying to generate a particular set of life circumstances—or, on a subtler level, a better state of mind—so that we can finally accept ourselves. We think that if only we acquire this or that set of conditions, *then* we'll be able to be fully present. But if our unconscious attitude is to always look to the future for acceptance, then of course that time will never come.

On the fruitional side, the focus is on being—on surrender, acceptance, and immediacy. But this is only part of the story. Over any collection of moments, a stream of experiencing takes place. Upon investigation, this stream of experiencing seems to have an evolutionary quality. Our universe, evidence suggests, actually *is* an evolutionary process. So while at any moment there is *being*, over time, there is always *becoming*. You can't have one without the other. If we focus only on acceptance and immediacy, we may ignore historically conditioned patterns that are causing harm to ourselves and others. I've worked with a number of spiritual practitioners who are able to generate very spacious states of mind but who avoid dealing with basic human concerns like work and relationship. Just like the concepts of "high" and "low"—neither of which would exist without the other—being and becoming codefine each other. They're relational. The Buddhist point of view is that *all* experiencing is relational. Our world appears to be made up of independently existing things and phenomena, as well as of independently existing selves observing and interacting with these things. Upon investigation, though, we may find that everything we experience depends on many complex conditions; that the more precise we are in our attention, the less evidence we find of anything having some permanent objective existence. In practice, the fruitional view simply returns over and over again to the present moment—to "being." What we find there turns out to be pretty much the same thing, pretty much all of the time. We might feel anxious, we might feel activated, we might feel sort of sad—but after a while, we realize that all these things are simply our human nature. Our humanness is all we are going to find in our immediate experience. From the point of view of development, or "becoming," we're always interested in evolving our endless stream of immediate moments into a better experience. So we look for different ways to improve ourselves and our circumstances, which is also very important.

If we combine these two apparently irresolvable but actually cocreative views into one image, they might start to look like a spiral staircase. The fruitional view would be the circular aspect: we're always revisiting the same issues over and over again. In practice, we say, "Well, I'll probably work with this sadness, this loneliness, this feeling of abandonment until I die. I'm going to keep coming across it again and again, so I might as well develop

FIGURE 3.1   SPIRAL STAIRCASE

a relationship with it. I'm going to practice feeling it, to see if it's actually a problem." The developmental view would be represented by a line, taking us from here to there. We're trying to improve our lives, to create upward momentum. "I understand where my abandonment feelings originated, and I'm going to stop trying to have relationships with unavailable partners." Combined, the circular motion and the line start to represent an ascending spiral. The vertical axes are our deeply embedded issues, which we keep having to deal with. But we can intersect these basic themes at increasing levels of maturation. We're walking in a circular pattern, but things are evolving simultaneously. We continue to encounter our core vulnerabilities, but hopefully at greater and greater levels of awareness and skillfulness.

HOLDING CONTRADICTORY ENERGIES SIMULTANEOUSLY

So how might we apply these apparently contradicting approaches in our everyday lives? When I work with clients, I often invite them to consider a two-step sequence. The first step is that of acceptance—becoming willing to accept the way things are. This represents the fruitional approach; we stay present with reality as it is. From that ground of acceptance, we can then ask how we might improve our situation or experience, which is the second step. Marcie was interested in this experiment, so I asked her, "How would it be to accept your partner and your relationship as if they are the way they are—as if they're never going to get any better?" I wasn't actually suggesting that would be the case. Who knows what will happen in the future? Her partner could leave her, or he could die, or they could get married and have kids. We just don't know. Instead, the point of the question was to direct her awareness to what it would *feel* like if no improvement were on the horizon. I was deliberately inviting an experience of claustrophobia—taking away any little exit that would allow Marcie to avoid committing to her immediate experience.

Some clients actually respond with relief to such an idea—"Gosh, I'm exhausted from always trying to make things better." But Marcie, like a lot of my clients, responded with a type of panic. "I can't accept the way things are," she told me. "His behavior isn't okay. Our relationship isn't as good as it needs to be." In the discussion that followed, however, it became clear that she was really saying, "I am choosing to be with him, I haven't chosen to end the relationship, but I have a complaint. So I'm not going to be fully engaged until things change. Until then, I'm here in the relationship, but I'm not *really* here."

"Here but not really here" describes a lot of us in our relationship with life, in general. We could all ask ourselves, "What would it be like if this is it, if life never gets any better than it is at this moment?" Again, the point of the question is to watch our emotional response. What would it be like to be completely committed to this present reality? Because, in fact, that's all there is to experience right now, even if it doesn't match up to our preferred conditions.

That's not the end of the story, of course. If we want to improve our situation, to evolve our circumstances, we should go for it. We should definitely give it a try. But if we try to improve ourselves without first accepting our circumstances, the effort may feel very serious. It may feel like our lives—or, like Marcie, our emotional well-being—hang in the balance. If, on the other hand, we've already accepted things as they are, then any efforts at improvement can be understood as being about practical issues or perhaps even be experienced as *play*. We're doing it for enjoyment. We're doing it because we *choose* to, not because we *have* to. We've already accepted that our lives are the way they are, so there's nothing at stake here. Our life circumstances are fundamentally workable just as they are.

Let's say you live in a home with a basically sound structure. There's running water and heat, and the roof doesn't leak. It may not be a palace, and the yard may not be as beautiful as the neighbor's, but it's adequate. You have a bed, a bathroom, and a kitchen—the basic setup. You don't really *need* anything more. Can you imagine living here just as it is for the rest of your life? If so, any improvements you might make—remodeling the kitchen, adding a sunroom, doing some landscaping—would be for pleasure and increased functionality, rather than out of necessity. These changes are not a requirement; nobody's well-being is at stake. You've already accepted that the house is complete just the way it is. But for the pleasure of it, you'd like to know what it would be like to have a nicer kitchen and a prettier yard. So you save up some money, and you hire the right people, and you make some improvements for fun, for satisfaction.

Of course, this idea applies to our own personal work as well. Imagine that you could really be committed to who you are in this present moment, without qualifications. Any work you might choose to do—be it therapy, spiritual work, yoga, what have you—would basically be for practical reasons, for a sense of satisfaction. It's not necessary. It's just a choice. Down the road, you might extend your motivation, seeing that doing your personal work would benefit others as well. But that's not the initial motivation. In fact, most of us are trying our best to take care of ourselves, which is the appropriate place to start, in my experience. But either way, any improvements you make to your own state of mind are a sort of added bonus. They are not necessary, because your life is workable just as it is, right now.

Developmental and fruitional . . . becoming and being. The apparent contradiction between these two energies points us toward a larger question: how can we hold contradictory energies simultaneously, with no fantasy of resolution? That's a question I often ask my clients in terms of their actual emotional work. Take, for example, the question of whether we actually want to wake up. If you're reading this book, you probably have the idea that you want to experience more freedom. But you're considering the idea that you are already and always free. So why don't you experience more freedom? Some people blame themselves or society. Some identify themselves as seekers, putting wakefulness into the future. Some feel frustrated. But perhaps it's simpler than all that—maybe we all have deeply contradictory feelings about waking up. Maybe we have already intuited that the experience of open awareness provides absolutely no support for personal identity, no security, no rewards, no recognition. That doesn't sound so good. We may have, legitimately, deeply contradictory feelings. We want more freedom, but we also want security. But perhaps this is not a problem to be resolved. Paradoxically, we may find an actual experience of greater freedom when we hold both of these human concerns at once, with no fantasy of resolution. If we try to identify with "freedom" and make our wish for "security" wrong, we just push our security needs out of awareness, where they will be enacted unconsciously, perhaps as an experience of feeling stuck on our path. What would our experience be if we gave ourselves permission to feel that we want to be free *and* that we don't want to be free, with no resolution, ever? For an experience of freedom to be always present, it can't take sides. It has to be a freedom that includes feeling stuck, that includes any and all experiencing. As humans, our minds seem to work dualistically, always dividing reality into this and that, good and bad, self and other.

Dualistic experience is not the problem; taking this experience seriously and trying to resolve it is. The unconditional acceptance of our human experience as we find it to be is at the heart of the fruitional approach.

Upon deeper investigation of such contradictions, we find that our "sense of self"—our awareness—turns out to be somewhere in the middle. We're actually unable to say that we feel only this way or that way. We can't identify with either side of our feelings, because both are true. Very organically, we end up in an irresolvable middle ground. Buddhism is sometimes referred to as the middle way or the middle path. That doesn't mean we take half of this and half of that and end up in a homogenized compromise; instead, it means we hold the totality of both at the same time. We develop the capacity not to take refuge in any one position. As a result, we end up in this open middle ground where there's no support for personal identity and no objective confirmation that we're ever doing anything the "right way." Obviously, from an egoic point of view, this can be quite disturbing, especially at first. But the benefit is that we are able to just show up without a preconceived formula about how to live our lives. We begin to experience the reality that every moment is fresh. It's open. We don't know what's going to happen, and we don't know the right way to do this or that. We can't even come up with a resolved feeling about things that are important, like whether we should stay in a particular relationship. We always have contradictory feelings. Learning to hold contradictory energies can be a very powerful support to a fruitional view. And in fact, on a subtler level, holding both the developmental and the fruitional views, without taking sides, is itself congruent with a fruitional approach, which finds "not knowing" at the heart of all relative experiencing.

One of the interesting considerations that arises when we talk about holding contradictory energies is that we still have to act. Every second, we are choosing to take some sort of action in the world. (Even if we're choosing the action of *not* acting.) And every time we act, we are representing only part of our experience. So once we understand the inherently contradictory nature of our experiencing, it quickly becomes clear that none of our choices for behavior or life circumstances will capture the genuine complexity of our feelings. If I choose to spend my money on this car, I don't get to buy that one. If I live in Seattle, I don't get to live in Florida. If I decide to split my time—spending my summers in Seattle and my winters in Florida—then I don't get to experience year-round weather in either location. There's a certain loss of complexity whenever we translate our feelings into behavior. We never get to represent both sides of our feelings in the same moment. Loss and limitation are inseparable from choice. We don't get to choose any one thing without, by implication, choosing *not* to have ten thousand other things.

This can seem like a problem because, in our culture especially, many of us believe we should be able to have a life without disturbance or limitation. We've talked about the fact that our cultural idea of freedom is an absence of limitations. So naturally the fact that we cannot have a life without limitation is disturbing to some of us. It's especially disturbing to those of us with histories of toxic loss—divorces, self-absorbed parents, or a family always relocating because of business or the military. When we have had very difficult experiences of loss, especially when that loss happened to us as children, we often feel significant resistance, even panic, about taking responsibility for choosing the specific type of limitation we will have to deal with. Many people end up using ambivalence as a form of defense. "I can't make up my mind," we tell ourselves. "I'm so confused. I go back and forth. I procrastinate. I just feel paralyzed when I have to decide." In many cases, these behavioral styles turn out to be defenses against taking conscious responsibility for the experience of limitation and loss that happens every time we make a choice. But as we've discussed, the experience of freedom can also be understood as arising from an unconditional commitment to the truth of our experience. Surprisingly, then, the experience of freedom turns out to be inseparable from a commitment to experience loss and limitation. When I'm working with clients who are facing a difficult decision—whether to continue or end a relationship, try a new career, move to a new city—I often suggest that they count on having second thoughts or regrets, regardless of their choice: "If I stay, I'll be disturbed. If I move on, I'll be disturbed." Once we are clear that any choice we make will never represent all of our very real and valid feelings, we can make decisions based on criteria other than the avoidance of disturbance. We can either experience disturbance in the service of neurosis or experience disturbance in the service of sanity.

GENERATING, AND CHALLENGING, THE EXPERIENCE OF BEING DIVIDED AGAINST ONESELF

When I'm working with clients, I hold these contradictory views of development and fruition at all times. I do not use a particular formula; at any moment, there's choice about what issues we work with and which view we work from. That said, I have found specific techniques and practices helpful, and I would like to share them with you. The intention of each of these views is the same: to dissolve the experience of there being any split or division. In developmental work, we're dissolving the apparent split between the conscious self and the unconscious or repressed self, while in the fruitional view, we're dissolving the apparent split between personal self—including all relative experience, both conscious and unconscious—and the larger context of nonpersonal awareness.

One way to approach this work is by understanding how, through progressive levels of disconnection, we can generate the experience of a divided self. This creation of a sense of being a "self divided against itself" requires great effort, creativity, and intelligence. We should be clear, though, that intelligence is not the same as wisdom. As discussed, this sense of a divided self is probably a necessary and inevitable consequence of our efforts to take care of ourselves as children. As adults, however, what was once healthy is now out of date but continues to be maintained without awareness, or unconsciously. The first and most basic level of disconnection is an **attitude of fundamental aggression** toward the truth of our experience. This attitude is one of refusing to accept our immediate, direct, noninterpretive experiencing as it is. Many teachers have said, in a variety of ways, that the basic cause of unnecessary suffering is wanting reality to be other than it is. In chapter 1, we discussed the three styles of fundamental aggression: positive, negative, and neutral.

The second level of disconnection is a **dissociative relationship** to our immediate embodied experiencing. Fundamental aggression is an attitude. We begin to put that attitude into practice through an ongoing dissociation from the obvious truth that we are embodied, impermanent, vulnerable beings. We'll focus on this specifically in chapter 5, when we discuss embodied awareness.

As a third level, we add a **continuous stream of self-referential commentary** to whatever we may be experiencing. As discussed in the previous chapter, we have an experience, and then, in a fraction of a second, we make up a story about how that experience has to do with our "self." We may pass judgment: "I like it" or "I don't like it." We may ask, "How does this experience relate to me? How does it reflect on my worth as a person? Can I ignore it, or is it relevant to me?" We do this thousands of times every day.

As a fourth level of disconnection, we **link moments of experience** to one another, creating an impression of continuity as the domino analogy suggested. Just as we're more likely to be absorbed in a book or movie with a good narrative, we maintain an experience of being a self-absorbed, continuing "self" with familiar narratives. What's even more fascinating is that we appear to be both the subject and the object of these stories. This linking practice continues and strengthens our sense of being a separate continuing self that *relates to* life, rather than being an *expression of* life. We discussed this process in chapter 2.

As a fifth and final level, we **stabilize a state of chronic struggle** by maintaining the claim that there's something really important that has to be fixed about "us" or about life. Now the narrative has become a cliffhanger. "Am I worthy of love? When will I finally heal my childhood wounds? How can I enjoy my life when there's so much suffering in the world?" Of course, the more significant the problem, the more significant we feel. Usually this very important problem presents as some kind of threat even to our survival. Only when it is resolved can we risk being fully present and engaged with our lives. This experience of maintaining chronic struggle is discussed in detail in chapter 4. At this point, we have achieved a very reliable and stable sense of disconnection from the always-open, not-secure, disturbing, and vulnerable reality of our human experience.

Once we have some understanding of how we generate the experience of basic division or dissociative split, we can then challenge the process. It's helpful to keep in mind, though, that we will almost certainly encounter very contradictory feelings about doing this work. Most of us identify deeply, and somewhat unconsciously, with our familiar senses of self. While we genuinely want relief from the suffering that this inaccurate self-absorption creates, we will probably feel quite anxious at some point if we actually begin to dismantle the fascinating drama of "our significant self."

These levels of dissociative practices are sequential, with each serving as the foundation for the next. Therefore, when challenging this process, it would seem to work best to start at the most relative level and work inward. In actual practice, I jump back and forth quite a bit, but there is a general sense of progression or movement. For example, a client may be identified with a struggle about how it's wrong to feel selfish. Until this is worked with, it will be difficult to go deeper into that client's immediate embodied experience of selfishness and even harder to practice kindness to this feeling. So even though I may work with any of these levels at any moment, I generally start with a client's claim of being in a state of struggle first and then move inward as the client is ready for deeper work.

Each level of dissociative practice actually implies its own antidotal practice, which usually involves doing the opposite of what we are used to doing. It may be helpful to use my work with a client to illustrate each of these antidotal practices. Keep in mind that in actual sessions, the work would not be so linear.

I recently met with Vance, a client who had moved from Chicago to Boulder in the past year. In his early thirties, Vance had become aware of a recurring experience of feeling unfairly criticized in his work and even of being attacked by his bosses. "I exhaust myself at work, and they still find fault," he told me. "I go out of my way to be friendly with my supervisor, but she's still rude to me." Vance is describing a familiar type of struggle, which probably had origins in his childhood experience. He told me, "My father drank a lot and was always angry. I tried to never upset him, but he always found something to yell at me about. I just wanted him to be proud of me." His struggle oscillates between his hope that somehow he'll get what he wants and his fear that it's hopeless. In a young, unconscious way, Vance is trying to resolve these contradictory feelings—sometimes believing that he will achieve his hope for safety, love, and recognition, and sometimes collapsing into a depressed belief that he will never get what he most wants. Rather than immediately offering encouragement—for example, by working on skills that might help him avoid attacks and get the approval he wants—I invite Vance into a variation on the worst-fear technique mentioned earlier. My intention is to first disrupt the *chronic struggle* that he has been using as an unconscious way to stabilize a familiar sense of self. Struggle requires a polarized split in our experience, which we could call *our hope* and *our fear*. It's then fueled with the fantasy that somehow we will get rid of our fear and achieve our hope. One way to challenge this very stable psychic process is to invite one's fear first into awareness and then into acceptance. It's hard to struggle when we're willing to feel and take ownership of what we've been trying to avoid.

I invite Vance to say out loud, "I give myself permission to feel that I will be attacked and will never get the love and approval that I most want, perhaps for the rest of my life." I make it clear that these are *feelings* that Vance already has been living with his whole life, not predictions about the future. I find that saying fears out loud, in the presence of another person, is much more impactful than saying them silently and privately to ourselves. Acknowledging our fears this directly is much more exposing and vulnerable, which then allows a more direct assessment of whether something bad is actually happening to us. This is not a one-time practice; it must be revisited many times if we are to develop an experiential confidence that feeling what seems so threatening does not actually harm us.

To address the fantasy of resolution, I explored with Vance the view that he may have these contradictory feelings—his hope *and* his fear—for the foreseeable future, just as he has had them most of his life. But, do they really need to be resolved? Why not learn how to respect both feelings—he, in fact, does carry a painful feeling of not being safe and not getting the love and approval he wants; and he, appropriately, has the hope of feeling safe and loved. Both feelings are valid. Can he commit to allowing both to coexist? Can he tolerate a more complex sense of self now that he's an adult?

As Vance relaxed his unconscious identification with "I am the one who will always struggle to get the safety and love that I will never get," we were then able to address the level of *linking moments of experience*—that is, how he continually constructed a narrative that, while familiar and therefore safe-feeling, was creating a lot of unnecessary suffering. Often it's helpful to first offer some reframes to the client's story before challenging the story making itself. The first reframe is usually to place the difficult feelings in a historic, developmental context. If Vance is telling himself that the problem is his boss, then he'll want to work with the issue in that relationship. But if he can see his painful feelings as having been with him all his life, as probably having their origin in his experience as a child, then he'll be more available to work with the issue as located within himself, as his own core vulnerability. Another helpful reframe is to present all of our out-of-date survival strategies as an expression of our health, our best efforts to take care of ourselves. Another is to offer the view that, whatever happened to us when young, if we want to strengthen our sense of being an adult, it's important to practice an attitude of complete responsibility for working with our experience, regardless of how it might have been shaped by our history. A next step at this level is to challenge *any* story about our experience, however positive. Here the practice of immediacy is very powerful. As Vance shared the drama of his struggles at work, I often interrupted to ask, "Excuse me, but what are you actually experiencing right now, without any interpretation?" Vance would at first appear a bit flustered or irritated, but he would then pause and pay attention in a way that, at least for a moment, would undermine his identification with his narrative. Over time, this practice revealed subtler and subtler levels of experiencing. But at first, it simply served to loosen his unconscious fascination with the story he was telling himself.

Beneath the stories we tell is our tendency to continually add *self-referential commentaries* to whatever we may be experiencing. We challenge this level of our "disconnection practice" by removing any claim that our experience is about *us*. This is a very strange idea to many of us, but as we become less identified with our interpretations *about* our experience and participate more *in* our experience, we may find no inherent evidence that anything we experience is actually about us. As Vance was able and willing to stay more in his immediate experience and less in his stories, he began to realize that his drama of victimhood was really serving as a defense against deeper feelings of anger.

"You know, I'm just now getting how angry I am at my father for always yelling at me and putting me down," he would say.

"How would it feel to just say 'I'm angry,'" I asked him, "with no explanation at all?"

Vance reported that it surprisingly felt even more powerful to do this. I then suggested that he drop the "I am" part of it and just say "angry" and feel angry. What was it like to feel the intensity of that emotion, the energy of anger in his body? To respect it and value it, without the need for it to be about anything—even about him? Any intense emotion is actually an expression of aliveness. But we diminish that raw intensity and aliveness when we make the experience about us—wanting either to get rid of it, if it's negative, or to hold onto it, if it's positive.

A very reliable, deep, and pervasive strategy of disconnection is to *dissociate from our immediate embodied experiencing.* When we leave our bodies, it's very easy to feel captured by our historic dramas. When we're vague about what we're actually feeling in the moment, it's easy to interpret our experience in ways that are most familiar to us but that may no longer be serving us. The antidotal discipline is that of embodied immediacy, returning over and over again to our embodied, sensation-level, noninterpretive experiencing. This is not an achievement but a practice we might commit to for the rest of our lives. Because we are only living in each present moment, we may find the most reliable sense of being supported by life in the truth of our experiencing, and not so much in our preferences or theories. With the practice of embodied immediacy, we will always find clarity and support. We may not find what we want to find, but we *will* find what is actually true in this moment. That's what we can count on, and that's what there is to work with.

As Vance and I worked together, I would regularly invite him to bring his attention to his immediate sensation-level feelings, with no interpretation at all. He would describe a tight throat, pressure on his chest, a sick feeling in his belly. But he discovered that although it was anxiety provoking to intentionally stay with these sensations, there was no evidence of any harm or damage. Although this practice is often disturbing, it is exactly what cultivates the confidence that all of our experiencing is workable and not actually a problem. To be clear, I'm not suggesting that we take on some new belief system of "There are no problems;" rather, we can practice discriminating between our actual immediate experience and our interpretations about this experience and find for ourselves which is most true.

Our most basic practice of disconnection—*our fundamental aggression to the truth of our experience*—is challenged by the dual disciplines of awareness and unconditional kindness. These two disciplines are major themes in this book and are discussed in a variety of ways. As is true of all of the antidotes, our understanding and capacities will probably increase with practice. But to work with any issue, we must first bring it into awareness. And as we become gradually more aware of all the ways in which we refuse to accept reality as we find it, we become more aware of how much unnecessary suffering we are creating for ourselves and for others. In turn, our motivation to practice unconditional kindness increases spontaneously and organically. In my work with Vance, once his awareness of a deeper level of experiencing became familiar, I introduced the view of being kind to whatever he might feel.

"When your boss criticizes you in a meeting," I would say, "you can expect to feel anxious and angry. What would it be like to say *yes* to those feelings?" Vance was increasingly able to see that these difficult feelings were not being done *to* him, but were experiences of his own vulnerability. He reported that he was more and more frequently catching himself in his commentaries, asking himself what he was feeling that he didn't want to feel, and then doing his best to be kind to these feelings—to be his own best friend.

I have used selective aspects of my work with Vance to illustrate the process of challenging the ways in which we construct the experience of disconnection. He and I also, of course, worked with family-of-origin issues, other core vulnerabilities, the question of whether it was healthy for him to remain in his current job, how to cultivate healthy boundaries and conflict skills, and so on.

It may be helpful to summarize the ways in which we practice and generate the experience of disconnection. Creating the sense of being a divided self builds on each successive level. The antidotal practices with which we might deconstruct this drama are used from the bottom up in Table 3.1 (next page).

WHY ALTERNATE BETWEEN DEVELOPMENTAL AND FRUITIONAL WORK?

As I've said, in my work, I alternate back and forth between developmental work, such as exploring family-of-origin issues, gender training, and the impact of various life experiences, and fruitional practices, such as embodied immediacy, noninterpretive experiencing, and unconditional kindness. In a Western way, I look at our capacity to set boundaries, communicate what we want, have constructive conflict skills, have a more realistic sense of self, and learn to listen. All of these developmental practices are very valuable in increasing our tolerance of experiential intensity. As long as we are still trying to take care of ourselves with the strategies we created as children, we tend to continue a child's basically defensive attitude toward intense experience. As we update these strategies and base them on current reality, however, we relate to difficult experience from our current adult capacities.

When we work only developmentally, though, it's very common to focus so much on our history that we end up believing that some wound or unresolved issue in our past is somehow *causing* our current difficulties. We might then unconsciously postpone being fully engaged with our lives until we have resolved that issue. But how can something in the past *cause* something now? Perhaps what we call a "wound" is actually a refusal to stay fully present and embodied with very disturbing feelings that are only arising in this moment.

TABLE 3.1

The Five Levels of Disconnection and Their Antidotes

	Disconnection	Antidote
Level One	An attitude of fundamental aggression toward the truth of our experience	The dual disciplines of awareness and unconditional kindness
Level Two	A dissociative relationship to our immediate embodied experiencing	The practice of embodied immediacy (bringing attention to sensation-level experience, with no interpretation)
Level Three	Adding a continuous stream of self-referential commentary to whatever we may be experiencing	The practice of removing any claim that the experience is about us; feeling the raw aliveness of emotion without making it a part of a story about our "self"
Level Four	Linking moments of experience to one another, creating the impression of continuity	The practice of first reframing stories to support personal responsibility and health and then practicing immediacy to help deconstruct any story, however positive
Level Five	Stabilizing a state of chronic struggle by maintaining the claim that some problem of survival-level significance has to be fixed	Worst fear technique: invite what we don't want to feel into awareness and acceptance; practice holding contradictory feelings, with no fantasy of resolution

While Western therapy can result in an endless project of improving our experience, there are those clients—especially spiritual practitioners—who try to do *only* fruitional work. In that case, the problem can become something we call "spiritual bypassing." This is where we learn to dissolve any sense of disturbance into spaciousness and immediacy. In this moment, there is no problem, and so actual dysfunctional patterns of behavior can be dismissed as "a story about our experience." This may bring immediate relief, but it often means we are not engaging with some very real, very messy aspects of the human experience. We may "wake up," so to speak, but that doesn't mean we suddenly become skillful. Just because we have woken up does not mean we suddenly know how to speak Swahili and play the piano. Neither do we suddenly know how to have satisfying human relationships or how to handle our conditioned history. If we experience some degree of wakefulness but then go off to live in a cave alone, we are less likely to get captured by everyday problems. But if we want to live in society—if we're going to be a parent, a partner, a teacher, or somebody trying to be of benefit to others—it's very important to do the developmental work to process our "characterological" issues. Because even though we might not feel identified with those issues anymore, the people we relate to may still be profoundly affected by our unresolved reenactment behaviors.

So, for those of us who want to wake up for the benefit of both ourselves and others, it's important to remember that part of being of benefit is to clean up our own act. We work with the patterns of our conditioned history, so that we are not causing undue harm to those around us.

We could say that each of these two views addresses half the story very well and the other half not so well. Together, they can be used in a very powerful, complementary way. Developmental work supports our fruitional path: reducing drama, taking better care of ourselves, and acting as an adult help us relax our chronically contracted attention and feel more able to investigate our immediate experiencing. Fruitional practices support our developmental work: dissolving our sense of being a divided, problematic self helps us feel less identified with and invested in our familiar survival strategies and more able to tolerate the anxiety that's inseparable from challenging them. But even more powerfully, we can use these possibly contradictory-appearing ways of understanding as an opportunity to stay in that open space between. We can investigate the disturbing territory we find between *this* version of reality and *that* version of reality, which we find whenever we try to grasp what's most true in our experience. We may find that we can best accommodate all of our experiencing when we're not identified with any of it.

THE GRAVITATIONAL SHIFT

As I mentioned earlier, at a certain point in the journey, we may experience a shift in our experiential center of gravity. On one side of this shift, we still have a certain amount of struggle, which is appropriate. We have to make an effort because our default position continues to be that very confusing, painful experience of being a problematic, divided self. So we actually do need to work on that. On the other side of this gravitational shift, however, our baseline, default position is to be open toward, relaxed about, accepting of, and at home with the truth of our experience—whatever it happens to be, whether we like it or not. In discussing this shift, Carl Jung used the metaphor of leaning back in a chair. If you're leaning back and you relax your effort, up to a certain point, the chair will return to where it was. It will fall back to its original position. But if you continue leaning back and cross the center of gravity, then a relaxation of effort will result in the chair falling over backward. The leaning is the same all the way through; nothing about the process changes. But at a certain point, the display becomes really different—almost the opposite.

Similarly, we could imagine climbing a steep mountain. We have to apply a lot of effort, or struggle, to climb up that mountain. If we relax our effort, we might metaphorically slide back down to where we began. Once we've reached the peak, however, and are heading down the other side, our work isn't to struggle anymore. Now it's to cooperate with gravity; it's to relax. We come down the hill by relaxing and letting gravity and our bodies cooperate. In a similar way, as we shift from experiencing ourselves as divided and problematic, to experiencing ourselves as already fully present and workable, there is a dramatic dissolution in the sense of struggle and of unnecessary suffering. We cooperate with ourselves; we find ourselves to be our own best friend, regardless of what's arising. As we cooperate with ourselves, we cooperate with life, and strangely enough, we begin to experience that life is cooperating with *us*.

PRACTICE **FEELING THE SUPPORT
THAT'S ALREADY PRESENT**

This short, guided meditation can be helpful for cultivating the sense of psychic shift that we have been talking about. If you have time, I recommend that you record yourself reading the script out loud and then play it back. Alternatively, you could ask a friend to read it to you. Be sure to pause after each line break so you can experience the meditation.

Sit down and relax. Make sure you feel comfortable. Wherever you're sitting, put attention on what you can feel in your body. Notice the weight of your body as you begin the meditation.

Feel the seat, the chair, the cushion, or the floor that you're sitting on. Feel how it is supporting you.

You don't have to do anything to deserve that support. All you have to do is feel it. Feel your body as it is resting on the earth. What is it like to have that support—support that you don't have to earn or purchase? You don't have to perch on your chair. The chair will support you.

Become aware of your breath. Feel that your breathing is supporting you. It doesn't matter if you're neurotic or sane, a good person or a bad person, happy or sad. Your breath is supporting you, regardless. It may not last forever, but for right now, your breath is supporting you.

Your body is supporting you. Remember all of the incredibly complex systems that come together to form your body. Your skeleton . . . your muscles . . . your mind. Your body is supporting you; you don't have to do anything to deserve support from your body.

The planet is supporting you. There's a workable range of temperature . . . the atmospheric gases are in just the right proportions. Gravity is working well . . . the seasons are working. You don't have to do anything to deserve any of that support. It's already present. Relax into the reality that you're already being supported. Perhaps not perfectly, but adequately.

You could imagine that even this crazy society is supporting you. There's food in the grocery store and gas at the pumps . . . people generally follow the law . . . the streets are paved . . . and the electricity works. It's not perfect, but even society is supporting you in its own way. You don't have to deserve it. Society is still going to be operating.

Allow yourself to feel that sense of support. It's always present. You don't have to do anything to deserve it or create it.

See what it would be like to relax into a state of well-being in this moment. Rest in the unconditional experience of well-being and support. You don't have to do anything to make it happen. All you need to do is relax into the way things already are. ▪

We don't have to do anything to deserve this ongoing sense of well-being, of relaxation, of unconditional support from life. We don't have to fix our life circumstances. We don't have to improve ourselves. We don't have to heal anything from our history at all. This sense of well-being is always present—we just have to remember to discipline our attention. It has to occur to us to look for it. It has to be a priority, actually. Interestingly, as we explore this practice, we may find resistance. Despite our claim of wanting relief from our suffering, we may discover an almost addictive investment in the entertainment of our familiar struggles and dramas. But if we care to, we can train ourselves to step into this state of well-being, relaxation, and support at any moment. And it's my experience that, if we do this more and more frequently, the experiential shift we have discussed is likely to begin to arise. We will actually start to have a sense of confidence that a good state of mind—a state of unconditional well-being—is always available. We don't have to resolve our neuroses or take care of our financial situation or settle our relationship or be in good health. Nothing is required. We don't have to do anything at all except look for it, because it's always there.

4

EXPERIENCING ANXIETY AND STRUGGLE

JEROME WAS A LAWYER in his late forties. He arrived at my office in a shirt and tie, on his lunch break from his job as a junior partner at a local firm. Despite his well-put-together appearance, he had come to see me because he felt unsuccessful at work and in relationships with women. Upon further discussion, he reported that he was not as assertive as he wanted to be, and he was feeling a lack of aliveness and effectiveness in his life as a whole. He found it hard to be himself when he was dating women, and at work he tended to placate or please. He worked more hours than his colleagues, doing what he could to avoid conflict. But the results were leaving him unsatisfied and frustrated.

I asked Jerome to imagine what it would be like to assert himself more effectively in any of these parts of his life—to stick up for himself in a conflict at the office or to disagree with a woman he was dating. He laughed nervously and said that even the thought made him feel uncomfortable. So I dug a little deeper and asked him what he would have to feel if he were to say "no" to a colleague.

Rather than answering the question, Jerome started rationalizing his passive approach. He started talking about the potential consequences of initiating conflict—how he didn't want people to be mad at him, didn't want to hurt their feelings, hated being yelled at, and just wanted people to get along with each other. I invited Jerome back to the present moment and asked him again what he was feeling in his immediate experience. Once he put his attention on his body, he was able to say that he was feeling tightness in his stomach, a little nausea, and a generalized nervousness. A couple of times he returned to his concerns about the consequences of conflict, and each time he was surprised when I pointed out that he had left his immediate experience yet again. He wasn't even aware of his own impulse to dissociate from his immediate experience of disturbing sensations and to jump into interpretation. Each time, I guided him back to the present moment.

I asked, "What sensations do you feel in your body as you imagine leaving your job at five o'clock and not taking work home for the weekend?" I was not, of course, suggesting that he actually leave the office at five o'clock; we were not discussing behavioral changes at this point. I was simply using a hypothetical situation to see what energies or feelings might arise if he were to face a situation he had been avoiding.

It didn't take long to discover that the feelings and sensations he had been avoiding at work were the same feelings and sensations he was avoiding in his relationships and in other unsatisfying areas of his life. They were sensations of anxiety—tightness in the chest, a faster heartbeat, a sense of nausea, a feeling of suffocation, and so on. These same feelings would come up whether he imagined conflict with potential partners, setting boundaries at work, speaking honestly with his parents, or disagreeing with a friend. It turned out that his behavior in each of these situations was crafted to avoid the very vulnerable, very disturbing experience we call "anxiety."

ANXIETY AS A NATURAL RESPONSE

For most of us, anxiety is an incredibly difficult experience to work with. It seems we have a collective societal fantasy that we're not supposed to feel anxious. Often we will relate to our experience of anxiety as evidence that there must be something wrong with us or our lives. We don't feel comfortable when we're anxious, and other people don't feel comfortable around us. Anxiety feels like a problem that needs to be fixed.

But in my experience, anxiety is a completely legitimate and valid, if not pleasant, aspect of being human. Each of us has to learn to work with anxiety skillfully because it is part of our everyday experience. I know that I feel anxious every day. Maybe it's because I wasn't paying attention as I was driving and I swerved out of my lane, or maybe I find myself wondering if our kids are okay. I might be anxious about some conflict with my wife or nervous about paying a bill. I may feel anxious with no obvious explanation. I don't think I've ever met anybody who doesn't experience anxiety as an ongoing part of life. So anxiety is not a choice; the choice is how we relate to it. Do we attack this disturbing experience with fundamental aggression—trying not to feel it, making it wrong, or distracting ourselves? Or do we approach anxiety with an attitude of commitment to, and acceptance of, this disturbing experience? Because anxiety is real; it's us. It's not some alien feeling happening *to* us. A life without anxiety is not an option.

A NOTE ABOUT ANXIETY

> For the purposes of this chapter, I'll be talking about what
> could be called "emotional" or "existential" anxiety. I'm
> not talking about the kind of anxiety that results from
> brain chemistry imbalances, hormones, or other medical
> problems. These biologically based experiences of anxiety
> usually need biologically based interventions: regulating
> sleep, experimenting with diet, making sure we exercise,
> possibly even medication. These interventions are all very
> appropriate. But here we'll be talking about the type of
> anxiety that we all live with—anxiety that doesn't seem
> to be caused by a neurological or hormonal problem. The
> anxiety of everyday human experience. ▪▀

When we're feeling anxious, generally we sense that there's
some sort of impending threat. Intense physical sensations arise,
which energize us and focus our attention on the search for danger. There is often a sense of imminent catastrophe, which is
interesting because often we can't even name what it is we're
anxious about. Anxiety is an immediate response to a *possible* threat, which is different from fear. Fear is an immediate
response to an *immediate* threat. For example, if we're hiking in
the forest and suddenly hear a loud noise, we'll likely feel some
fear. If we're hiking and we feel anxious, on the other hand, it's
because there's a *possibility* of danger—we're worried about what
could happen, rather than what *is* happening. In this way, anxiety serves almost like a preparation for our survival response. It's
getting us ready for the possibility of danger.

Both fear and anxiety are at the center of our biology. These
basic survival responses have certainly been around much longer
than we as humans have been on the planet. Our species probably wouldn't be here if we didn't have fear and anxiety. If our

ancestors had felt only peaceful and happy, sunning themselves on a rock all day, some wild animal probably would have eaten them up. The threat response is a necessary part of the evolutionary process. Perhaps for the same evolutionary reasons, anxiety seems to be very contagious. For example, if a single bird in a flock gets startled, in a fraction of a second, the whole flock will take off. The same goes for a herd of deer or a family of prairie dogs. Interestingly, it's not that different among humans. Most of us have had the experience of becoming anxious simply because someone we care about is feeling that way. If a loved one feels angry, jealous, or confused, we usually don't feel the same feeling. For some reason, we can keep more distance, probably because these feelings are not a signal of an imminent threat to our survival. But the anxiety response is deeply embedded in our makeup, which makes it very contagious and very difficult to work with.

It's difficult to work with anxiety because we seem to be biologically wired to avoid it if at all possible or to escape from whatever is triggering it. If anxiety were a signal of real imminent danger, this would of course be an intelligent response. We would want to get away from the danger as quickly as possible. But as modern humans, we experience life beyond the biological level of physical survival. We're having emotional, cognitive, social, and spiritual experiences, too. And when there is disturbance on any of these levels, we seem to respond in a fraction of a second to the possibility of a threat, as if it were a biological signal. Evolutionarily, it's better to be safe than sorry. And because we don't take the time to examine this anxiety in detail, we react as if our literal, physical survival were at risk. What has become clear through Western developmental work is that most of us learn to organize our survival strategies around the avoidance of certain feelings, thoughts, and sensations—especially those associated with intense levels of anxiety.

ANXIETY AND OUR DISOWNED FEELINGS

From the Western perspective, anxiety is basically a developmental phenomenon. In the first years of life, we're subjected to intense emotions and sensations that we're really not capable of processing. These intense, energetic, emotional experiences threaten to overwhelm our very fragile sense of self, our ability to function; thus, they can provoke intense anxiety in us. To disconnect from the anxiety, we quickly construct internal fences to separate our conscious experiencing from these disturbing emotions. These fences—or defenses—may include repression, regression, projection, intellectualization, dissociation, and so on. Whatever our style, we're basically trying to get away from the perceived threat. In the process, we sacrifice a part of ourselves—the part that's feeling disturbed. We cut off from those emotions, so that our more conscious sense of self can operate relatively free of anxiety. As we have discussed, however, the cost of doing this is a fundamental sense of being divided against ourselves. We create a character structure: a positive self—sometimes called "ego," which is associated with the ability to function and survive—and a negative "not-self," created out of the disturbing energies we're not willing to feel. When young, this anxiety-avoidance strategy is healthy and intelligent. It's very appropriate and very creative. In fact, it requires incredible discipline to learn how to not feel what we're actually feeling in a consistent way. But by organizing our character structure around the avoidance of these unworkably intense feelings—such as grief, rage, and fear—we paradoxically place these worst fears at the center of our sense of self.

This is what Jerome, the client we met at the beginning of this chapter, had done. Over the course of a handful of sessions, Jerome started to examine the possibility that what was common across all the problem areas in his life was the avoidance of anxiety. He discovered that the anxiety he felt was pretty much the same in all of these areas; there wasn't a different anxiety for relationship and another for work, for example. He started to see that the experience of anxiety had been part of his life—perhaps for his whole life. He remembered feeling it as an adolescent, when applying for law schools and when taking the bar exam. He could even remember feeling anxious when he was left home alone or when his parents would fight. Once he recognized that he'd been feeling anxious off and on for as long as he could remember, he became more open to the possibility that anxiety was a valid, necessary part of his human experience—even if it was one he didn't like!

To help him become more tolerant of his own anxiety, I had Jerome close his eyes and do a visualization. I asked him to stretch his arm out as far as it could go and imagine that his hand was holding the experience of feeling anxious. I had him try to get as far away from it as possible. Of course, his anxiety would still be part of him; he can't actually leave it behind. In the visualization, I suggested he try walking forward while attempting to leave the anxiety behind. The anxiety is still in his hand; so if he's not willing to bring the anxiety with him, he will end up walking in a circle. I had Jerome visualize himself just rotating around and around that central feeling, all the while pretending it wasn't there.

This is what happens to all of us when we divide ourselves against feeling certain emotions or sensations. We're walking forward through life as if things were settled and taken care of, but secretly massive amounts of our awareness, intelligence, discipline, and creativity are going toward making sure we never have to be aware of our disturbance. Ironically, the result is that we begin to organize our lives around the central feeling we're avoiding. We end up walking in a circle when we think we're moving forward. If we're lucky, by the time we're in our thirties or forties, we start to wake up to these repetitive, habitual patterns. We become curious about and sort of mystified by why we keep re-creating the same painful dramas over and over. We can see that the behaviors are not to our benefit, but we don't seem to be able to stop them.

This is when we need to investigate the possibility that we are basically maintaining these patterns as a ritualized avoidance strategy. We're behaving almost like a planet rotating around the sun. The very experience we've dedicated our life to not feeling—be it loneliness, lack of worth, abandonment, anger, or dependency—has become the center of our sense of self. And this sense of self is not a very positive, workable one. In fact, we relate to this core sense of self as quite problematic and threatening. By the time we're adults, our efforts to avoid the immediate experience of anxiety can result in a state of subtle but chronic anxiety.

Jerome wanted to challenge his historic conditioning, but to do so, he had to commit to going into his worst fears and dissolving his avoidance strategies. He had to recognize what he didn't want to feel and bring it back into immediate, embodied experience. This practice unfortunately doesn't make the difficult experience go away—Jerome will likely feel disturbed by conflict for the rest of his life. It does, however, leave us free to engage with our lives more spontaneously because we're willing to have those feelings arise at any moment. We learn that we can feel them and they aren't going to kill us. Gradually, we gain what I think of as the *confidence of "so what?"* "So what if I feel uncertain and confused? So what if I feel victimized or dependent? So what if I feel hurtful and alone and selfish? So what?" They actually just turn out to be feelings—feelings that can be worked with, feelings that don't have to be acted upon.

From a Buddhist point of view, our commitment to not feeling disturbing emotions gives rise to a very convincing sense that we have some central, essential nature. Our lives indeed seem to be formed around something, and that something feels deeply problematic to us. By practicing our avoidant strategies over and over, day after day for decades, we become experientially convinced that there must be a central point around which our life revolves. The centerpiece of our being is composed of our core vulnerabilities, which are perceived as problematic. Our life revolves around a problem. And that problem must be our secret self, because it's always been there and never seems to change.

Oddly enough, this belief serves us, because it means we don't have to consider the possibility that there is no center to our lives and no independently existing self. Instead, we can spend our lives in therapy or spiritual practice, trying to somehow heal or take care of the seemingly solid problematic self we've created. At this point, we might attempt to improve our experience of the problem through Western therapy, or we might try to experience "no self" through spiritual practices like meditation. But we're still motivated by a fundamentally paranoid attitude that there is some problem needing to be fixed. But when we actually recover what has been disowned and bring it into our immediate embodied experience—and see that it's not going to kill us—we begin to dissolve our sense of having an essential self. We discover that, absent a central struggle, we have no center to our life at all. We just show up each moment and deal with our life as it happens.

BINDING OUR ANXIETY TO A SPECIFIC ISSUE

As we've discussed, when we stabilize our efforts to not feel anxious, the result is a sense of being divided against ourselves. This, in turn, generates distrust in ourselves and a sense of having a basic flaw, as well as many of the issues commonly worked with in psychotherapy.

Anna Freud coined the term *signal anxiety* to refer to the function played by anxiety in preparing us to defend against inner threats. She saw this kind of anxiety as a signal that previously unconscious material was threatening to be experienced consciously. Similarly, we can understand anxiety as a signal that there is something we've been pushing away that needs to be integrated. Something has been disowned; maybe we ought to check it out?

Chronic anxiety is the result of our ritualized refusal to stay fully embodied with our present experience. One of the strategies we use when we refuse to experience whatever it is we've been pushing away is called *binding anxiety*. Binding anxiety arises when we identify our anxiety as caused by a particular issue. We tell ourselves a story about a particular threat, which binds our anxiety to that localized issue. We sacrifice this part of ourselves as if it were a symptom or problem, as if it were the cause of our anxiety. By apparently containing our anxiety within a specific problem, we create a sense that the rest of our life is free of anxiety. This also gives rise to the fantasy that we could have an anxiety-free life if only we could solve that problem. "If there's a cause to my anxiety, there must be a solution. If only I had enough money, had children, were single, were enlightened, then my anxiety would be solved." In truth, if we actually solved this "problem," anxiety would continue to arise. And so, unconsciously, we actually make sure that we never solve our favorite problem. Or if we do, we find a new problem, a new explanation for our anxiety. Otherwise, we'd have to face the fact that inexplicable anxiety will continue to arise, off and on, as long as we are sensitive, embodied, biological beings.

A client of mine, Patty, had been married for twenty-four years before divorcing once the children left for college. She'd recently begun dating again, and it was bringing back a lot of bad memories from her younger years. After having been married for so long, she'd forgotten how anxious she'd always been around men she was seeing. Even as a teenager, she'd feel uncharacteristically shy and nervous when out on dates and had a hard time being herself. She came to see me because she was so distressed by this problem and wanted help getting underneath it. Of course, she didn't much like what I had to say! I suggested to her that perhaps by focusing on this repetitive, apparent problem, she was distracting herself from a deeper vulnerability. She could pin her generalized human anxiety on the issue of dating. "I'm anxious because I have a date this Friday night, and I don't know if I should cancel," she could say. "I'm afraid I'll get a panic attack. If only I could meet the right man, so I could stop dating. Then I wouldn't be anxious. Because dating is the cause of my anxiety. I'm really not that anxious in other parts of my life." Like most of us, Patty believed that the generalized anxiety she felt about being human was bound up in this one familiar issue. In our discussions, it became clear that during her marriage, she had not been free of anxiety; instead, she had explained her anxiety as being caused by her natural concerns about her children, finances, and so on.

Patty, of course, probably had some very real history about her relations with men, perhaps beginning with her father. But her history is in her past. It is not causing the present anxiety, even though it may be *triggering* it. But now that she's an adult, it might be useful for her to learn to have a relationship with anxiety as anxiety, without explanation. I worked with Patty on developing a willingness and ability to stay present with her anxiety whenever it might arise. While not easy, she found that she could do it. She also began to see that a refusal to stay embodied with her own disturbance was a type of self-abandonment. This refusal to be intimate with herself made it feel very threatening to explore the possibility of being intimate with a partner. She took on the practice of including the experience of anxiety as a valid part of any experience of intimacy. She started counting on it, rather than treating it as a problem to be solved before a relationship would be possible.

Most of us would rather do what Patty was doing—projecting all of our anxiety onto one single issue. We don't seem to be ready to welcome anxiety into our everyday lives as if it were a necessary, valid experience. We may understand that anxiety has served for hundreds of millions of years as a useful signal of imminent threat to survival. But who wants to be aware of feeling that their survival is threatened? That experience is very disturbing. Therefore, we have a strong motivation to get out of that anxiety. If we can escape our anxiety, then we will feel safe.

But just because we feel unsafe doesn't mean there's a real threat, and just because we feel safe doesn't mean that we actually are. Some types of therapy, in fact, emphasize the need to feel safe in order to work with one's vulnerabilities. It seems true for many situations that a specific environment is needed for specific work, just as we want a sterile operating room for an operation. I don't have expertise in working with trauma, but my sense is that feeling safe is very important when investigating traumatic organization. Although this safe environment is very accurate as a temporary experience, it may be easy to then think that feeling safe is a requirement for engaging with one's life. But there is another possibility, which is to develop a confidence in our willingness and ability to experience our fear, anxiety, and negativity and to work with whatever may arise at any moment.

Perhaps a confidence based on our own capacities will be more reliable than a feeling of safety that is dependent on circumstances we really have little control over.

BINDING ANXIETY IN GROUPS

The phenomenon of binding anxiety can also be seen at a group level, whether that group is a social network, a work team, or a spiritual organization. Most groups are not very conscious of, or skillful in dealing with, the anxiety that's guaranteed to arise when a number of people relate to each other. Therefore, it's almost inevitable that any group will experience a scapegoating process. In the same way that we compartmentalize our anxiety and tell ourselves that it's about one particular issue, a group will unconsciously and frequently select a subgroup to feel an emotion or energy that the other members don't want to feel. Perhaps it's anger or sadness or a fear of being left out. The subgroup is usually made up of the person or people with the greatest unresolved issues—and weakest boundaries—around the particular energy the group doesn't want to feel. In a very powerful, unconscious process of induction, this person ends up expressing, for example, not only her *own* anger but also the anger of the rest of the group. The rest of the group gets to feel relatively free of anger and, therefore, of anxiety. Meanwhile, this one person or subgroup appears to be the problem. Just as Patty believed dating to be the cause of her anxiety, the group begins to think, "If only we could get rid of this person, then our group would be great." Often the next step is to actually get rid of "the problem"—that is, the person holding that energy for the group. But, of course, once that happens, it's only a matter of time until the group starts to experience anger arising somewhere else. The anger is still there in the group; if they are not willing to acknowledge it, feel it, and work with it at the group level, a new subgroup or person will be chosen as the next location of the problem.

This is also a very challenging issue in working with families. As a family therapist for social services in the 1980s, time after time I would meet with families that would be unconsciously scapegoating a child. Because young children are like psychic, emotional sponges, they tend to absorb whatever their parents have repressed and won't deal with. The child then tends to identify with that energy and act it out. The parents can then enable the child to continue acting out what they don't want to feel while punishing or rejecting the child for being that way. ◾

COMMITTING TO THE EXPERIENCE OF ANXIETY

When we investigate the experience of anxiety, the Western approach takes the experience itself as its starting point. What triggered the anxiety? How can we work with it? How can we make it go away? How can we improve our circumstances so we don't have to feel so anxious and divided? As discussed, a Buddhist approach suggests that how we *relate* to the experience of anxiety is even more important than the details of that experience. If we start by taking our experience at face value, we're starting from the assumption that this experience has its own real, objective existence. If what I am feeling has an independent reality—that is, if such a "thing" as "anxiety" exists—then there seems to be a subtle but powerful implication that the self who is *aware* of this anxiety must have its own independent reality, too. "Anxiety" and "I" must be two fundamentally separate things. There is, as discussed previously, the vivid appearance of a self, seemingly with its own essential nature, relating to a world made up of separate objects, feelings, thoughts, and so on. Without examination, we are understandably likely to take this appearance as an accurate experience of reality. This perpetuates our sense of being a small, separate, alienated self, living in a vast, impersonal universe. This significant, alienated, problematic self seems so vivid that we believe it's a representation of reality. Since it so obviously appears to be there, it *must* be there. And so, of course, it makes sense to protect and improve this self.

This could be called the egoic process—the process through which we generate and maintain the experience of a solid, continuous, significant and personal self. Unfortunately, this project of selfhood is never going to be truly successful. As much as the Western approach might improve our ability to engage with our lives, in reality, everything is always changing. We can never solve our lives. Life is not a thing that can be broken and then fixed. Life is a process, and we can never solve a process. We can only participate in this process, either consciously or unconsciously. We aren't going to find the perfect formula and then coast our way through life. We can't make pain go away, although we can reduce unnecessary suffering significantly. The more deeply we investigate, the less we can grasp or even know this apparent self that Western psychology takes as its foundation. From the Buddhist perspective, the nature of life—and of our own mind—is basically open. There is no foundation; no ground to stand on. We can consciously participate in this open nature, but we can't know it.

On a subconscious level, we seem to understand this. We sense that we're identifying with a self that cannot be located. The inevitable consequence is a pervasive and chronic anxiety. Our efforts to feel safe and comfortable are constantly being undermined by the evidence of our actual experiencing. Anxiety, from a spiritual path perspective, can therefore be understood as the *accurate perception of the basically open nature of life, as seen from the reference point of egoic process.* The egoic process is that aspect of the self that, quite understandably, wants to feel comfortable, happy, safe, secure, and in control. When faced with the reality of how open everything actually is, that part of us basically freaks out.

From this point of view, we can see that anxiety is actually a necessary part of our path. As we move in the direction of waking up, increasing our tolerance of more and more awareness or open mind, we will inevitably experience anxiety. At some point or another, anybody committed to a spiritual path may find it important to commit to the experience of anxiety as an approximation of an open state of mind. This is not because reality is itself anxiety producing but because the inevitable engagement of a "personal self" with nonpersonal reality will be experienced as a threat to this self—that is, as anxiety.

When I say "committing to our anxiety," I mean doing the difficult work—difficult because it goes against both our biology and our cultural conditioning—of training ourselves *not* to try to escape our anxious feelings. It even means to learn to appreciate them, explore them, feel them, and see for ourselves whether they are as much of a problem as we think they will be. If anxiety is not a problem and if we understand that it's actually an essential part of our path of waking up, then we might want to practice this attitude of commitment. "I am ready to feel anxious at any second," we might say to ourselves, "and to work with the energy of anxiety for the rest of my life. I give up my fantasy of a life free of anxiety."

The anxiety we feel often seems to be associated with particular circumstances. If my wife is significantly late coming home, or if I have to go to the doctor, or if my daughter is not speaking to me, I will likely feel anxiety. But if I look more closely, I see that each of those situations is forcing me to acknowledge how open my life actually is. Yes, my wife might have gotten into an accident. Yes, I could have undiagnosed cancer. Yes, it could be that I'm a bad father. All of those things are completely possible. There's no guarantee of happy endings, and we are always aware of that on some deep level. But such circumstances, it turns out, become reminders of the fundamental openness of our lives in general. Underneath the particulars, we're anxious because these life dramas force us to acknowledge that we don't actually know what's going to happen. We have no way of really controlling our circumstances, which, from an egoic point of view, is very uncomfortable.

If we examine our experience more broadly, we may discover that we can't actually answer any of the most important questions about our lives. Do we really know who we are? Do we know the meaning of life? Do we know how to have healthy intimacy? Do we know how to parent our children without passing on our unresolved issues? Do we know what happens when we die? Do we even know if we should be doing this type of work or living in this town? Upon investigation, we find that we don't know anything that's really important. (A lot of us don't even know what we want to eat for dinner tonight.) If anxiety is our egoic response to the truth of not knowing—of openness—then we really might want to consider committing to the experience of anxiety, because it's not going anywhere.

THE METAPHOR OF *BARDO*

I find the Tibetan Buddhist concept of *bardo* to be a useful metaphor for learning to tolerate the experience of openness and anxiety. From a traditional religious perspective, bardo is a series of experiential realms that consciousness enters after death. Each realm is less open, more solid, and more contractive than the one before it. When awareness can finally tolerate the degree of openness and anxiety of a particular realm, then that's the realm in which it reincarnates. Its tolerance for openness determines where it will stay; it can't incarnate into more openness than it can handle.

Personally, I have no idea what happens when we die; I'm more interested in applying the metaphor of bardo to the way our minds work on a daily basis. We could consider that, moment after moment, we are incarnating into—identifying with—particular states of mind. We're incarnating into certain attitudes, positions, beliefs, and roles. For example, when working as a therapist, I take on a deep identification with that role. I've found that this role actually supports a greater tolerance of open mind than, let's say, when I'm in conflict with my wife in my role of partner. Even within my role as therapist, I may be captured by a variety of states of mind, depending on my tolerance of anxiety and openness at any given moment. When I recognize the feeling of being captured, I have learned to ask myself, "What more open experience am I refusing to participate in right now?"

From this point of view, our practice is to gradually learn to metabolize—to contain and process in our embodied experience—more and more anxiety. That way, over time, we can integrate more and more experience of open mind or awareness into our daily life. As we gradually become more and more able to go deeply into our anxiety—rather than be stopped by it—we discover that it's not a problem. We then have more frequent moments of open awareness. Gradually, we find that the familiar ups and downs of daily life are being held in an environment of openness. And we find that this actually changes the meaning of our familiar experience. We find that "form," experienced as inseparable from awareness, is not only workable, but may even be blissful. ▪

From both the developmental and Buddhist views, we're now left with a dilemma: *acknowledging* the truth of our experience will often require feeling our *immediate* anxiety, but *resisting* the truth of our experience results in *chronic* anxiety. Either way, we will feel anxiety. Rather than looking more deeply at this disturbing dilemma, our usual unconscious response is to try to avoid either choice. We do so by manifesting symptoms that appear to explain and bind this anxiety. As "symptoms," we can claim that the cause of our anxiety is an aberration. We *acknowledge* that there *is* anxiety, but we *resist owning it* as a necessary part of life. We can then involve ourselves in the project of seeking relief from these symptoms through a variety of means. But if we were to successfully resolve these problems, we would lose the distractive function they provide. At that point, we might actually have to examine the root cause of our anxiety. We would then be faced with our worst fears. From the developmental perspective, this would mean facing our core emotional vulnerabilities. From the fruitional perspective, we would face raw, immediate experiencing, which provides no support for personal identity. So we have two choices. We can avoid the truth and instead experience the exhausting, but partially unconscious, disturbance of chronic anxiety, or we can commit to the truth and live with the conscious disturbance of emotional vulnerability, with no support for personal identity. Until we train ourselves to rest in the embodied experience of anxiety and disturbance—to find out for ourselves that we are not harmed by it—and to understand that these difficult experiences are completely legitimate and valid parts of life, we will unconsciously look for some way out. We'll be searching for some resolution or, at least, some reliable distraction.

POLARIZING DRAMA AS DISTRACTION

A common response to this dilemma of anxiety is the creation of polarized life dramas—with fear on one side and hope on the other. We represent the disturbing truth of our experiencing as a fear and our wish to have a safe, comfortable, undisturbed life as a hope. When we add the fantasy of resolution to these contradictory, apparently mutually exclusive experiences, our attention is successfully captured. The struggle between these two becomes a distracting drama.

There is so much anxiety associated with our fear of openness that finding a resolution usually takes on apparently survival-level importance. We really seem to believe that the outcome of this drama will determine our worth as a person or the viability of our lives. Let's say that I feel unworthy of love. It's a horrible feeling to have, and it goes way back in my life. I want to collapse or explode in rage whenever I feel this feeling. Naturally, I imagine what it might feel like to be truly loved, and then I begin to behave in ways I hope will give me that feeling. I'm kind and generous; I'm helpful and avoid conflict. This fear of feeling unloved (which I already live with) is countered by the hope that someday I'll feel loved in the way I want. *Then* I'll be able to start living my life. *Then* I'll be okay. Until then, there's a lot at stake. This is a really significant issue: my worth as a person is on the line.

This polarized drama is fascinating to us, yet it does not resolve anything. I already feel unworthy of love. It's a historic issue, deeply conditioned, and it's unlikely I ever will get rid of it. So rather than trying to escape it, another possibility is to experience it—to commit to feeling this very difficult vulnerability, to let myself feel unworthy of love and then see if I'm harmed. But that's not our instinctual approach. The closer we get to our core vulnerabilities, or to the truth of openness, the more we feel an annihilatory panic. So we unconsciously opt for the experience of polarized drama to avoid having to face the truth of our experience. And in doing so, we create an incredibly resilient and stable psychic structure: struggle.

THE NATURE OF STRUGGLE

Having come up with this strategy of struggle, we've developed a pretty effective defense against feeling raw, embodied, unexplained anxiety. *Struggle* can be defined as "a continued effort to resist force or to free oneself from constraints." The core struggle for most of us is that we want things to be different than they are. We don't want to feel fear and other intense negative emotions. We don't want to become sick and die. We don't want the incomprehensible violence in this world to continue. But negative feelings and difficult circumstances are inseparable from the complex reality we are all expressions of. *Neurotic struggle,* then, could be understood as "a continued effort to resist reality or to free oneself from its constraints."

Imagine finding yourself in prison, unjustly accused, convicted, and sentenced to life without parole. How would you relate to such an injustice, to the fact that you're going to be in prison for the rest of your life? You might struggle against that reality, against the unfairness of it, but that wouldn't get you out of prison. In fact, it's possible that you may end up feeling even more claustrophobic and enraged—basically, in hell. The struggle would, however, serve to distract you from the deep grief and powerlessness that you would have to feel if you actually acknowledged the truth of your situation.

We might say that all of us are, in fact, imprisoned—in the constraints of body, gender, our history, our race, and life circumstances. And most of us distract ourselves from that imprisonment through struggle. That way, we don't have to consciously participate in what it's like to feel claustrophobic, imprisoned, powerless, and constrained by reality. Instead, we can hold on to our fantasies of a life without limitation. So neurotic struggle has a function; it serves a purpose. Until we're ready to be present, embodied, and kind toward the truth of our experience—which is very disturbing on a certain level—we will have an investment in maintaining neurotic struggle.

To be most effective, a strategy for resisting reality will have several features. Most basically, it will operate at an unconscious level. After all, if we're aware of what we're defending against, it's not such a great defense. In a more sophisticated way, we can acknowledge our experiencing without actually working with it. For example, I work with many people who in some way or another say, "Yes, I really want to work with that issue. I really want to get to the depth of things." They are acknowledging that they have core vulnerabilities, and they claim to want to work with them. But often there's some excuse. "I'm not ready for it yet." "It's too scary." "My life circumstances are too busy; now's not a good time." "My partner doesn't support me doing this work." The truth of their reality gets mentioned but never really encountered. They claim to be unable rather than unwilling.

A good strategy for resisting reality will also be vague enough to be used in a variety of circumstances. If getting the promotion I want could prove my worth as a person, I'd lose my drama if I got that promotion. But if my worth requires that I get the love I want, then there's no end to that project. There will always be some qualification or disappointment available.

Another feature will be that this strategy for resisting reality is self-perpetuating, meaning it has its own life. We don't have to keep attending to it once it's set in place. This is the elegance of struggle. We have an unconscious investment in making sure it continues, because we need to maintain its avoidant functions. So we refuse to acknowledge reality, which gives us some immediate relief. But disconnecting from what's true creates the ongoing experience of alienation and feeling problematic. This, in turn, generates chronic anxiety, which provides a continuing sense of imminent threat. That threat activates our distrust of ourselves and of life, which then justifies the need to avoid reality. Avoiding reality, we then feel alienated and disconnected, which starts the cycle all over again. In this way, struggle is an incredibly complex and effective way to *pretend* to ourselves that we're dealing with our lives without really doing so. It allows us to believe we're trying to solve our problems, while simultaneously guaranteeing that no change will really take place.

THE THREE LEVELS OF STRUGGLE

Struggle operates on three distinct levels: content, process, and basic. The three levels work simultaneously, though they seem to have a sequence to them. If we are committed to the path of waking up, our energetic investment tends to progress from content, to process, to basic. This progression could also be understood as a movement from disowning energies, to owning energies, to experiencing energies without either owning or disowning.

Struggle at the Level of Content

The content level of struggle focuses on specific fears and disturbances. It's about improving the story of one's life by eliminating the problems that seem to threaten us, even while unconsciously maintaining these problems as distractions from deeper realities and vulnerabilities. From a therapeutic view, this level addresses "preneurotic" experiencing, or how we handled our lives before we achieved the capacity of a reliable repressive or dissociative function—before we stabilized our neurotic strategies. For most people, that achievement takes place around four, five, or six years old. Before this achievement, we, as young children, are really at the mercy of whatever inner, relational, or environmental circumstances may arise. We are like a leaf on the wind, a cork in the ocean, always in danger of feeling overwhelmed by influences over which we have no control. But with neurotic organization, we create reliable ways in which to limit the degree of intensity with which we have to deal. Most of us have adequate levels of neurotic defenses, but the content level of struggle addresses all of the disturbance that continues to arise, despite our best efforts to not be aware of what we don't want to feel.

When young, we develop our basic strategies. For example, we might train ourselves to not be aware of our anger and boundaries and learn to cue off others' needs. Or we may disconnect from our grief and dependency and learn to act as if we're self-sufficient. As adults, we use denial, distraction, stress management, exercise, meditation, or any number of other methods to try to soothe our anxiety. Most of us unconsciously spend much of our time and energy using these strategies in an effort to create life circumstances that will feel safe, supportive, and positive and that won't provoke anxiety. Unfortunately, one of the consequences of this approach of eliminating problems is that the more successful we are at cocreating life circumstances that seem to guarantee safety, the more likely it is we will start to feel stagnant or deadened. We're no longer engaged with the spontaneity and unpredictability of things, and often we no longer feel fully alive. It's like living in a gated community. It's comfortable, but something's missing. What we often end up doing, then, is "hiring" a partner who is the representation of the "other"—of whatever it is we are trying to repress. The benefit is that we feel more aliveness; it gives us some relief from this safe little world we've created. But the flip side is that this person appears to be a threat to our safety and comfort, so we end up with a very complicated, ambivalent relationship toward that person. Or we might do some extreme sport as a way to feel alive, perhaps even in an addictive way, not realizing that the very intensity of our sport can make the rest of our life appear even more dead.

In a Buddhist view, the content level of struggle can be seen as us working with a story about what we're trying to possess, avoid, or ignore. Each of these options represents one of the three styles of fundamental aggression discussed in chapter 1. In the beginning foundational practices of Buddhism, there is a strong focus on removing oneself from problematic circumstances. We may leave our social life, even our family, and go to a monastery. We may make use of many rules, called precepts, which support our cultivation of a calm, stable state of mind. Many beginning practices emphasize positive behavior and training ourselves to replace negative thoughts and feelings with those that are positive. At this stage, the content of our experience is what we attend to and try to change.

What's in common at this level for both a therapeutic and a Buddhist approach is an often-unexamined attitude that our state of mind is mostly determined by inner and outer circumstances, which we are unable to resist. And so it makes sense that to improve our state of mind, we must improve those circumstances. In both of these views, we're still trying to manipulate our lives so we feel safe and secure. At this stage, the goal of relating directly to open awareness is seen as a possible future achievement. For now, or so the story goes, one's sense of self is too problematic. This content level is characterized by a continuing struggle to eliminate problems and heal wounds, dissolve obstacles, and feel good about ourselves. This struggle is accepted without examination. "Of course," we think, "that's what it's all about. My whole life is about trying to feel good and avoid feeling bad." We're still focused on our life circumstances as the cause of our difficulty and anxiety. When things are going well, we feel okay; when they are going badly, we feel anxious. It's a little bit like being a child at the mercy of a parent's mood.

Struggle at the Level of Process

At some point, we may achieve the capacity to feel stable enough, safe enough, and self-contained enough that we no longer feel we're always at the mercy of our immediate circumstances. This accomplishment—the accomplishment of neurotic organization—has incredible benefits. But one price tag of this is a stabilized sense of discomfort that's not associated with any specific content at all. It comes from feeling divided against the "dangerous" parts of ourselves. As we discussed earlier, this division leads to ongoing or chronic anxiety. The good news is that, at this point, enough confidence has been gained that we can take on the project of recovering experiential ownership of that which has been disowned. We feel some degree of trust in ourselves; we feel adequately intact. Because of this, we can now risk relating to "other" in a more confident way, and we transition to the process level of struggle. Having committed ourselves to recovering ownership of our difficult vulnerabilities, we now focus on how we relate to these experiences.

The process level of struggle is the realm of most Western depth therapies. The basic intention is to make conscious that which has been unconscious or, on a subtler level, to cultivate a more open and receptive attitude toward what we don't want to experience. In most cases, therapy at this level is focused on an exploration of what got repressed when we were young and, more importantly, how this is still being repressed today. While we continue to work with content, the central issue becomes how we engage with our experiencing, rather than what we are experiencing. Acceptance of self becomes the focus, more than fixing the self. And because we are not so invested in solving an endless display of content-level problems, we are now able to investigate patterns of experiencing. We discover that it is our out-of-date patterns that perpetuate our young survival strategies and that what perpetuates these patterns is our current refusal to consciously participate in our core vulnerabilities. While we may deal with specific thoughts and emotions, we're actually working with recognizing how we continue to dissociate and with learning ways in which to tolerate more experiential intensity. As discussed previously, a very effective way in which to maintain our repressive strategies is with ritualized struggle. Our conscious experience is either our hope or our fear, and our repressed experience is the opposite—either our fear or our hope. If I grew up in a family in which anger was either prohibited or very destructive, I would be smart to disconnect from any of my own feelings of anger. Growing up, I might believe that I "struggled with anger." Perhaps I struggled with my own anger, expressed in explosive episodes about which I felt ashamed, or with the anger of others, such as a succession of partners with anger issues. As an adult in therapy, a major part of my work would be to recover a conscious relationship with this disowned aspect of myself. I may find that what I've struggled with is not anger but my repression of my anger. It might help to understand my history, to learn skillful ways to express my anger, and so on, all in service of learning how to have an adult relationship with anger.

Bringing repressed material into awareness allows us to feel more integrated, less divided. Of course, one problem is that we will never make all of our experience conscious. Research over the past twenty to thirty years consistently suggests that as much as 95 percent of what we experience never arises into conscious awareness. A massive amount of experiencing, processing, and decision making is happening without our conscious participation. So even if we become receptive to our unconscious experience, I think it's extremely unlikely we'll ever be fully aware of everything we're choosing not to feel. If feeling whole requires that we no longer repress experience, then the Western approach to this level of struggle is an unending project, and in some cases, Western therapy does in fact seem unending.

From the Buddhist view, the process level of struggle can be seen as working with the tendency to subtly define and orient ourselves based on our experience of *relationship,* especially with emotional energy. I may be taking my sense of self from the quality of my emotional relating, from how well I deal with difficult feelings, or by how much equanimity I am capable of feeling when disturbed. Struggle may now be based on the hope and fear I bring to my relationship with *other*—whether it be another person or the "other" of my own psyche. I hope that I will feel clear and generous in relating to myself and to others. I fear that I will feel envious and arrogant. I struggle to feel open and calm whenever I'm actually feeling closed and agitated. Reducing struggle at this point requires taking ownership of the full range of my feelings, like them or not, and learning that feelings have no necessary connection to behavior. I am able, at first as a practice, to relate as a dignified and considerate person, regardless of how I'm feeling. As an adult with repressed anger, my practice at this level might include returning over and over to my immediate experience of anger, slowly discovering that what was once, in fact, unworkable is now quite workable. But recovering disowned anger is not the real point. Rather, the point is to stay present with all of my experiencing—pleasant and scary—with no agenda of understanding, healing, or resolving; just participating in whatever arises. Buddhist practices at this level are basically generic, not issue-specific. I relate to whatever arises with awareness, embodied immediacy, and unconditional kindness, cultivating a resilient relationship with all experiencing. My efforts are to improve the quality of engagement, regardless of content. The patterns of relating that I work with are the familiar ways in which I escape from open immediacy into the attachment, anger, and ignoring expressions of fundamental aggression. I wouldn't be doing these practices, though, if I already experienced myself as whole, complete, not problematic. I am still splitting off from these parts of myself as if they were somehow not me. While it's much improved, a sense of split remains.

In both views—Western and Buddhist—there's an increasing sense of confidence at this level. But there still remains an identification with our conscious experiencing as "I" and with other persons and certain aspects of ourselves experienced as "not I." This generates an ongoing sense of tension and anxiety, which we continue to avoid with dramas of struggle about relationship. We continue a subtle investment in the project of improvement. We continue to be in a struggle to feel more fully alive, more embodied, more present, and more wakeful. All of those things are wonderful. But beneath the display, there's still some sense of being a project—as if who we are in this moment is somehow deficient or not quite okay yet. We still are claiming that we can't yet show up fully and engage in our lives just as we are.

Struggle at the Basic Level

The basic level of struggle concerns the way in which we're unconsciously using the unending display of our experience as a distraction from the nature of open mind. While we may have given up the fantasy of an only-positive life and relaxed our project of only-positive ways of relating to our experiencing, we still find a tendency to escape from the non-personal nature of open awareness into our fascination with our personal relative experiencing. To return to the metaphor of the movie, when we're captured by a movie, we lose any sense of awareness of the environment within which the movie is being shown. The more fascinating the movie, the more completely we are captured. And what seems most magnetizing about a movie is the sense of a problem, or struggle, with some very significant resolution to be decided. The same goes for our daily lives. We seem to be fascinated by the endless stream of thoughts, feeling, hopes, fears, and perceptions that make up the display of our minds. This fascination is unconsciously used as a distraction from awareness—or whatever we want to call that larger context of open intelligence and perception. Again, we avoid that open experience, because it has no qualities that can ever be grasped and provides absolutely no support for personal identity—which makes it very disturbing to our project of continuing our sense of being a significant self.

This basic level of struggle is usually not addressed by mainstream Western therapies, because within that view, the belief in an objectively existing self remains largely unquestioned. Developmental psychotherapy is organized around the effort to improve one's experience of the self; it's pretty straightforward. Not so from the Buddhist view. It's at this basic level where the fruitional view really begins, focusing on the question of how the relative experience of form and limitation is related to the absolute experience of open mind and freedom. Buddhist practices are really an invitation to drop our fascination with *what* we are experiencing and attend to the already existing *awareness* of our experience. Awareness is already always present. In fact, awareness is inseparable from the content of our experiencing. So there's no future goal, no project, no struggle for achievement. There's just a shift of attention or perspective, over and over.

THE THREE LEVELS OF STRUGGLE IN CLINICAL PRACTICE

Having described these three levels of struggle—content, process, and basic—perhaps it would be helpful to give some examples of how this may actually show up in my office. It's very common at the beginning of therapeutic work for someone to be looking outside of themselves either for the cause of their problems or for their solution. Because we have very little control over others, even over our own feelings, this strategy guarantees struggle at the *content* level. This happens for everyone, but in my experience, it's most vivid in relationship work.

When a couple first comes in, often each is blaming the other for their experience. "If only he would be more sensitive and emotionally available, I could be happy." "If only she would stop telling me what to do, we would have peace." Unconsciously—or, in some cases, quite consciously—the solution they have in mind is for their partner to change so that they don't have to feel disturbed. This conclusion is often accompanied by a helpful list of what's wrong with the other person. In most cases, each is hoping that I will validate their position about their partner and that their partner will "get the message" that they need to change.

What most couples don't understand is that by placing the cause of their disturbance outside of themselves, they're assuming a powerless child/victim position. This position itself is the main source of their distress. In the meantime, they're missing an opportunity to learn how to deal with their *own* disturbance. They're basically saying, "My life would be so much better if only you would be who I want you to be and not who you are." That is, of course, a formula for chronic conflict—and for some very destructive experience in relationship. At this content level of struggle, the basic therapeutic intervention is to introduce the practice of personal responsibility. When working with a couple in conflict, I will continually interrupt, reframe, ask questions, tell jokes—all with the intention to make it increasingly difficult for the couple to maintain their drama of blame and struggle. When struggle with one's partner is not so believable, we are forced to recognize our struggles with ourselves. Realizing that we are having feelings we don't want to feel is already a first step in relating to these difficult feelings as possibly workable. By practicing personal responsibility, we can become curious about the fact that our disturbance seems to be something we've lived with our whole life. Perhaps we can remember feeling unloved as a child or like we had to be the junior parent. We start to realize that the issue we've been blaming our partner for causing is actually something we have within ourselves; it just happens that it's being triggered very intensely in this relationship—which is what relationships do. But the other person is no longer seen as the cause and thus will never be the solution.

If all goes well, the client and/or couple begin to think, "Well, seeing how I'm stuck with these difficult feelings, maybe I should investigate them and learn to work with them. Perhaps I will feel more personal power if I stop putting my well-being into somebody else's hands, since I have no real control over how that person behaves."

This shift marks the transition into working at the *process* level of struggle. This is the work that most therapists do: trying to dissolve the stabilized struggle between what we consciously *want* to feel and what we are unconsciously afraid we will *have* to feel—the latter of which inevitably gets triggered by our partner, our coworkers, our children, and our lives. When working with a couple that is willing and able to make this shift, I tend to alternate going to depth with each person's disowned vulnerabilities. This allows each partner to witness what fears and strategies their partner may be experiencing and perhaps to realize that their partner's issues really have nothing to do with them.

As mentioned, working at the content level—that is, helping clients to have "good" experiences—could be understood as doing "preneurotic" work. This work has to do with giving clients support and calming their anxiety. Working with clients at that preneurotic level requires the therapist to be very supportive, maybe even a bit of a cheerleader. Without confronting them too much, the therapist teaches concrete life skills and takes the role of a soothing parent. But as clients move out of this content level of struggle into the process level, things begin to shift. They start to realize that their unresolved issues—their vulnerabilities—are their own responsibility to work with. At this point, the therapist transitions into what is called "uncovering" work. Here, the intention is to bring up exactly what clients don't want to feel.

Many people begin therapy with the unexamined agenda that they only want to feel happy—"Why can't our marriage feel positive and supportive all the time?" But if they progress in their work, most clients, somewhat naturally, shift into a willingness to examine whatever is arising. They begin to realize that if their project is "to feel happy," then that suggests that they actually have not been feeling happy. So maybe working with what's true in their experience will be more productive than trying to ignore it. They become willing to look into their own unconscious material and take responsibility for their own experience. This is the point at which clients become ready to practice the attitude of being an adult. They're saying, "Oh, this sucks! I hate the way I feel when my partner behaves this way. It's hard, but you know, I get it. It's really my issue, isn't it?" At that point, the therapeutic work is to continue bringing up anxiety-provoking issues so that they get the opportunity to investigate for themselves whether the anxiety they're feeling is actually a problem. As they discover that the panic associated with a disowned feeling is not really a reliable signal that their survival is threatened, their need for the protective function of struggle gradually dissolves.

Some people I work with continue forward, making the transition into investigating the *basic* level of struggle. While it's usually those who have some sort of spiritual practice, sometimes I'm surprised. I've had many clients who seem naive about therapy and spirituality who become immediately curious. "What is the nature of awareness? What has been aware of all this drama I've been going through?" It's almost like a little lightbulb goes off or there's a spontaneous shift of perspective. They start saying, "Hey, this is really interesting! If I check into my experience, I can feel that my awareness is undisturbed even when I'm disturbed." So while it's not the usual therapeutic territory, some people—and I can never predict who—seem to have an instinctual resonance with the basic level of experiencing and want to investigate that experience further. I may then point out when clients have resolidified their sense of self in some way and are taking their drama seriously, interrupt a narrative and ask what is aware of their experiencing in this moment, invite them into an embodied sense of not-knowing when there appears to be some dilemma, join in the sense of well-being that arises when they drop their fascination with problems and struggle, and present a larger context of seeing their work as really being for the benefit of all.

RELAXING STRUGGLE

Working in either the therapeutic or Buddhist context, all of these levels of work involve the same intention: relaxing struggle. When we relax our struggle, the apparently significant dramas we create begin to dissolve. As we gradually allow our various hopes and fears to coexist, we find there is, in fact, no resolution necessary (or even possible). Experiencing our worst fears doesn't kill us, and experiencing our greatest hope doesn't save us. Both are only transient energies. Each arises, dwells, and falls away. Being willing to consciously participate in negative and positive feelings equally, we begin to cultivate an attitude of nonbias. Being open to all experience, we can't really identify with preferred experience and reject difficult experience. We discover that not knowing who we are does not make us dysfunctional. On the contrary, it gives rise to the experience of freedom, unconditional confidence, and openheartedness.

On an even deeper level, relaxing struggle may give rise to an experience of empty nature. As discussed earlier, the appearance of solidity is actually *maintained* by struggle, which is based on fundamental aggression toward reality. So as we relax our struggle, the immediacy of our experience becomes more and more vivid. With less chronically contracted attention, more and more moments of open awareness are consciously experienced and integrated into our ongoing experiencing. It doesn't mean that we lose our capacity to plan for the future or remember the past, and it doesn't mean that our familiar issues no longer arise. It just means that now there's an experiential dialogue going on at all times. Our thoughts, plans, and strategies—our hopes and fears—continue to arise. Simultaneously, awareness, which has no quality of problem to it, arises more and more frequently. We find that we can hold deeply contradictory experiences at the same time, which makes it difficult to take any version of reality too seriously.

As we do this work, we may find that our habitual patterns may actually serve as a reminder to direct our attention to the experience of openness. Complaints give rise to a sense of what could be called "natural perfection." This doesn't mean that everything is perfect; it just means that at any given moment, there is no alternative reality. At any given moment, this is it. Reality is what it is. Whether we're feeling anxious or calm, the moment is perfect in the sense of being complete and whole; nothing is missing. In the next moment, things will change. As we commit to and welcome the experience of anxiety as an approximation of open mind, we begin to see for ourselves whether it's an accurate signal that our survival is at risk. We become more engaged with and aware of our own embodiment, which is the subject of the next chapter. And as we relax our struggle, our habitual distrust of ourselves and of life starts to give rise to spontaneity and a sense of effortless well-being.

5

EMBODIED AWARENESS

IN THE LAST CHAPTER, we met my client Jerome, who had come to me complaining of a chronic, underlying sense of anxiety. A major theme in our work was to help him develop the ability and willingness to step out of his interpretations and into his immediate experience. Once he could relate to the sensations he was feeling in the present moment, he could find out whether the experience of anxiety was actually harming him, whether he had to continue unconsciously organizing his life around avoiding this experience.

The same approach is relevant to all of our intense feelings, not just anxiety. We can practice staying embodied with our grief, rage, joy, fear, sexuality, confusion, or depression by bringing our attention out of interpretation and into sensation. When we do this, we are bringing our attention out of our history and into what is most true in the immediate moment. Our conditioned history is what's waiting for us in our interpretations. For example, historically when Jerome felt a tight, nauseous feeling in his gut, it was a signal of danger. Like most of us, when these sensations arose, he would unconsciously jump out of his embodied vulnerability and into his interpretation. The interpretation that would be waiting for him, given his history, was that he would be attacked if he didn't immediately soothe, accommodate, and avoid conflict with the other person. It told him he needed to do anything necessary to not feel separate from that other person.

But as Jerome was willing to stay at the sensation level, he found that none of his sensations were an accurate signal of imminent attack in the present. He may have noticed shallow breathing, a rapid heartbeat, a constricted throat, or a swirly energy in his chest. (Sensations are different for different people, but most of us seem to experience our embodied vulnerability in our torso.) Although disturbing, he found that the sensations he felt were basically neutral in nature. They were an expression of aliveness, and they were not permanent. They were always in motion, always changing. If he could stay out of interpretation, then they had no significance. They didn't mean anything. They just were this alive, vulnerable, disturbing experience.

Jerome was learning to hold the developmental view—working with his story, his history, his conditioned patterns of behavior—and the fruitional view, which directs our attention to immediacy. In my work with him, as with all my clients, I focused especially on what it means to practice *embodied* immediacy. After all, we're all embodied beings. It's not possible to *not* be embodied. All of our experience is embodied experience. The practice of immediacy is not meant to increase our awareness *of* the body as if it were somehow separate from us; rather, it's to relax into awareness as being experienced *through* the body, to allow our conscious minds to surrender into the experience of what it means to be an embodied being, right now.

I've been in many types of therapy over a lot of years, all of which have been valuable in different ways. While some therapies focus on body experience, the traditional Western approach is to talk about emotions and thoughts. I can't remember any mainstream therapists ever being curious about what sensations I might be experiencing as we explored important issues. But I have also been fortunate enough to have experienced a lot of body work: Rolfing, massage, core energetics, breath work, and other body-based modalities. For me, all of those experiences were useful, but most were separate from awareness practices. What I've found over some time is that focusing on bodily sensations can be a powerful practice in both dissolving unnecessary neurotic suffering and in inviting more frequent moments of open awareness. We're going to investigate that in this chapter.

EMOTIONS, AFFECTIVE AROUSAL, AND SENSATION

When researchers attempt to document all the possible emotions human beings can have, they come up with a variety of lists describing many different emotions. However, cross-cultural research suggests that there are probably only six or seven fundamental states of *affective arousal,* or basic biological feeling responses to life. These states have been described as anger, happiness, sadness, disgust, fear, anxiety, and surprise. And even these states of affective arousal seem likely to be strongly influenced by context and culture. The implication is that emotions are strongly interpretive. We experience some form of affective arousal—say, anxiety—and then we interpret it. We might feel a tight stomach, our heart may be beating fast, or our breathing may be shallow. Depending on what the circumstances are, we might interpret those sensations as nervousness (if we're awaiting medical results, for example) or excitement (if we're meeting up with a lover). In that way, for every basic state of affective arousal, there may be many different interpretations, with each interpretation resulting in a different emotion. But underneath both lies an even more fundamental layer of experience: raw sensation.

Our thoughts carry our interpretive history, but our strongly interpretive emotions do as well—often in even more powerful and less obvious ways. When we focus on sensations, though, we're putting attention on something more basic and more fundamental than emotions and thoughts. Whether we're talking about evolution or individual human development, it seems accurate that physicality comes first, followed by emotionality, and then the capacity to use thoughts and symbols. From this point of view, sensations are very reliable, very human, and basically impersonal—that is, they aren't heavily shaped by personal history. Interpretations, on the other hand, are often deeply shaped by our patterned, conditioned history.

Obviously there's a circular process that happens—thoughts trigger feelings and sensations, which then can trigger more thoughts. And feelings and sensations trigger thoughts, which can then trigger more feelings and sensations. Some forms of Western therapy, such as cognitive behavioral work, tend to focus on thoughts as a point of intervention. But my interest—especially from a fruitional point of view—is to seek out what is *most* accurate at any given moment. What is *most* reliable? What can we count on? What can we rely on for support? In my experience, what we can most consistently count on for support in our lives is the truth of our immediate experience. This doesn't mean that whatever we experience in the moment is "true"—we can have distorted, mistaken perceptions, even hallucinations. It just means that our immediate experience is what's always available; it's where we begin.

By *support*, I mean the experience that we're standing on ground that's really there, that's not theoretical, and that we can engage with our life without constantly questioning ourselves. We feel a confidence that our experience is reliable, even when different than others' experiences. Especially in our culture, support is often thought to be synonymous with positive feelings. When I have good feelings, I tend to take that as evidence from life that I'm on the right track, that I can trust myself. If I feel clear and engaged, I feel supported by life. If I feel confused and depressed, I feel shaky and that something's wrong. If I ask for support from a friend, I usually want him to help me feel more positive. But of course, life isn't only positive. Given our predisposition for "positivity," any time we have to deal with negativity, we tend to interpret this as evidence of a problem. We're understandably not committed to the experience of negativity. Yet, if we continue to go beneath this experience, we may find that much of what we call "negative" is actually interpretive. If we stay at the sensation level, it's possible we won't be able to find any problem, nothing inherently negative. We may discover that what we take as negative actually comes from our attitude toward our experience rather than anything innate in that experience. The more we consciously participate in sensation-level experiencing, the more we're able to commit equally to experiencing both positive and negative feelings.

In my experience, what we discover when we are able to stay with both positive and negative experience is that life is already supporting us. Actually, we find that it is our willingness to commit to all of our experience, regardless of our preferences, that supports us. It's very common that we feel that "something's missing" from our lives. So we search for love or security or enlightenment or whatever. But what's actually missing is our full participation in our ongoing, immediate experiencing. *We* are what's missing. When we are fully engaged in our life, regardless of whether we like or don't like what's present, we no longer have the drama of something missing. We will always have limitations; our relative experiencing is a collection of limitations. But our feeling of being supported or not, full or not, is a direct result of our openness to life, and I find that staying with our sensation-level experience gives us immediate evidence that it is workable to be open. We ask if we're a "glass half empty" or a "glass half full" type of person. Actually, the glass is always completely full, just not of what we think we need or want. The glass is full of water and of air. Our life is full of experiences we like and those we don't like.

I want to make clear that we're not talking about taking sides between sensations and interpretations. Both are very valid. Our lives wouldn't work very well without interpretations. But in this particular type of work, where we're interested in the experience of freedom, feeling at peace with and supported by life, learning to keep our hearts open to others, it seems to me that familiarity with and access to our sensations can be very useful. We can then have an experiential dialogue between our immediate, embodied, sensation-level experience and our interpretations of that experience. This allows us to find out for ourselves, at any moment, what's actually most true right now.

For example, over the years I've heard many clients tell me their *interpretive stories* of emotions such as loss and abandonment. I've heard many claim that they *feel* abandoned. But no client has been able to point toward an actual *sensation* of abandonment. In fact, no client has turned up a sensation of guilt or low self-esteem or shame or any of the many difficult human emotions. When I work with clients who have, for example, abandonment issues, I frequently invite them to consider letting themselves feel abandoned. Then I ask, "What are the sensations right now that you're aware of? What is it like to feel abandoned? Where's the intensity in your body?" Some people have access to their sensations in this way; some don't. But if the client does, they will often say something like, "Well, my stomach's very tight" or "I have this heaviness in my heart" or "I feel flushed in my face" or "My body wants to sort of curl up." I then encourage them to investigate whether there's a problem with those sensations. Is it killing them to feel a tight stomach or a heavy heart? Do they think it's giving them cancer? Do they think they're becoming dysfunctional or that the world is going to come and attack them? Where's the evidence that there's any problem whatsoever in feeling this intensity in their body? Or, even, where's the abandonment in those sensations? If they stay at the sensation level, without interpretation, where's the abandonment?

This line of inquiry doesn't make the issue of abandonment go away, but it begins an experiential dialogue. If that same abandonment experience gets triggered at a later date, the client may remember—either spontaneously or as part of a deliberate practice—to ask, "What's beneath this abandonment? What is even truer in this moment than that emotion? Do I have to take this experience as if it's the whole story, as if it's a description of reality? Because if it's the whole story, of course I have to *do* something about it. I have to get rid of it or work through it or something. But if the emotion is not what's most true, then I might have to experience it, but maybe I don't have to make it go away or heal it."

In the practice of embodied awareness, we are asking ourselves, "Is it killing me to feel this disturbance?" In Western culture, for those of us with fortunate circumstances, 99 percent of the time it's not. But we should remain open to the possibility that it might be. If the sensation is one of persistent pain that might be associated with a medical issue, we should go to a doctor. We shouldn't just say, "Well, this pain is just because I'm being aggressive to my vulnerability," and then die of a ruptured appendix!

Similarly, it's important to recognize and work with the well-researched relationship between stress and our health. Many serious physical conditions have an important emotional component. Embodied immediacy is not a spiritualized, reductionist approach. Rather, it's an invitation to hold a more complex understanding in which both in-the-moment and over-time experience is appreciated.

In the developmental approach, we're usually placing our experience in the context of past, present, and future. If we're trying to understand how our parents' divorce left us with the vulnerability of always feeling abandoned, we may not need to know what our tight stomach feels like. But if we're approaching our experience from a fruitional point of view, our practice is to return—over and over and over again—to embodied immediacy. Our practice is to cut interpretations and see what's most true in the moment. If we're not paying attention to our sensations, we will probably be captured by our historic dramas. They are fascinating. They're very convincing in their appearance. But for those of us dealing with abandonment issues, a fruitional approach—not *instead of* the developmental approach, but *in addition to* it—is to question what's happening right now. "What does it feel like to feel abandoned?" I often go through the same sort of questions with clients: "Is it killing you? Is it harming you? Where's the evidence of abandonment in your sensations? You have this heavy heart. You have this feeling of yearning. Your throat is tight. Where in any of those sensations is any evidence about your worth as a person?"

If clients are willing and able to investigate in that way, they often come to the same conclusions. "I don't like those sensations. I wish I didn't have them. But I actually can't find any evidence of harm." At that point, I often encourage people to perhaps say out loud, just to see what it feels like, "I give myself permission to feel like an abandoned person, off and on, for the rest of my life." It sucks to feel abandoned; none of us likes it. But so what? Now that they know it's not harmful—and that they are, possibly, stuck with it—can they actually commit to having this experience?

These core vulnerabilities are embedded at very, very deep levels. But if we're willing to commit to this experience—because we have investigated it ourselves and have found no evidence of harm—then maybe we can get on with our lives, instead of putting them on hold until we no longer feel abandoned. At this point, we commit to our core vulnerabilities as being inconvenient but valid parts of our life, not problems to solve before we can have a life.

DISEMBODIMENT AS A REQUIREMENT FOR NEUROSIS

As we've seen, both the experience of neurosis (in the developmental approach) and the experience of being an alienated, significant self (in the fruitional approach) seem to arise from and depend upon a sense of a basic split. From the Western point of view, this split is a disconnection from our deeper vulnerabilities. From the Buddhist point of view, it's a disconnection from our always-present awareness. If we return to the idea that neurosis is always a substitute for experiential intensity—and if we understand that intensity is always experienced in the body—it makes sense that to avoid experiential intensity, we have to leave our bodies. We have to dissociate from our immediate, embodied experience, because that's where the intensity is found. And where do we go? We can escape into activity, into numbness, into a variety of distractions. But most reliably, we go into interpretive states—our stories and dramas. Those dramas have their own type of intensity, but it's a familiar intensity. In fact, upon investigation, it turns out that all of our myriad stories are basically the same drama played over and over again. If we were to watch a scary movie over and over, it might still be scary on some level, but we would know deep down that we could handle it. We would know the beginning, the middle, and the end; even though it might feel scary, it's not a new threat.

Most of us recycle our basic dramas continually as a way to distract our attention from our immediate embodied experience, which is fresh, unpredictable, not contained in a formula, and which can thus feel genuinely threatening. In fact, as it turns out, disembodiment is a *requirement* of neurosis. Neurosis itself is an avoidance strategy, and it's very difficult to sustain any avoidance strategy if we're aware of what we're avoiding. Such a strategy wouldn't serve its function! So we must disembody in order to maintain our neurotic struggle. To say that disembodiment is a requirement of neurosis is not to imply that simply being aware of embodied experiencing is enough to dissolve neurotic organization. I've worked with a number of clients who have had training, perhaps as an athlete or as a dancer or as part of a spiritual practice, and who are able to tune into sensation-level experience and still maintain their neurotic strategies. Embodied immediacy is a capacity, a ground, from which we then can investigate our vulnerabilities, our conditioned patterns. We first bring ourselves out of our identification with our interpretations. Then we discover for ourselves if our disturbance is harmful. Then we explore a relationship with our fears and our pain. Then we practice unconditional kindness to these difficult experiences. These practices tend to cultivate a deep confidence in our ability to work with whatever we may find in each moment, whether positive or negative. We then have the choice of intentionally investigating what we have organized our lives around avoiding, usually for decades.

Embodied immediacy is not a solution; it's a way of experiencing or a capacity that we bring to the hard work of challenging and slowly dissolving our variety of strategies for avoiding fully wakeful engagement with ourselves and with life. In my experience, challenging these strategies from a ground of immediate, embodied, noninterpretive confidence can be much more powerful than only challenging these strategies with more current and accurate interpretations.

In my developmental work, I tend to deal with symptoms. We look at specifics, such as guilt or sexual inhibitions or a fear of failure at work. We take the perspective that these specific issues have their origin in historic events and, thus, can be worked through. Often this perspective is very accurate. But in order to get to the heart of *all* neuroses—the underlying process that gives rise to the variety of neurotic symptoms—it's helpful to take the fruitional approach. This approach doesn't concern itself with specifics; instead, it is generic and simple. The fruitional approach is to dissolve neurotic organization by first reembodying, in a conscious and openhearted way, and then bringing this attitude of open confidence into relation with any and all of our experiencing, however intense. It doesn't matter what specific symptom we are investigating. It doesn't matter what our history was. We're just returning to immediate, sensation-level experience, over and over again. Of course, this isn't the easy route on a moment-by-moment basis. It's much easier to avoid disturbance and experiential intensity than to embody it. In every moment, neurosis is much easier than sanity. But in the long run, neurosis actually leads to a deterioration in the quality of one's life.

When we use neurotic avoidant strategies, we may get some momentary relief, but the intensity we're refusing to relate to doesn't go away. So we're not learning how to work with that issue. Instead, we generate a sense that there's something about us that's unworkable. Our efforts to escape difficult feelings have their own disturbance, because they're not based on what's really true. We then try to avoid those disturbances. We still have the actual intensity we're avoiding, but now we have an extra layer of unnecessary suffering in addition to that. As a result, we don't handle our lives very skillfully. So although it's hard to implement in the moment, over time, sanity actually leads to an improvement in the quality of our lives. It puts us into contact with what's true so that we can learn how to deal with deep and often difficult issues—even if they don't go away.

SANITY: A COUNTERINSTINCTUAL PRACTICE

Many of my clients find themselves a little puzzled about why they're so invested in neurosis. They're sitting in my office because consciously they want relief from neurotic struggle, after all. Yet when I present practices for reembodying in their vulnerabilities, they quickly get more perspective. Most of us are far more comfortable with neurosis than sanity. Who's not more comfortable avoiding intense disturbance than participating in it? We're never going to *want* to practice sanity, because it's so difficult. Doing so requires discipline to reembody into sensations that were associated with the survival-level threats we had to deal with as children. We've trained ourselves to take the easier, safer-feeling way out. After all, our young strategies were survival strategies, not quality-of-life strategies.

Imagine you're hiking, and you have the choice to hike down the mountain or to hike up. You might choose to hike upward, because you know the reward will be a better view, but it's going to require more effort and even pain for you. The easier way would be to walk down. The problem, of course, is that if you continually step down, at the end you're down! There's not as much to see, not as much potential. In a similar way, we exhaust our potential by always taking the immediately easy step into neurosis. Even seeing this doesn't change our experience that in every moment—and we are only living in each moment—it is easier to avoid disturbance than to embrace it. Understanding this, we can then appreciate the view that *sanity is actually a counterinstinctual practice.* It is not an achievement; rather, it is a practice, never resolved, always requiring more effort in the moment than the practice of neurosis. We can't wait until we feel safe to practice sanity. We can't wait until we're in the mood to practice sanity. It'll be a long wait.

The work of embodiment, then, requires discipline. It's not easy to go into our anxiety, our tight stomach, the panicky feelings in our torso, or that tight throat we hate to feel. Most of us need to get a glimpse of what life could look like from the top of the mountain, when we are no longer identified with our neuroses. There has to be an intention. We need to understand the view, to see why it might be to our benefit to do this difficult work. It helps to meet a mature, wakeful person who might be an example of what's possible or to read a book that inspires us. But for our efforts to be sustainable, we must come to our own understanding of why it makes sense to take on these counter-instinctual practices.

To help my clients develop this understanding and intention, I often ask them to identify one issue in their lives that is especially difficult for them to deal with. Perhaps it's loneliness or claustrophobia. Perhaps it's a sense of being unloved or of being smothered. They may choose guilt, overwhelm, or exhaustion—whatever repetitive issue feels most problematic for them.

Once they've identified their issue, I suggest, as an emotional exercise, that they accept that they are likely to feel this way for the rest of their lives. Regardless of circumstance, regardless of what does or doesn't change in their lives, no matter how much work they do on themselves. I might even suggest a mini-dialogue along these lines: "Perhaps I am going to feel this way, off and on, for the rest of my life. I certainly have felt it for a long time, maybe all of my life up until now. There's no evidence that it's just going to go away. I've been to therapy. I've done spiritual practice. Maybe it's time to actually explore the possibility of having a relationship with this experience that I don't like? Maybe that would be a new approach, instead of my increasingly sophisticated attempts to make it go away." Although this exercise may sound depressing, it's actually an expression of confidence in oneself—in one's ability to participate consciously in the full range of human experiencing.

Through this type of mini-dialogue, we are giving up the child's wish for a safe, protected, happy life—an infantilized life—and committing to an adult life. We're committing to a willingness to experience and work with whatever is true, whether we like it or not. And very frequently, when clients are willing to stay engaged and embodied with their worst fears for a few moments, they are surprised to find some relief, even humor, in finally acknowledging experientially what they have been trying to not feel for much of their lives. They get a glimpse of what it might be like to not experience themselves as problematic.

PRACTICE GIVING YOURSELF PERMISSION TO FEEL YOUR FEAR

If you would like to try this practice, decide which feeling you're going to work with. Ideally, you will choose an underlying issue that you really don't like to feel—something like abandonment, shame, low self-worth, dependency, guilt, anger, or anxiety.

Once you've decided on your issue, take a moment to settle in. If you're sitting down, feel the weight of your body in the chair. Then begin to pay attention to your breath, feeling both the inhale and the exhale. Once you're present, start dialoguing with yourself.

Say out loud, "I give myself permission to feel [this feeling that you really don't like to feel] off and on for the rest of my life." Accept this feeling as if it were already a legitimate part of who you are. As you invite this feeling, try to bring your attention out of any interpretation into whatever raw sensation is happening. For example, many people find that the torso is the location where they feel emotional intensity. Check it out and see if there's any agitation there. Perhaps you feel numb from the neck down; perhaps there is some sense of tingling in your hands, or aching or fullness or lightness somewhere in your body. Perhaps the experience permeates your whole body. Or maybe you don't have any awareness of sensations except behind your eyes. It doesn't really matter what you discover. The point is to be willing to direct your attention toward your experience at the level of sensation.

Next, ask yourself whether this sensation you're feeling is actually a threat in any way. Are you going to die from feeling a ball of pressure in your stomach or a hollowed-out chest or a heavy heart? Is the burning sensation in your solar plexus actually dangerous? Will the tension in your belly or your throat actually constrict you enough to kill you?

If you find that experiencing these sensations is not harmful, even if they are disturbing, then experiment with a commitment to having a relationship with these sensations, perhaps for the rest of your life. What feelings arise when you think of this? What sensations?

The point of this exercise is to see for yourself whether it is, in fact, a problem to feel the sensations you've organized your life around not feeling. ▪

THE PRACTICE OF EMBODIMENT

As I've mentioned, one of the experiences I have historically dissociated from is that of dependency. If I were to do this exercise as I present it to my clients, I would invite in the experience of dependency. What does it feel like on a sensation level to be a dependent person? Immediately, I notice a sense of grief—a sadness that seems to be located in my chest. There's also a sense of collapse, as if part of my body wants to fall apart, along with a little tightness in my stomach.

My next question is, "So what? Do any of these sensations harm me? If I stay at the level of sensation, applying no interpretation at all, is there any evidence about my worth as a person? About my being worthy of love or not?" The answer is, I don't find any. Right there, in that moment, I suddenly have an immediate confidence around feeling dependent. I don't like to feel that way, and I probably won't change my style of self-sufficiency. But suddenly it's not so much of a threat. It doesn't really matter if I feel dependent or independent. Along with that clarity seems to come a certain type of relief.

If you find this practice of interest, you might consider building it into your daily life in some way. It might just be thirty seconds in the morning or at night before you go to bed. It's not a big time commitment, but in my experience, it can be very powerful. Over time, we can gradually bring into direct relationship our historic claim that it's really dangerous and bad to feel a certain way with the immediate experience that there's no evidence of threat or harm. That experiential investigation has to be done thousands of times, of course; we have to do it over and over. We are dissolving the tendency to accept, without investigation, that it's a threat to feel dependent or guilty or alone. At the same time, we're developing an embodied confidence that says, "So what? I'm ready to feel that way at any second. I've done this thousands of times now, and it hasn't harmed me yet."

I often suggest that my clients take this practice of embodied immediacy into their daily lives, ideally finding some structure to remind themselves to practice. I'm of the opinion that practicing in small moments throughout the day is probably more effective than doing a concentrated hour of practice, even though both seem to be helpful. If someone can practice immediacy once a day, great! But like most things, the more we practice, the better we get. So if we can remember to do the practice twenty times a day, things will probably move along quite a bit faster than if we remember to do it once a week.

A simple, practical way to approach embodied immediacy is to notice any moment that we're aware of our own avoidant behavior. Common avoidant behaviors include obsessive thinking, emotional reactivity, feeling too busy, running a story about how somebody's not treating us well, feeling complaint or resentment, or any of our familiar dramas. Anytime we notice such behaviors, we could ask ourselves, "I wonder what I'm experiencing in my body at the sensation level right this second?" When we are in a familiar avoidant energy, there is almost always a more vulnerable, sensation-based experience that we're trying not to feel at the same time. Why not just train ourselves to use our disturbance as a signal to wake up and pay attention? To be curious and ask, "What am I feeling right now that I don't want to feel? And is it a problem?" Just stay at the sensation level—no interpretation. We're not trying to heal it or even understand it.

Our normal way of operating is to relate to our embodied sensation from the perspective of our interpretations. We feel something, and then we immediately—and usually unconsciously—categorize and define it in relationship to our conditioned history. I may say something harsh to someone, and my stomach tightens. Depending on my history, I may interpret that response as, "I've been mean, and they won't like me. I should apologize profusely" or "I'm just defending myself from their attack, and if they don't like it, that's their problem" or "I'm feeling upset, but I don't know what just happened. I should just leave." The point of staying embodied at the level of sensation is to establish some confidence in the workability, intelligence, and aliveness of our immediate, embodied, *nonconceptual* experiencing. From that ground, we then explore and relate to our concepts and interpretations—and therefore to others—in a fresher, more present way.

It's important to say again that interpretations are in no way wrong or a problem. Concepts are very important. We need to be able to think conceptually in order to live more than biological lives. To recognize patterns, to plan for the future, to imagine possibilities—all require thinking. This book you are reading is using ideas as a way to suggest the value of noninterpretive experiencing. To me, the point is to move more and more in the direction of *choice*—spontaneous, immediate choice between our concepts and our embodied immediacy. That way, we can decide in the present moment, "Do I want to use interpretations right now, or do I want to stay in and use immediate, nonconceptual experience?"

Different situations call for different skillful means, but most of us are way out of balance on the side of taking interpretations too seriously. While perhaps less-literate societies would do well to take on a corrective practice of applying more interpretation to their experience, we in the Western world might want to do the corrective practice of embodied immediacy so that we actually experience more choice in our day-to-day lives.

PRACTICING EMBODIMENT IN THE CONTEXT OF ANXIETY

If you'd like to take the concept of embodied experiencing into an even more intense experience, consider our discussion about anxiety in chapter 4. Anxiety is difficult, pervasive, and connected with survival-level response. How can we truly learn to work with anxiety without first training ourselves to stay embodied at all times? Even though it is very valuable to practice reembodiment with our historically conditioned issues, it may be even *more* valuable to do this very difficult practice of staying embodied with our moment-by-moment experience of anxiety. As discussed, anxiety from a therapeutic view is usually seen as a signal of deeper, not fully conscious vulnerabilities pushing into our awareness. By escaping from our anxiety when this occurs, we tend to perpetuate the assumption that these core issues are indeed unworkable and a threat. By doing so, we perpetuate our young conditioned beliefs and strategies, unconsciously continuing our experience of being a powerless child.

Imagine you're a parent whose child believes there's a monster in the closet and who is ritualizing their life to avoid being torn to shreds. The child really believes that she is avoiding the closet *because there's a monster inside.* You can see that, actually, your child is convinced there's a monster *because she is avoiding the closet.* Your job as a parent is to help your child find a way to open the closet and see what's true, however scary this might be.

By training ourselves to remain present with our anxiety, we have the opportunity to discover that it's our avoidance of our core vulnerabilities that gives them the appearance of being a threat; there is nothing inherently harmful in these vulnerabilities themselves. We begin to live as adults, basing our lives on what is currently true, rather than as if we were children, basing our lives on what used to be true. The price tag: a commitment to anxiety as a valid, workable part of one's adult life. From a Buddhist view, anxiety is a direct perception of the already-open, vast nature of life, of our own minds, but through the filter of egoic process. Escaping from anxiety is escaping from open mind and into some version of self-absorption. Staying embodied with anxiety trains us to gradually tolerate the experience of openness, to find that the sense of a personal self basically serves as a defense against the initial anxiety of experiencing open, nonpersonal awareness. The price tag: a commitment to anxiety as long as there is egoic process. ▪▪

REEMBODIMENT AND TRAUMATIC ORGANIZATION

One specific—and potentially problematic—version of this embodiment work has to do with traumatic organization. Trauma can be understood as our response to intensity that overwhelms our system's capacities for processing and integration. Because this experience is not integrated, it tends to be compartmentalized and largely unconscious. I try my best to be aware of the potential for trauma in my clients. Yet trauma seems to be very encapsulated. It's almost like an energetic cyst in the emotional system, and there's often not a lot of warning when you're getting close to it. Neurotic organization, on the other hand, is very integrated and pervasive. Within a couple minutes of working with a new client, I usually have a pretty intuitive sense of their avoidant style. But often I don't see the traumatic organization until it actually gets triggered.

Every once in a while I get really surprised by a client's trauma. If it becomes clear that the traumatic organization is significant, I generally refer the client to a therapist who specializes in trauma work. The fruitional work is, after all, very intense. It invites people to go immediately into their deepest disturbances. If somebody has enough resilience, that's fine. But if not, it can trigger very intense reactivity. I offer this as a word of caution. No style of therapeutic work is a good fit for everybody, and the work I'm discussing is really best suited to those with at least neurotic levels of organization. It's not particularly appropriate for people with preneurotic organization, those who would be called borderline or psychotic, or those with pervasive traumatic organization.

When we feel traumatized, threatened, or overwhelmed, it's like getting an injury. When we were children, our young systems often could not process or metabolize the intensity of emotional threats to our survival. Just like a hurt knee will get stiff and frozen as a form of protection, our emotional system seems to protect us from having to be too aware of what we can't handle by compartmentalizing these experiences until they are immobilized and encapsulated as traumatic organization. Even when the injury to our knee has healed, the immobility that has protected it will tend to continue. Similarly, on an emotional level, many years later, after the trauma itself has long passed, the structures we created to protect ourselves will tend to persist.

Thirty some years ago when I started this work, most therapists talked about trauma as if it were still present in one's system. But since that time, what I believe to be a more accurate understanding has been growing. This new understanding says that it's actually the traumatic organization—our protective strategies—that persist over time, even after the event or disturbance has passed. But just like a healed knee will hurt as it regains its full range of motion, so is it painful to unwind traumatic organization from our bodies. Our bodies have been stiff for quite a while; they're tight. As we loosen up, there will be pain and associated panic, which might seem like a step backward. But it's just like watching a movie with our legs crossed and discovering one of them has fallen asleep. Before we notice it, it's numb, and there's no pain. But if we want to recover use of it and walk out of the theater, we have to allow circulation to come back in. Often that means an uncomfortable pins-and-needles experience for a period of time. In the same way, reembodying—especially around traumatic organization, but even in more manageable levels of overwhelm—is often a very disturbing experience.

The trauma work that I think is most congruent with the fruitional approach has the therapist helping clients very, very slowly reenter their body. It's important to do this at a slow pace to avoid retraumatizing the client. So while the same principles apply to working with traumatic organization as with more basic neurotic organization, I do think it's very helpful to find a practitioner who specializes in trauma when there are these intense issues to be explored.

THE RELEASE OF STORED ENERGY

An analogy that seems helpful in understanding reembodiment is to imagine that, as children, we actually learned to anesthetize ourselves. Let's say as a child, I was in a tough situation that I couldn't get out of. I couldn't go find new parents or move away from home, for example. That situation would be like having my hand on a burning stove and not being able to move it. What, then, would be the next best thing? To numb up my hand. It's still going to be injured, of course, but at least I won't feel so much pain.

At some point, I become an adult and am now able to make my own decisions and take care of myself. Unless I put attention back on my hand, it will remain numb, and I might leave it on the stove. I'm not even aware of the hurt, pain, and damage that are taking place. For this reason, as adults, it's very important that we dissolve the anesthesia almost all of us had to learn to apply as children. If I were going into surgery, I would want anesthesia. I don't want to stay embodied and present while someone cuts open my stomach. I would much rather be numb.

But when the surgery is over, it's very important to come out of the anesthesia. If you've ever been through an operation, you know it's not exactly pleasant as the anesthesia wears off. But we have to go through the pain, or we'll never be able to feel again.

The work we're doing is the work of coming out of our historic anesthesia—out of our sense of split, dissociation, and repression. This is the work of the fruitional approach. It goes right to the mechanism of neurosis, skipping right over the content. The work of focusing on sensations is also something like that of meditation. In fact, in Buddhist meditation, the mindfulness of the body is the first of the four mindfulness practices. It's a practice common to almost every form of Buddhism, though there are a lot of variations. When we attend to sensations, we're taking our attention away from our drama. Just as we return to the breath in meditation, when we put our attention on sensation, we're removing it from our discursive thinking. We're interrupting our identification with our story by attending to something that's very difficult to make a story out of.

With some types of body-centered therapy, the invitation is to stay embodied and then listen to the message that our body is trying to give us. Such therapies are valuable work. But the fruitional practice of immediacy is different. We don't listen for any sort of message. Maybe there *is* no message. Maybe it's just immediate experience. We don't necessarily need to be making meaning about it.

As we stay embodied—without interpretations—and attend to sensations, it's my experience that suppressed and constricted energy begins to release. It's almost as if our attention, our kindness toward ourselves, experientially validates that energy's right to manifest. As a result, it can arise into consciousness. If a child who was habitually ignored or repressed was then attended to with curiosity and kindness, it's likely that he may act out unpredictably for a while. When stored energy is released, it's often disturbing. Sometimes the energy might be expressed psychologically, as emotion or a painful memory. Other times it might be expressed somatically, through physical symptoms. But as this energy is validated by our attention, it develops a life of its own. It's as if more movement becomes available.

As a therapist, I never know where that movement is going to go. If I'm working with an individual and she starts loosening up her constrictions, I don't know whether she's going to have the outcome she is hoping for. If a couple starts to loosen the ritualized dynamics that have kept them in pseudo-security, I don't know if they'll stay together. So this work isn't about knowing what the outcome will be. Instead, it's about a commitment to our aliveness and openheartedness, as well as a confidence that however we choose to engage with our life from this ground will probably be what's most accurate and useful for us, most in alignment with our aliveness.

THE CONFIDENCE OF IMMEDIACY

The more we stay embodied with our moment-by-moment experience, the more confidence we have that we can work with whatever arises. The more we have dissociated—as a way of gaining security or stability—the less we're in touch with what's actually true at the moment. And the less we're in touch with what's most fundamentally true, the less confidence we have. It's a paradox: the more we avoid immediacy and intensity so that our lives feel more stable and workable, the less confidence we have in our ability to work with ourselves and our lives.

When we stay embodied, on the other hand, we start to develop unconditional confidence. This is the confidence of knowing that, whatever happens, we'll be willing to work with it. Not as a theory, but because we know from experiential evidence that we're going to be present with whatever may arise. We're actually working with our situation, our sensations, and our lives—moment after moment after moment. As a result, we start to develop a continuity of awareness. We can see and feel that we can stay present through all of those experiences, with no gaps. We discover that there is no such thing as a static, permanent experience; our sensations are always in motion. As such, there's nothing to hang onto. There's no interpretation we can make in this moment that is going to necessarily fit in the next. But we find that our awareness of this stream of experiencing is always there. We find continuity in *awareness,* not in what we are aware of experiencing.

As we remain embodied, what we discover is that all intense experience seems to have a wavelike life of its own. Intense emotional experience begins, builds slowly or quickly, peaks, and then dissipates. We begin to feel some disturbance—sadness, anger, fear—and as the intensity of our experience increases, we tend to feel panic. On a biological level, this panic feels like a signal of some threat to our survival. On a historic level, these feelings were probably too much to process and stay with as children. Usually, unconsciously, we escape our immediate sense of panic by leaving our bodies and taking refuge in some familiar dissociative strategy. While this action gives some immediate relief, we're not learning how to work with our difficult experience. As adults, most of us actually have the capacity to stay present with a great deal more disturbance than we had as children. But until we discipline ourselves to do so, we tend to reenact and take as necessary our young survival strategies. And most of these strategies are based on the conviction that we are not capable of tolerating too much emotional intensity.

To discover just what our current capacity for tolerating experiential intensity might be, we must stay present and embodied, even while our instinct is to escape. Our practice is to learn to ride this wave of intensity, remaining embodied even while our panic is telling us, "Get out, get out, we're going to die." The practice is not to manage the intensity, not to heal it, not to understand it; rather, it is to consciously participate in the sensation-level experience of it.

Without a commitment to remaining embodied, we tend to apply our particular style of fundamental aggression to any experience that feels too intense. We try to fix it, collapse, or pretend it's not happening. Or in biological terms, we go into fight, flight, or freeze responses. Perhaps in a social situation, someone tells a joke at my expense. A rush of embarrassment arises; I feel hot, exposed. Without discipline, I might respond by attacking the person speaking. I might want to say something self-deprecating. I might reach for a drink or just feel confused. With discipline, however, I might allow myself to feel my intense discomfort, be curious about it, not go into any story about it, and watch while the intensity peaks and then dissolves all by itself. When we can train ourselves to let our intense experience have a life of its own, we discover that there's no such thing as a permanent feeling. It's actually when we try to avoid our feelings that we tend to "solidify" them and make them appear significant.

One view is that it is precisely what we refuse to consciously participate in that gets stuck in our physical and energetic systems. With this understanding, we gradually dissolve our historic conditioning by consciously welcoming as immediate sensation, with no interpretation, any and all of the disturbing experiences we have refused to feel while growing up. Staying at the sensation level supports this process, because it helps us see that there's actually no real threat. The experience may be scary or overwhelming, but that's actually not a problem. We begin to have an approximation of what, in Buddhist jargon, is called the experience of self-liberation. We see that our experience is self-liberating—it takes care of itself. We don't have to do anything with our experience. When we stay embodied, our experience simply arises, dwells, and then falls away.

PRACTICE ARISE, DWELL, FALL AWAY

The more we discipline our attention to be present with our immediate noninterpretive experiencing, the more clearly we see that all of our relative experience—our thoughts, feelings, sensations, perceptions—arise in an endless and never-resolvable display. Resisting this reality generates unnecessary confusion and suffering. Bringing our experience into alignment with this reality gives rise to clarity, relaxation, and a more skillful engagement with our lives. So it may be helpful to investigate this view.

As an exercise, you can experiment with relating to all of your experiencing just as you relate to music. When listening to music, you may participate fully in each note, without hanging on to notes you like or adding commentaries to notes you don't like. You cooperate with the flow of experience. In a similar way, you could choose to observe the flow of your thoughts, feelings, and sensations, practicing an attitude of nonintervention. As you allow your experiencing to have its own life, you may find that it's impossible to know where a thought, a feeling, is originating. It appears, it displays itself briefly, and then it dissolves. What becomes of that display is impossible to know. An experience arises, out of who knows where. It dwells, manifests, briefly. Then it falls away, dissolves into who knows where.

All of your experiencing, without exception, has this quality. Even your experience of the observing "self" has this quality. Even your commentary as you do this exercise has this quality. As you practice this attitude of *engaged nonintervention,* you may find that all of your experiencing simultaneously has the characteristics of vivid appearance, while lacking any continuing essential nature. Experience "liberates itself" not only through its ever-changing flow; it is inherently free—free of solidity, permanence, and conceptual meaning. ▪▪

EMBODIED IMMEDIACY AND SKILLFUL ACTION

One of the benefits to developing the confidence of embodied immediacy is that it gives rise to a sense of choice. It supports the cultivation of what the Buddhists call *skillful means,* which refers to how we engage with whatever situation is arising. If we dissociate from intensity out of panic, we usually go into a primitive, conditioned, fight-flight-or-freeze response. In that situation, our choice is limited; we'll pretty much do the same thing we've always done—whatever feels familiar and safe. When we can allow intensity to have its own life, however, we find we can try all sorts of things. For example, say your kids just disturbed you. Instead of yelling at them—which is many a parent's conditioned response—perhaps you're practicing staying embodied. You let the wave of intensity rise and fall. Once the impulse to escape from disturbance passes, you could then experiment with a variety of responses. You could talk to them about their behavior, joke with them, apply logic, let the whole thing drop, or implement behavioral consequences—however you choose to respond. At this point, your engagement with your life can actually be informed by the present-moment situation. A familiar summary of this work is to *move from reaction to response.*

When we're coming from a panicky place, trying unconsciously to get out of our immediate embodied intensity, then our responses are basically going to be attempts to get out of our feelings as quickly as possible. We tend to react, biologically, as if our survival were threatened. We react, historically, from our young, out-of-date strategies for taking care of ourselves. On the other hand, the more we can stay embodied without interpretation, the more grounded we feel, the more access we have to our current adult capacities. We learn to expect our panic, to not be captured by it, to not behave as if our survival were at risk. We actually learn to be grounded in our panic. We discover that the more confident we feel in our own experience, the more intimately we are able to engage with another person's experience. This discovery is especially powerful in intimate relationships. We find that we don't feel so threatened by our partner's disturbance. We're embodied with our own experience, so we can be with our partner in his or hers. We expect to be disturbed by our partner, rather than hoping that we won't be, and we develop the confidence that this will be workable—perhaps not pleasant, but not something we must avoid or solve.

If we approach somebody from our own dissociative, avoidant state, that other person's version of reality can feel very threatening. Because we're not participating in our own reality, the other's reality appears to be more valid and powerful. It's easy to then slip into a black-and-white response, where we cue off of our sense of the other's feelings and thoughts. The two basic ways we do this are (1) to go into a state of merger, where we become an extension of that person's reality, or (2) to go into a state of reaction, with a lot of distance between our reality and his or hers. We'll talk about these strategies more in the next chapter.

EMBODIMENT AND WORKING WITH EMOTION

So far we've covered several steps or suggestions for exploring a relationship with our immediate, sensation-level, noninterpretive experiencing. To summarize, first, either as a formal practice or in response to some disturbance, we recognize an impulse to escape from some feeling, thought, or interaction. We then direct our attention out of our usual stories about what's happening to our immediate, sensation-level, noninterpretive experiencing. Because we often find some degree of anxiety or panic, we investigate our automatic assumption that there is some threat. Is there actually any evidence of harm, damage, or problem in our sensations? Is there any evidence about our worth as a person or the viability of our life? Can we even find such apparently real emotions as shame, abandonment, or guilt? When we find no actual problem in what's most true in our immediate experience, we gradually develop a trust that it's safe and workable to stay in relation with this experience. As we cultivate a willingness to be in relationship with ourselves at all times, regardless of what is arising, we then practice being kind to all of our experiencing, regardless of whether we like it or not. We begin to understand that being unconditionally kind to our experience is being unconditionally kind to ourselves, to our own vulnerabilities.

But that's not where the practice ends. If it's of interest, we can return to whatever emotion or thought seemed to trigger the disturbance in the first place. But now, rather than using our often-problematic interpretations or concepts as our ground, we can investigate the difficult emotion or thought from the confidence of being grounded in our immediate, embodied, noninterpreted sensations. Attempting to understand and work with our sense of shame, for example, is a different experience when we have discovered that there is no objectively existing shame.

I recently saw a client named Jennifer. Jennifer was in her early thirties. She had been married for just a few years when she had an affair with a coworker while on a business trip. Although she had admitted everything to her partner and he had forgiven her, a sense of trust had been lost between them. She reported feeling a great deal of shame about the incident and the damage it had caused her marriage. Rather than try to help Jennifer get relief from her experience of shame, I invited her to go as deeply as possible into her actual immediate experience of this difficult emotion. To make this investigation, I invited her to stay at the level of sensation and report what she was feeling. She said she felt a heavy emptiness in the space where her heart should be, as well as a churning in her lower belly. I asked her whether, with no interpretations, she could locate a sensation she would call "shame." She paused and felt her body, but said she couldn't pinpoint which one of those sensations was the sensation of shame. This is, of course, because there is no such sensation—I've never found one, anyway. Her use of the concept "shame" was an interpretation pulled from her conditioned history to explain the physical sensations she did not want to feel. By turning her attention back toward her immediate, embodied awareness, however, she was able to see that shame was a label she was adding herself. And by staying in relation with these disturbing sensations, Jennifer was able to determine for herself that they were not harming or damaging her in any way. In other words, it was workable to feel these sensations that she was interpreting, without evidence, as shame.

Of course, staying at the level of sensation doesn't make shame go away. We are always thinking and interpreting, and it's intelligent to do so. If that's the case, then what's the point of feeling our embodied immediacy? The point, as I mentioned earlier in this chapter, is choice. Jennifer could, if she wanted to, choose to explore her experience of shame at having an affair. But if she then found herself starting to get captured by her story of shame—taking it too seriously—she now had a ground she could return to of immediate, sensation-level experience. She could explore her experience of being a bad person; she could explore her experience of being a completely workable person; she could explore the complex experience of having both feelings about herself.

I gave Jennifer a practice to work with throughout her week. First, she would notice whenever her shame came up—whenever she started thinking, "Oh God, I was such a fool. I made such a mistake. I hurt my partner so much. I'm bad, and I deserve punishment." She could then ask herself, "What am I feeling right now, in this moment, that I don't want to feel?" She could then practice directing her attention to her sensation-level experience, with no interpretations at all. After checking to make sure there was no harm happening, she could then practice opening her heart to her disturbance. Over and over, Jennifer's discovery was that the sensations were not actually shame. They were a tight stomach and an aching heart, but they were not shame. And these sensations carried no evidence at all about her worth as a person. In fact, as Jennifer was able to practice kindness to her own vulnerability, she discovered a much more complex emotional experience. She found grief and fear and anger, as well as shame. She realized that she was using the formula of shame as an unconscious way to avoid the disturbing reality of having complex and contradictory feelings. This, in turn, helped her see this as a reenactment of her childhood strategy of needing to blame herself for real but overwhelming relationship experiences with her parents.

This practice shows us how to step out of our identification with our interpretations and step into our immediate experience. There we find out for ourselves—so it's not somebody else's theory—*what's most true.* Since we're only living in the present moment, that's probably where we're going to find what's most true—especially when dealing with intense emotions.

For Jennifer, it was most true that her stomach was tight and her heart hurt. It wasn't as true that there was shame. This practice can be applied to any emotional experience—be it guilt, abandonment, selfishness, low self-esteem, or what have you. The fact that these emotional interpretations are not what are most true doesn't make them go away. It's actually very helpful to explore our conditioned history in order to recognize our recurring patterns of experience and to realize how powerful the momentum of these familiar dramas can be. By doing so, we become increasingly able to expect familiar issues to be activated, not take them to be caused by current circumstances, and to develop a repertoire of skillful means to use with them. But I find that an ability to stay present and embodied with our vulnerabilities supports this investigation of our historic issues. Discovering that we can participate in our fears, and even bring kindness to them, allows us to go deeper into them, and often new understanding arises out of this new confidence.

By taking part in this practice, we gradually build confidence that our worst disturbances, our greatest fears, our most vulnerable issues are in fact completely workable. There's no inherent problem about any of those experiences, even though they are disturbing. From that ground of workability, we find that we can proceed much more quickly on exploring our issues than we do when we try to explore those issues from only the interpretation level. This is especially true when we're experiencing some type of emotional reactivity. Our interpretations in those cases are usually a disguised emotional process and expressions of our young survival strategies.

If Jennifer had previously developed the capacity just to stay open to her experience of shame—to experience it as just that, an *experience*—she might have discovered that underneath her inter-pretation was a feeling of raw and intense aliveness. Not many of us have this capacity, however. Almost all of us unconsciously relate to interpretive emotions, such as shame and guilt and aban-donment, in a self-referential way. It's as if these energies reflect our worth as people. This drama of self-worth seems so important that usually our inquiry stops here. We believe this issue must be resolved, which prevents any deeper investigation. This self-referential or self-defining aspect is hallucinatory, actually; it's not at all true. But it's the experience that most of us have. It's by staying with our often intense underlying sensations, devoid of interpretation, that we begin to recognize these seemingly very personal emotions as impersonal energies with interpretations attached. At that point, we begin to experience a new level of freedom: the ability to be with whatever disturbance might arise, even our worst nightmare, with commitment and kindness.

EXPERIENCING THE BODY AS A CRUCIBLE

As we stay embodied—as we gain more confidence and clarity and become more willing to experience very intense states—we find that transformative change is possible. Not only is embod-ied immediacy helpful in the moment, but this practice also may help us gain more access to awareness and clarity over time. I like to think of the symbol of the crucible from the Middle Ages. On the surface, alchemical transformation was about changing ordinary material into gold. Yet for some people, alchemy was also about something much deeper. It was about the spiritual path of transmuting confusion into wisdom, neurosis into sanity.

Symbolically, you would put the ore into a container called a crucible. Then you'd really crank up the heat. The material in the crucible would become so hot that the impurities would begin to separate from the pure essence—the gold. Following this metaphor, we might consider that transformative change requires learning to use our own body as a crucible. A good crucible has a certain set of properties. It can withstand a lot of heat without melting; it is strong enough not to break; and it must not chemically interact with what's in it. In a similar way, the more we can learn to hold and experience intense energy in our bodies, the more likely we are to invite transformative change. Yet for obvious reasons, most of us take intensity as a threat. In our culture, the two basic choices for working with intensity are repression or discharge. When repressing our experience, we push it out of our conscious awareness, ignore it, retreat to our thinking, and pretend it's not happening. When discharging, we process our disturbance by talking it out with a therapist or friend, exercising, or yelling and screaming. The basic intention is the same: to get the disturbance out of our bodies, out of our awareness.

In this way, becoming a crucible—inviting transformative change—is counterinstinctual. Rather than repressing or discharging, we investigate the possibility of feeling flooded with intensity and doing absolutely nothing about it. With practice, we discover that we don't have to push it away; we don't have to release it. Instead, we can train ourselves to tolerate very, very intense sensation. As a result, we develop the freedom and confidence to stay present and engaged in any situation, because we know we'll be able to work with whatever comes up.

As we stay more continually present and engaged, we see more clearly. "What is a problem, and what is not? Do I have to respond to this situation? What might be to my and others' benefit here? What is the sane aspect of my experience, and what is the neurotic aspect?" On a subtler level, more and more frequent moments of conscious participation and awareness allow us to reduce our reliance on formulas and dramas for the sense of continuity. We also may find that our discipline of embodied immediacy gives rise to an increasingly powerful sense of "presence," a sense of engagement, confidence, and equanimity.

Several years ago I went through a period when I was frequently waking up in the middle of the night with intense panic. I tried different strategies to get rid of it or to go back to sleep. Then it occurred to me that maybe I just needed to lie there and feel the panic. I allowed this really, really disturbing experience to happen. I remember it felt like molten iron flowing through my body. But even though it was intensely disturbing, I discovered that it didn't harm me. The more attentive I was, the more the panic seemed to have a life of its own. I never understood it—I didn't even try. I just let it be there and stayed present to it. After a while, it didn't happen anymore.

The attitude of being willing to feel flooded with intensity at any moment actually gives rise to a very strong confidence—confidence in our capacity to be present and engaged and to keep our hearts open. I've found the practice to be very valuable, both personally and with my clients.

EXPERIENCE AND THE "SELF"

Alan Watts, who described himself as a spiritual entertainer, had a very interesting way of talking about embodied experiencing. His approach was that our experiencing actually *is* our self. It's not that there's a self that's experiencing things; the experience is everything. To explain this view, he gave some everyday examples. We can say "It's hot today" or "It's night-time" or "It's snowing." As if there is an "it" that's hot or an "it" that's snowing. Obviously there's not an "it" that's snowing; there just happens to be snow. In a similar way, we may say "I'm happy" or "I'm sad." But perhaps there's no "I" that is happy or sad. Perhaps there's just the experience of happiness and sadness happening. Dōgen, a thirteenth-century Zen master, said, "Mindfulness of the body is the body's mindfulness." He was, I believe, pointing to the same understanding. There's no "I" being mindful of our body; there's only our embodied experiencing happening.

Awareness is an inherent aspect of our embodied experiencing. The concept of a "self" who's separate from that experience is a story or drama, an artifact of conceptual thinking, language, and culture, with as much reality as the "it" that snows. Awareness is inseparable from experience, and this awareness turns out to be nonpersonal. The more we can stay embodied at the sensation level, the less evidence we find to support our fascination with this drama of personal identity.

From the fruitional view, open awareness is—already and always—the ground of our experience. It doesn't really matter if our experience is clear or confused; awareness is always there. In my experience, we tend to have greater access to this experience of openness when we attend to raw body experience rather than to mental experience. Sensation is less distractive, less personal, and less fascinating. It's more straightforward—cleaner, in a certain way. This is why my work with clients involves a constant alternation. We work with the developmental view, exploring our interpretive, conditioned experience, because that's the vivid display of our lives. Yet over and over again, we return to the fruitional practice of embodied immediacy. At the level of sensation, there's no interpretation. There's an immediate aliveness, an immediate reality that is trustworthy in a way that no interpretation ever could be.

If you were to take just one thing from this discussion, my hope is you'd feel a curiosity, a willingness to experiment with the fruitional practice of embodiment; that you'd investigate for yourself whether going through all your history, all your story, is truly necessary to dissolve neurotic organization. Perhaps instead, you can cut right to the root of what gives rise to and sustains your sense of basic split through the practice of reembodiment. For just as dissociation is a requirement for neurosis, so reembodiment is an antidote.

There is no place that's more fertile or useful to begin practicing this principle than in the crucible of intimate relationship. Much of my practice is devoted to helping individuals and couples navigate the extremely difficult experience of relating to others, especially intimate partners. For this reason, in the next two chapters, we'll continue exploring the intersection between the developmental and fruitional views within the provocative, irresolvable arena of relationship.

6

ALL RELATIVE EXPERIENCE
IS RELATIONAL

I'VE WORKED WITH RELATIONSHIPS a lot, both personally and professionally. I'm a licensed marriage and family therapist, and I see about half individual clients and half couples. I think the reason I'm so drawn to and interested in this work is because my own experience of relationship has been so difficult, rich, and provocative. I don't think there's any likelihood that relationship will ever resolve into a nice, settled experience for me. It's incredibly alive and therefore disturbing—apparently for both me and my clients.

My wife and I met in the Masters of Buddhist and Western Psychology program at Naropa University in 1977. We got married two years later; we've been together quite a while. I think it's accurate to say that I have experienced being disturbed in this relationship every day of the nearly four decades we've been together. (She assures me that it's been the same for her.) There she is, just being herself, and I'll have a sudden surge of irritation, impatience, anger, or critical feelings. If I look beneath that initial feeling, I usually find feelings of sadness and grief. Just by being herself, my wife is almost guaranteed to touch some sore spot of mine. She's not *causing* that sore spot. By her proximity, she pushes against my tender spots, my vulnerabilities. Of course, every day, I also have feelings of comfort, appreciation, and affection. But those aren't the feelings that most of us find hard to work with.

As I've said before, my style tends to be one of wanting to feel more in control, competent, self-sufficient, and independent. Anytime somebody who's important to me is not behaving in my preferred style, it's very activating. Just through a process of resonance, we feel what those close to us are feeling. When these are feelings that we are trying to disown, it's disturbing. I find that it's difficult to have the feelings I've spent most of my life trying to not feel—dependency, loss of control, and so on—get triggered every day.

Recently I had the opportunity to work with just this type of feeling. My wife and I have twin daughters who are currently in college. One weekend when they were home from school, one of our daughters was so upset with her mother that she was refusing to speak to her. This is naturally a very disturbing experience for a mother—to have her daughter refusing to communicate. I kept telling my wife to let it go, that this type of behavior is typical for nineteen-year-old girls and was not a reflection of her capacity as a mother. But she was feeling incredibly hurt and upset. The degree to which my wife was affected by our daughter's silence was very disturbing to me because it revealed her dependency. The longer the silent treatment went on, the more activated my wife got—and the more irritated I became. I wanted her to take a more objective view and behave more independently, as I would have done in the same situation. The fact that my feelings of irritation were being triggered directs my awareness toward exactly what it is I have to work on. If I want to free myself of my own conditioned history and be able to show up confidently in the present moment—choosing my life as an adult rather than reenacting my childhood—I must learn how to be with feelings of dependency.

For many years I tried to resolve or eliminate my relational disturbance. At some point, however, I decided to change tactics. Basically, I was exhausted from my project of creating the life I thought I deserved—a life without disturbance. It just wasn't working. I decided to commit to what I was already feeling but didn't like; to investigate and see for myself whether the disturbance triggered in me by my relationship was actually the problem I was claiming it to be. This approach is, of course, very resonant with my Buddhist training. In the Tibetan Vajrayana lineage, everything is welcomed as valid. We don't dismiss any experience. I've found this inclusive approach to be very useful both in my own marriage and when I'm working with clients.

THE DISTURBING NATURE OF INTIMACY

Our society's idea seems to be that relationship is supposed to be a refuge from our difficult lives. Our cultural expectation, reflected through the media and in terms of relational norms, is that intimacy is supposed to be warm, supportive, and continually sexually passionate. Perhaps we'll hit a few bumps at the beginning, but then we're supposed to sort of coast from there. I just don't find much evidence that this is accurate. I do think that some couples are very lucky. Just like an individual might win the lottery, some couples win the relationship lottery. They genuinely have very positive, passionate, easy relationships, which continue in this way over decades. But the majority of people I've worked with and known socially struggle with intense disturbance and vulnerability, which get brought out into the open by intimate relationship.

We might consider the difference, though, between what we want and what is to our benefit. Most of us would probably choose a life without pain, never getting sick, being independently wealthy, children who never drove us crazy, and so on. But health is not synonymous with positive experience. Wisdom is not the same as happiness. And freedom is definitely not dependent on feeling good.

From a Buddhist perspective, a fortunate life is one with "the right amount of suffering," as long as we are willing and able to work with and learn from our difficult experiencing. The path of waking up appears to require contrast, discovering that it's impossible to be identified with any one version of reality, any one formula. At the same time, it seems very helpful to learn how to moderate the degree of intensity we engage with. Not enough disturbance is comfortable but is unlikely to bring into awareness what we must work with. Too much disturbance is likely to take us into a dissociative or even retraumatized state, in which it is very hard to stay present. In exactly the same way, a fortunate intimate relationship can be understood as one with "the right amount of suffering." But for our relationship with our partner to actually be fortunate, we must discipline our relationship to our own difficult experiencing. This means that we must do the counterinstinctual work of bringing awareness, embodiment, and kindness to exactly what we don't want to feel. We have a choice about how we relate to the disturbance of intimacy. If we want an intimate relationship to only be a source of happiness and comfort and security, I think most of us will end up feeling disappointed—maybe even bitter or victimized. Instead, we might consider relating to our experience of intimacy as one of the most powerful vehicles for personal and spiritual growth that we, in our culture, have access to, as our culture doesn't really seem to have many options in terms of viable spiritual paths.

There are many understandings of what a spiritual path involves. One view says that our normal, socially familiar experience is not the whole picture. Most of us feel ourselves to be very small, finite selves in an incomprehensibly vast and infinite universe—and then we die. How can we find meaning, joy, and openheartedness in these circumstances? Most spiritual paths offer a variety of ways to help us see through this appearance of alienation; to experience our actual identity with the mysterious vast nature of reality; to experience ourselves as expressions of the universe, rather than as its observers. Because this is not easy work and it usually progresses through certain stages, it is usually presented as a "path." Understanding and working with intimacy as a path is one of the best ways to challenge ourselves to grow—or to "wake up," from a Buddhist point of view.

Another way of saying this is that intimacy demands authenticity. The closer we are to somebody, the longer we are with somebody, the more difficult it is to pretend that very deep grief, rage, fear, or panic is not being triggered in our relationship, and the harder it becomes to deny how powerfully our partners bring love and meaning to our lives, beyond what we can create for ourselves. In our relationships, we can choose either to acknowledge and go into our disturbances and vulnerabilities or to deny and avoid them. If we choose the latter, it's generally an unconscious choice on the part of both people. We unconsciously agree to ritualize the relationship in ways that allow us to stay together, while protecting us from too much vulnerability. But if we want to grow—if we want to wake up—it makes sense to me to use the never-resolvable disturbance of intimacy as an opportunity to gradually increase our tolerance for living in the truth of each moment, rather than constantly trying to live in the fantasy of our preferences; to use it as a tool to help free ourselves of our conditioned history, so we can live our lives as adults, rather than reenacting the survival strategies we developed when we were quite young and immature.

ALL RELATIVE EXPERIENCE IS RELATIONAL

While relationship with an intimate partner is often at the forefront of what we consider to be our "relationship issues," I think it may help to step back a bit and look at the context of relationship in general. Relationship is all around us. From a Buddhist perspective, everything we experience—other than pure awareness—is relational. In fact, in Buddhist jargon, we say that pure awareness is an "absolute" experience, while everything else is "relative." And from what I can tell, all relative experience is relational. Meaning that upon examination, we're never going to find any experience that has its own independent, essential nature.

Let me offer some obvious examples. You can't have high without low; there's no essential highness. The concept of "high" is only defined by the concept of "low," and vice versa. You can't have hot without cold, or light without dark, or left without right. In fact, we can't articulate any experience without contrasting it with something that it's not. This relative nature of all experience is somewhat of an alien idea in our culture. For at least the past two thousand years, the pervasive assumption of our culture has been that we have an independent, continuing, essential nature; that the objects of our experience have their own nature, independent of ours. But when we examine our experience beyond appearances, we find that everything is mutually cocreative. By this, I mean that everything depends on an incredibly complex number of conditions for its own appearance. To have conscious experience, we need sense organs. We also need material reality, whatever that might be, and we need to have our awareness. No one of those qualities can give rise to our experience all by itself. It's like steam or water or ice. None of these manifestations of H_2O exists independently of temperature. Or like building an arch: it's the tension—or the relationship—between the bricks that keeps the arch together.

In the same way, our experience seems to be defined by both what it is and what it's not. There seems to be a certain foreground/background quality to experience. As humans, we tend to focus on what's in the foreground, on what's moving. It's probably an evolutionary hardwiring that we have. But what's in the foreground is actually defined by what's in the background. Perhaps you are familiar with the vase-faces optical illusion (see Figure 6.1). Depending on how you look at the drawing, you

FIGURE 6.1 **VASE-FACES OPTICAL ILLUSION**

might see two figures looking at each other or a vase in between. Our experience flips back and forth from one to the other; we can't hold both the vase and the faces at the same time. Why? Because what is in the foreground is actually *defined by* what is in the background. That's the way our brains work.

In a similar way, our sense of *self* is defined by *not self*. If we lived in a reality without gender, we would not experience ourselves as male or female. We think of ourselves as uniquely human by how we are different from other life forms. Every appearance is a cooperation among an incredibly complex number of factors. To appreciate this, however, we need to really examine our experience. If we stop at appearances, it's going to seem that everything has its own independent nature. You and I are separate bodies, driving separate cars, doing separate things with our days. We each have thoughts and feelings the other can't ever really know. So, to understand that all experience is relative, we must hold both the appearance and the analysis simultaneously. We don't choose sides. We don't say, "Everything's just one big mess together," and we don't say, "Everything is totally independent." Instead, we acknowledge that everything appears to have its own independent nature and, upon examination, turns out not to have its own objective existence.

Recall the example of the rainbow I mentioned earlier in the book. It certainly looks like there's a rainbow in the sky, and it wouldn't make sense to deny this experience. But upon investigation, there is actually no independently existing rainbow there. It's a completely relational experience. Upon investigation, all of our experience, including the "experiencing self," is found to be completely relational in its nature. Just as it doesn't make sense to look for the pot of gold at the end of a rainbow that doesn't have an objective existence, it may not make sense to look for a "true self" with its own independent reality.

NOT TWO, NOT ONE

How might we relate to the assertion that our world is perhaps not a collection of independently existing "things"? That it may instead be an incredibly complex reality, in which anything that "is" is defined by, and simultaneous with, all that "is not"? One approach, which we discussed in chapter 3, is to increase our capacity to hold apparently contradictory ideas, thoughts, and feelings simultaneously, with no fantasy of resolution. As F. Scott Fitzgerald said, "The test of a first-rate intelligence is the ability to hold two opposed ideas in the mind at the same time, and still retain the ability to function." And Michael J. Gelb, author of *How to Think Like Leonardo Da Vinci,* named "sfumato"—or the capacity to hold contradictions and uncertainty—as one of Da Vinci's "seven principles."

We can also consider the idea that all of our experiencing is inherently without essential division; there is nothing we experience that is not an expression of our experiencing. This idea seems obvious, but most of us actually feel that we are somehow separate or disconnected from life, from others, and even from aspects of ourselves. From a Buddhist view, this sense of basic disconnection is illusory, maintained out of awareness, moment by moment, with great effort and creativity. One view of how we might generate this feeling of essential division was discussed in detail in chapter 3. But because of our unexamined feeling of separateness and even disconnection, we understandably think that we will experience "wholeness" when we can improve our feelings of connection. But just like "high" and "low," our experiences of "separate" and "connected" have no independent existence; they are heads and tails of the same coin. We can't be connected unless we're separate to begin with. We can't separate unless we're first connected. Perhaps we will have a better sense of our already- and always-existing wholeness as we learn to include feeling both separate and connected, at all times, as equally valid and necessary. It turns out that all apparent opposites are expressions of how our conceptual minds work, rather than accurate descriptions of a fragmented reality. Holding both opposites at the same time turns out to be a better approximation of the nondivided nature of our experiencing than trying to resolve which of these energies we should take sides with.

In the field of quantum physics, Niels Bohr proposed the principle of complementarity: Because reality is so complex, so basically unknowable, the best approximations of reality must allow contradictory descriptions and understandings. We can understand light as both a wave and a particle. I like my job; I feel drained by my job. I want life to be fair; I know that life isn't fair. I want to feel more alive; I want to keep the security of what's familiar. If I can tolerate the sense that there's no formula to count on, not even the formula of pretending that I have conflicting feelings that must be resolved, then I may find that it's possible to call on the full range of my experience as I engage with this incredibly complex life. Even more subtly, if I hold my contradictory experiences as equally valid, my "sense of self" is left in some open space in the middle of these positions. This may be a useful understanding of the Buddhist idea of "middle way"—not "half of this and half of that," but rather an open creative awareness that holds contradictory versions of reality, without a need to be identified with any of them. A Buddhist summary of this view is "not two, not one," meaning that it's not entirely accurate to say that everything is separate, but it's also not entirely accurate to say that we're all one. This is simple to say, but it requires a lot of work to gradually develop the capacity to hold this complex state of mind in an ongoing way.

THE FUNDAMENTAL EXPERIENCE OF RELATIONSHIP IS THE EXPERIENCE OF FUNDAMENTAL DISTURBANCE

Perhaps for all of us, the most fundamental location of this never resolvable, cocreated experience of relationship will be that of "self" and "other." This experience is inherently disturbing. There is some type of gap, or transition, between self and other that we can never cover over or bridge. We can never make our experience only about our self without some *other* intruding. I can try to create a world of control, tranquility, and order, but other people—or the weather or my own health problems—will mess things up. We can never make our experience only about others without our *self* intruding. I can try to be selflessly generous and to practice surrender and acceptance, but I will not be able to get rid of selfish thoughts or upsetting emotions. We cannot even draw a clear, straight line dividing self and other. When does the air we breathe change from atmosphere to part of our body? When does our language transition from being what we are given by others to become our own creative expression? At what point does our partner's behavior become our interpretation of his or her behavior?

It's very upsetting to not be able to create and count on a continuing, stable, reliable formula about who I am and how I should relate to my life and to others. Out of this upset—this accurate intuition that we will never have any solid ground to stand on—most of us unconsciously try to create and maintain our own formulas of certainty. Of course, because this fantasy of certainty is a defense against the reality of basic uncertainty, our efforts end up generating a subtle, but powerful, atmosphere of chronic anxiety. This chronic anxiety, in turn, fuels a continuing project of seeking resolution, which itself results in more anxiety. So it goes, in what can operate as a self-perpetuating cycle of unnecessary suffering and confusion.

The most obvious and unconscious strategy for not acknowledging the never-resolvable tension between self and other is to emphasize one or the other side of our experience, while erasing or ignoring the other side. From one perspective, we can focus on *self* and subtly invalidate *other*, which gives rise to an experience that life is basically about separateness. From another perspective, we can focus on *other* and subtly invalidate *self*, which gives rise to an experience that life is basically about connection. While either strategy may give us some degree of conscious relief, it never actually works, because it's not based on what's actually true. But this response to the inherent disturbance of relationship is so pervasive that almost all of us appear to enter adulthood consciously identified with either a style of separateness or of connectedness, while unconsciously disowning the opposite energy.

SEPARATENESS AND CONNECTION IN RELATIONSHIP

I find that the qualities of separateness and connection provide a rich, useful framework for working with intimacy and relationship. Almost all cultures have some way of talking about these two apparently contradictory energies. Many relate the truth of separation to masculine energy and the truth of connection to feminine energy. We might also call them *yang* and *yin* or *becoming* and *being*. Whatever words we use, we're talking about the tension or dance between these energies. While they appear to be contradictory, we also sense that they are inseparable in some way, that both are expressions of the basic nature of reality. Upon investigation, we find no independently existing quality of "connection" nor of "separation." It's easy to generate confusion when we believe that we can have one without the other. To be clear, we are not talking about "male" and "female" here. All life forms must have both the qualities of separateness and of connection. Any life form must have a shell or skin or membrane, must compete for resources, and must defend itself. And any life form is completely interconnected with its physical and biological environment. But in most human cultures, women seem to express connecting energy more obviously, whereas men seem to express separation energy more obviously.

The energy of separation includes a capacity to rest in one's existential aloneness, to have boundaries, to assert needs, to allow other people to have their own lives, to not feel inaccurately involved with others, to resist influence from the environment, and to maintain a familiar structure over time. A simple summary of this separate quality is "integrity." This quality reflects a certain sense of consistency and containment. We are willing to be ourselves and let others be themselves, while at the same time sticking up for ourselves. But of course, there are neurotic aspects to the separate style, as well. These may include a disconnection from others, a lack of empathy, the repression of feelings we don't want to feel, insensitivity, and a sense of isolation and deadness. At the extreme end, we could say that the expression of neurotic masculine energy is that of the perpetrator. Someone in that position is so dissociated from their experience of connection that they're able to treat others as if there's no commonality: "I don't need you, so it doesn't really matter how I treat you."

The energy of connection, on the other hand, includes the awareness that we're all interdependent. It's characterized by the qualities of empathy, accommodation, support, a willingness to welcome influence from our environment, and continual change. There's a willingness to let others' needs come first and to find our meaning and satisfaction in relationship. Anybody who's been a parent knows that it's important to be able, at any moment, to put our child's needs ahead of our own. This sense of connection and immediacy can be talked about as the experience of "aliveness." We feel the freshness of relating to "other."

In its neurotic aspects, the energy of connection may be characterized by a lack of boundaries, an avoidance of conflict, and a tendency to compromise integrity in exchange for approval, love, or security. The extreme expression is that of the victim, where someone puts relationship as such a high priority that they lose touch with themselves. The stance of the victim is the perfect complement to that of the perpetrator—it says, "I need you, so it doesn't really matter how you treat me."

In both cases, the neurotic expression of each style arises when there is a fundamental split—a disconnection from the opposite energy. As discussed above, this sense of a dissociative split comes out of our unconscious efforts to not acknowledge the inherent tension and disturbance of all relationships. Neurotic masculine arises when there is a disconnection from the always-present experience of empathy and connection, from the experience of other. Neurotic feminine arises when there's a disconnection from the always-present sense of basic aloneness and separateness, from the experience of self.

To experience the sane expression of either the masculine or the feminine, we must learn how to lead with one energy, without losing experiential contact with the other. Sane masculine energy arises when we can assert our separateness, have conflict, set boundaries, and know that we are alone in some fundamental way—all the while still keeping our heart open. We can feel connection and empathy with others, knowing that any conflict between us is most likely there because they're so important to us. Sane feminine energy leads with connection, communication, support, and empathy—all the while maintaining boundaries and personal responsibility. We understand that no relationship will work well if we lose touch with our fundamental aloneness and compromise our integrity.

In relationship, I find that it usually works best to lead with our experience of connection when things are friendly, going well, cooperative. Knowing that this relationship is not going to "save" us—that we will always have differences to deal with—we can still focus on our commonalities in the moment. We can let irritations slide, rather than keeping score. When both partners are leading with connection, it's the time for sharing our vulnerabilities, risking discussions about sensitive issues, exposing aspects of ourselves that we usually keep private. Healthy feminine energy allows us to stay present in our vulnerability precisely because we remain responsible for our own safety and integrity. When we're in conflict with someone, however, it seems to work best if we lead with the energy of separateness. We know we care about this person and that this person cares about us, but that's not what's being focused on right now. Conflict is the way we deal with our differences, after all, and that's really what differences are—evidence of our separateness. You can't have intimacy without conflict, because you're two separate people getting very close to one another. Conflict, by itself, is not a problem in relationship; problems arise from *unskillful* conflict. Healthy masculine energy can experience conflict without apology—working with the truth of interpersonal differences—precisely because we can feel our care for the other. We know that, paradoxically, the purpose of this conflict is to help us keep our hearts open. A lack of healthy masculine energy is one way in which many couples get into difficulty. They're having conflict, while unconsciously trying to reassure themselves of their connection. The refusal to keep it simple and just have "clean conflict" actually arises from a lack of confidence in our connection and contributes to the "sticky conflict" characteristic of codependent dynamics.

BALANCING RELATIONSHIP STYLES:
FROM UNCONSCIOUS TO CONSCIOUS

Tamara and Allan had been married almost twenty-five years, and their three girls were all finally away at college. They'd come to see me for the same reason many couples do. One of the partners—and it's usually the woman, but about a third of the time it's the man—is in pain because they believe they want more connection in the relationship. During our first session, Tamara went through a long list of efforts she'd made to get more emotional intimacy with Allan. She'd tried to schedule more time together, planning date nights and getaways. She had signed them up for a meditation class in hopes they'd discover a shared interest. She'd tried talking to him about his feelings, to no avail. In fact, it seemed that her attempts were resulting in the opposite response she desired. Allan seemed to get moodier and spent more and more time in his study, reading books and surfing the Internet. Finally Tamara had decided they needed outside help; a friend recommended they come see me.

As is often the case, my first suggestion did not land well. I suggested that rather than trying—unsuccessfully—to promote more connection with Allan, Tamara might use this difficult situation to explore and accept her experience of feeling alone and separate. Every balanced relationship, I suggested, includes both togetherness and separation. As long as Tamara was the voice of connection, there was no need for Allan to make any attempt at connection himself. Allan, like most (but not all) men, had a stylistic tendency toward wanting to feel separate. Tamara's emphasis on connection meant he could take as much space as he wanted, unconsciously aware that she would ensure there was closeness, so he did not need to exert himself to connect.

So many people who desire more intimacy and closeness with their partners would actually benefit from stepping back and getting comfortable with feeling alone. Naming what they want, yes, but not doing the work for both people. Tamara, like many partners who are holding the energy of closeness, had a habit of doing 90 percent of the work of connection. She was going overboard, continually trying to make things work even when she was feeling hurt and exhausted.

I have the view that a healthy, intimate relationship is one based on equity, with each partner making roughly the same amount of effort. Each will get what they want about half the time, and each will not get what they want about half the time. But if we have the habit of doing 90 percent of the work of connection, who are we going to find as a partner but somebody who specializes in doing just 10 percent? So one of the experiments I suggested to Tamara, which anyone in her situation might make, would be to step back to the 50/50 mark and see what happens.

Even though Allan was in the masculine energy position of wanting more separateness, I suggested he look to see if he also genuinely wanted connection. His answer was yes, but that Tamara's efforts were *too* much. She was so demanding, he said, that he needed to sneak away to his study just to be able to breathe. Tamara was always supplying the energy of connection, so Allan never had to. In fact, to maintain his own inner balance, he felt that he had to emphasize his separateness. He had not considered the possibility that by acting in such a separate way, Tamara never had to experience her need for separateness. Like a lot of people who hold the energy of independence in a relationship, he felt he had to withdraw in order to get the space he needed. What Allan didn't understand was that, as he withdrew, Tamara's impulse to close the gap between them and maintain a sense of connection got even stronger. And as she made more efforts at connecting, Allan would withdraw even more. This potentially escalating cycle is called "distancer-pursuer" dynamics in Western therapy.

Counterinstinctual as it might have been, what I suggested was that Allan experiment with initiating *more* contact with Tamara, just as I had invited Tamara to step back. I suggested he might suspend the thought that Tamara was trying to control and smother him and that perhaps she simply wanted the reassurance of connection. Over time, as Allan became more willing to initiate contact, Tamara reported feeling more willing to step back when he wanted some time to himself. And as Tamara was willing to allow Allan more time alone without conflict, he found that he could join her with less anxiety about feeling trapped or losing himself in her needs.

From the Western developmental point of view, our relationship styles originate in childhood. As we've discussed, they develop as part of our strategy to take the best care of ourselves possible, given our circumstances, gender training, and families of origin. There are many different scenarios, but very commonly, an adult who is identified with the energy of separation will have grown up with a parent with whom feeling connected was a problem. The parent may have been smothering or invasive or may have pushed away any attempts to be close. There are many possible situations and conditions, but the child's ongoing experience is that life works better as the child learns to take care of herself and not count on anyone being there for her. All children have to cue off of their parents. They are profoundly dependent, still very immature, and basically powerless. So very similar life circumstances can lead to very different strategies, depending on the parent's basic emotional stance.

In Allan's case, it wasn't a surprise to learn that he had a history of experiencing his mother as overinvolved, smothering, and controlling. To protect himself—his emotional integrity—he had to withhold relationship, but in a way that avoided obvious boundaries that his mother would attack. So he tended to overtly accommodate and agree in order to avoid conflict, but then he would not follow through. Instead, he would just disappear. This style of separateness was necessary for Allan in childhood because his mother claimed that she wanted closeness, but it was clear to him that it was about her needs, not his. Another child might learn a style of separateness from parents who didn't want to feel burdened by parenting or who were working long hours and came home exhausted. This child may have been rewarded for independence and self-sufficiency and, as an adult, be very proud of having a separate style. Of course, as children, we are profoundly dependent. So our strategy of wanting to feel only separate will never actually work. As an adult, we may find a "connecting" partner, as Allan did, to continue this drama of "trying" to be separate.

When an adult is strongly identified with a connecting style, that person usually will have grown up with parents with whom feeling separate was a problem. This is often the case when a child has experienced emotional neglect or has been through significant abandonment events. This may mean a parent who is overtly negligent, who is working three jobs because they're in poverty, or who got very sick and went into the hospital. Perhaps this child's parents got divorced and were very absorbed in that process, so they didn't have as much attention for the child. Whatever the reasons, when a child has a parent who's not emotionally engaged, it's very common for that child to learn to make the connection. If the child wants relationship—and, of course, as dependent young beings, we must have relationship—then that child will have to make it happen. Such a child is trained to connect, to be the one responsible for the connection. When no one is really available or interested in the child, the last thing that child will do is to assert any separateness. The child won't develop skills with boundaries or feel able to express anger and won't learn to assert needs effectively. As an adult, this person might mysteriously end up with a partner who is emotionally unavailable—because that's the kind of relationship the adult knows and understands.

Tamara is a good example. She was the only daughter of four children, whose parents divorced when Tamara was about eight years old, after several years of bitter conflict. She unconsciously responded to her own needs for security and love, which in fact were not being met, by taking on the role of being the family's caretaker. No one was there for her, so the best she could do was to be there for everyone else. She was trained to believe that relationships were about her doing all the work—about *her* making the connection. She "hired" Allan because he specialized in being emotionally unavailable and thus allowed her to play her familiar role as the never-really-successful connector.

Personally, I don't think it's necessary to go back and bring alive one's parent–child relationship in order to grow and transform through therapeutic work. But for many of us, it can be helpful to see the historic origins of our style in order to appreciate how deeply embedded our patterns may be. So I'm always curious about parent-child dynamics. But I can usually find in the present situation enough evidence to understand the basic themes of a client's history. Thus, if a client is not interested in, or is resistant to, exploring past relationship experiences, I don't find that to be a problem. Of course, my clients' histories do come up as context. And it does seem almost always the case that the style we bring to our adult relationships was the survival style we learned in our families of origin. These are not wrong styles—developing our coping strategies was the most intelligent, healthy thing we could have done, given our circumstances at the time. But now we're adults, and our style is now several decades out of date. We're still trying to take the best care of ourselves possible, but we're doing so ineffectively.

EMBRACING THE CONTRADICTORY ENERGIES OF SEPARATENESS AND CONNECTION

As we have discussed, all of life can be understood as requiring a never-resolvable interplay between two basic qualities: the truth that everything is separate and the truth that everything is connected. We can't really have life without these qualities, which appear contradictory but are obviously inseparable parts of the larger nature of reality. Given that, it also seems extremely likely that we can't have healthy intimacy without these apparently contradictory qualities. To translate into practical terms, healthy intimacy requires that we value not only our sense of connection with our partner but also our sense of separateness. Most of us genuinely want to give and receive love, to share our life with someone, to go to depth, to have companionship. And it's also true that our partner is not on the planet to understand us, much less take care of us. The closer we get to anyone, the more we're guaranteed to feel hurt, off and on. Most of us don't really want to compromise our lifestyle to accommodate a partner. Most of us, I think, are cautious about trusting anybody on the planet with our core vulnerability. So to me, healthy intimacy requires this never-resolvable dance—a tension or friction—between the deeply contradictory feelings that we genuinely want to be close to our partner and we genuinely don't want to be close to our partner.

In our culture, however, most of us are taught that "intimacy" is synonymous with "closeness." So if a person says, "I want to be intimate with that man or woman," that person almost always means, "I want to be close to them." In fact, there is very strong pressure on couples to *only* be close. It's so strong that publicly, most couples try to present themselves as only happy, warm, supportive, and enjoying their relationship. They save their conflict for the privacy of their own homes. What I've discovered through my work is that there's a certain type of shame that many couples feel—shame that they're not meeting the cultural expectation that intimacy is supposed to only be positive and happy. Such couples carry the secret burden that they're not as close as they think they're supposed to be.

There are many pressures to only feel connected, most of which are not consciously articulated. Pressure to only want to be close to one another and nobody else; to always like each other; to be happy together; to be sexually passionate. This leaves most of us, as couples, in a type of dilemma—we have to deal with our truth of separateness, but we must do so unconsciously. Being separate persons in relationship is not negotiable. In fact, healthy intimacy *requires* a conscious relating to the truth of separateness. Yet as couples, most of us are left to deal with our need for separateness in an unconscious, often symptomatic way.

Because we consciously try to only be close, we unconsciously create a variety of symptomatic behaviors to put distance between us. Some very common distancing dynamics include chronic conflict that never gets solved, even though the issues are really not difficult to work through; miscommunication, even though we could really understand our partner if we tried; a loss of sexual intimacy, even though we still find our partner attractive; parent-child roles between partners, even though we know we're both adults; living parallel lives as we raise children, even while we claim we want more engagement; and so on. Many of us use some combination of these apparent problems as a way of regulating the dynamic balance of feeling connected and feeling separate. When we are feeling stressed or vulnerable or anxious or just want to be left alone, we will unconsciously call on one of these patterns as a sure way to get some separateness. That's unfortunate.

I think it's possible to have agreements that if we want to be close, we communicate and behave in that way. If we want to be separate, that's how we communicate and act, without needing any justification, blame, or apology. But in my experience that idea is not supported by our culture, and most of us experience feeling separate from our partner as evidence of some problem that needs to be fixed. So, many couples come to therapy believing that the difficulties in their relationship are being caused by a lack of closeness.

In over thirty-five years of private practice, I've worked with at least several thousand couples. I can only recall a handful of couples that have come in asking for help in being more separate. Probably nine out of ten couples want help in being closer. Other than a few who want help with parenting or the like, almost all the couples I see have the idea that there's a lack of closeness that needs to be fixed. Most haven't yet considered the idea that the problem is actually an overemphasis on closeness and a lack of consciousness that they are separate people and that sometimes feeling distant is natural and necessary.

This cultural pressure is also supported by the fact that as children, almost all of us had to put connection as a higher priority than separateness. We had to put the security of our relationship with our parents as a higher priority than our integrity. As a child we couldn't say, "No, I fundamentally disagree with you. I think I'll go find some other parents." Little children have to do whatever they must so that their parents will love them, protect them, nurture them, not abuse them, and not abandon them. As a result, from the time we are very, very young, we're all trained to compromise our integrity to purchase security. We enter adulthood with that training very powerfully conditioned. In my experience, it's usually not until we're in our thirties or forties that we actually have enough life experience, emotional resilience, and confidence in ourselves to consider putting our own integrity ahead of closeness. This transition is quite disturbing, of course, because most of us associate intimacy with closeness, and asserting our integrity makes the fact that we are different from others very clear. It's difficult to acknowledge the truth of separateness. It feels like we're risking loss of the relationship. But the separateness is already there; it's actually nothing new. What's new is that we're starting to work with it consciously.

UNDERSTANDING CODEPENDENT DYNAMICS

As we enter adulthood, we begin to discover how powerfully conditioned most of our experiencing actually is. This conditioning arises from our social and cultural experience, our gender training, our family of origin, unexpected life events, and so on. For example, traditionally women have been taught that their worth as persons comes from relationship, from their ability to be sensitive to the needs of others. While in some ways this is changing, on the whole, if a woman stands up as separate and independent—perhaps choosing not to have children, but instead to focus on career—she's often criticized as cold and not really feminine. Men, on the other hand, are taught that their worth comes from their ability to stand up as separate people. They're taught to go out into the world, take their hits, not complain, and not be dependent. If a man shows too much dependency or emotional sensitivity, he's often criticized as not being manly enough. As discussed, most of us also strongly shape our relationship styles in response to our parents' energy and behavior. As an accommodation to these many complex influences, we almost always seem to grow up learning to be identified with either a connecting or a separating style, with a disconnection from the other energy.

The complexity of our styles and the strength of the disconnection appear to operate along a continuum. In my experience as a therapist, it's extremely rare for somebody to come into adulthood without such a stylistic imbalance. I'm using the word "imbalance," because usually we're unconsciously disconnected from the opposite energy and don't really experience choice in how we relate. We tend to have a "one size fits all" approach, which, given the complexity of life and of relationships, works well about half the time and not very well about half the time.

Looking back at my own childhood, I believe that it was intelligent for me to disconnect from my feelings of dependence. As far back as I can remember, there's evidence that self-sufficiency and independence were more likely to get me the love and approval I wanted. I would guess that every time I showed a willingness and ability to take care of myself, I was rewarded. As a result, I entered adulthood with a conscious belief that I was self-sufficient and independent and didn't really need others. In fact, I put a fair amount of energy into making sure that was the case. I learned to cook, to take care of myself, and to handle my life skillfully. It wasn't until I was in my forties that I started to feel safe enough to realize how incredibly dependent I am as a person.

One of the first clues had to do with my relationship with my wife. It dawned on me one day that if I were truly independent, she wouldn't bug me so much. I wouldn't be so disturbed by her tone of voice, her behavior, or how she related to me. I wouldn't feel so warm and relaxed when she was kind to me. She had an incredible impact on my feelings; apparently, I was so dependent that my state of mind was profoundly affected by her mood and behavior. When I'm working with clients, it's often pretty obvious, pretty quickly, what style they have. If clients have a very self-sufficient style, like I do, I encourage them to say out loud, "Perhaps, secretly, I'm an incredibly needy, dependent person." The responses I get are very interesting! Often there's a type of disbelief or revulsion at the thought. If, on the other hand, someone specializes in always trying to connect, soothe, and accommodate others, I might suggest that they say out loud, "Perhaps, secretly, I'm an incredibly selfish, angry person." The response in this case is usually something like, "But that's so horrible! I don't want to be that way. That's a bad way to be." As we start looking into these organizations, we usually find that we've not only been suppressing half of the story—the half that didn't work as young children—but we've also often had to *attack* or *abandon* that part of ourselves to make sure it never comes up. We've had to sacrifice part of ourselves for the sake of our larger well-being. Because of this, many of us enter adulthood with a lot of judgment and even aggression toward that disowned half of who we are.

Another important dynamic to consider is that we all have been trained into the experience of relationship in which we, as children, are immature, deeply dependent, and without power. The "other" is the parent, not an equal. Mutuality is not even a possibility. We must learn to cue off the other's reality, compromise our integrity to purchase security and love, and remain private in much of our vulnerability. If we're able, we learn to read our parents' moods, anticipate their behavior, and try our best to be who we think they want us to be. Also, the younger we are, the more our experience of relationship is, appropriately, one of emotional fusion. Our most formative training in intimacy is that of learning how to relate within the energy of being merged with the other.

If we are fortunate, our experience as a powerless child is positive. If unfortunate, our experience is negative. But in all cases, we learn how to relate to the other from a subordinate, reactive position. Imagine, then, two adults coming together—each from this probably inescapable training in relationship as an experience of powerlessness, of needing to look to the other to have one's needs met. Although we look like adults and have adult capacities in other parts of our lives, in the arena of intimacy, we're like a child trying to have a relationship with another child. It's no surprise that most of us operate in our intimate relationships in a much less mature way than we operate in the world. We often treat our partners, and allow ourselves to be treated, in ways we would never accept with friends or colleagues.

With these understandings, we can begin to explore the phenomenon of codependency. We could say that pretty much all of us enter adulthood predisposed to codependent dynamics, some obviously more so than others. The basic dynamic of codependency is when one person chooses, or "hires," a partner to be the location of—to manifest—exactly those energies that the first person has disowned in themselves. The partner, in turn, has hired the first person to be the location of his or her own disowned energies. I've seen this dynamic with almost every couple I have known, whether socially or in my work as a therapist. People like myself, who grew up disowning our dependency, will mysteriously be attracted to and attract partners who specialize in connection. If it's a good fit, that connecting partner will be hiring the independent person to be the location of separateness. Now, this is actually a good division of labor; if it were a conscious decision, it would be fine. But most of us have a compulsive, unconscious relationship to our own style. We don't choose it, but we unconsciously maintain it, even when there's evidence that it's not working well. It feels as if our survival is somehow at risk if we don't.

A basic theme of codependent dynamics is that one person is the voice of connection, and the other is the voice of separateness. The connecting person will take responsibility for wanting more connection. The separateness person will take responsibility for wanting more space. At first, it seems like a really good fit. It's like we've found our missing half. For example, when I met my wife—who specializes in connection and dependency—at first it was, "Oh, this person is so playful and emotionally expressive and sensitive and nurturing!" After a few years, however, my fundamental aggression toward that energy started to come out. At that point, it was like, "Why doesn't she get a life of her own? Why is she such a leech? Why is she so dependent? Why can't she be more like me?" Likewise, at first my wife appreciated me being strong and confident. She liked that I was able to deal with the world competently and be a steady support without getting captured by my emotions. After a few years, however, the complaints began. "You're unavailable. You're insensitive. You used to want to be close. Why can't you be more emotionally engaged?"

This is a predictable theme in my work with couples. Some version of this drama will almost always be present. What we don't understand is that it's a setup. Initially we feel like we've found our missing halves, but there's a reason that half is missing: we've disowned it. It's only a matter of time until the fact that we're aggressive toward that part of ourselves will start to be expressed as aggression toward the very person we've hired to hold that energy for us. After a few years, most couples end up with a sense of polarization—even an adversarial attitude toward one another. It may not be there 24/7, but it's a theme that keeps arising and getting more difficult. Often we take the position that we don't really understand each other; we don't "get" each other. What we *actually* don't get is that we have hired our partner to manifest what we're not willing to be responsible for in ourselves. So in therapy, this is a lot of the work I do, addressing this "mutual projection process." It's not the whole path of intimacy, but it's a lot of the work that happens inside my office, because most couples seem to be dealing with it to a greater or lesser degree.

Team Neurosis

Codependency is basically an agreement between two people to ritualize a balance between closeness and separation. It's an unconscious effort to experience wholeness without having to take conscious ownership of what we don't want to experience in ourselves. So we look for wholeness in the relationship rather than in ourselves. Each person wants connection, but at the same time, neither wants to feel too vulnerable. So we get close, but then we each protect ourselves from a direct experience of these vulnerabilities by blaming the other for our own internal disturbances. That's the core of the problem: neither of us is taking responsibility for the never-resolvable tension within ourselves of having profoundly contradictory feelings about intimacy, and we're projecting the cause of this tension onto our partners. Since we're not acknowledging the tension inside of ourselves—that we want both closeness and separation with our partner—that tension starts to be experienced as if it were between the two of us. As a result, the relationship itself starts to feel problematic.

Without knowing it, each partner is actually using the relationship to serve a function—the same function that neurotic organization serves within the individual: to attempt to live a life without disturbance. We want to be close to somebody, and yet, at the same time, we don't want to feel the vulnerabilities that being close to someone reveals. We want to feel fresh and alive while not having to feel powerless, sad, angry, or whatever a spontaneous engagement with life may invite. But of course, it doesn't work in relationship any better than it works in our own private life. Once again, there's a dissociative split; a pretending that operates on an unconscious level. We're pretending that half of our experience is not here—it's in the other person. It's not who I am; it's *you*. In this way, I like to think of codependency almost like "team neurosis." It's serving the same distractive function, but it's a step more elaborate. We are once again removing ourselves from our immediate embodied experience, because that experience is actually disturbing. It's disturbing to be alive. It's especially disturbing to be alive in an intimate relationship.

Neurosis is organized to make sure that no resolution is found, so that it's distractive function is not lost. This means that our avoidant strategies must never be seen as out of date and as no longer needed. Codependent dynamics take this a step further. "Not only am I in my *own* personal state of never-to-be-resolved drama and struggle, but now I've involved somebody else—and that person has involved me. The apparent disturbance is not just inside me; it seems to be outside me as well, between myself and my partner." And just like neurosis, our unconscious investment in the codependent dynamic is to make sure it never is "seen through." If it were resolved, we would be threatened with having to be responsible for our own difficulties, our own emotional vulnerabilities. As long as we can point the finger at our partner and say, "You're the cause of my grief, rage, disappointment, and abandonment," our attention remains elsewhere. The more we behave, think, and feel as if our partner is the problem, the less likely we'll be forced to see our own deeply contradictory feelings. Most of us would unconsciously prefer to have our partner say "no" to our fantasies and then blame him or her, rather than have to say "no" to ourselves.

THE UNCONSCIOUS EXPRESSION
OF OUR "DISOWNED HALF"

When we find a good fit for our codependent dynamics, we enable each other in strengthening our claim that it should be possible to only have our preferred half of the complex reality of relationship. "I want more connection and engagement; you're the problem because you won't give it to me." "I want more separateness and freedom; you're the problem because you won't give it to me." However, because we all *must* have both energies, what we are disowning *must* continue to be expressed. When we routinely complain that there's not enough connection, we're really saying that we feel separate but that this feeling is a problem. Not appreciating the connection that is always there, because it doesn't fit our preferences, is actually the disguised activity of separateness. But now the fact that we are withholding relationship, perhaps out of hurt and pain, is expressed unconsciously and indirectly. I find the partners taking this role are often focused on what they're not getting, their feelings of abandonment or lack of engagement, communicating their disappointment to their partner, or retreating into the self-absorption of blaming themselves. Their behavior is actually reflecting their investment in feeling separate. If they really want to feel more connected, it's not complicated, because connection is always present. They can just join their partner's reality. They can focus on moments of engagement and mutuality and bring to mind feelings of being loved and of loving. Of course, they would have to acknowledge the complexity of intimacy—that this isn't the whole picture, that maybe this isn't their preferred version of connection.

People who claim they want more separateness are apparently feeling very connected, but they experience this feeling as a problem. Rather than focusing on the separateness, which is always there, always available to be experienced, they complain about demands being made or about how their partner is never satisfied or can't handle their life and must be taken care of. This is really just a disguised expression of their own dependency feelings; they are maintaining connection in the form of entangled conflict. This unconscious intention is often manifest as ineffective boundaries, allowing them to claim that they're trying to be separate but are somehow prevented from doing so by their partner. If they really want to feel more separate, it's not complicated. They must learn not to participate in unproductive conflicts, to have effective boundaries, to stop claiming that their partner is controlling them, and so on. Of course, they would then have to take full responsibility for their own disturbance.

In both styles, the unconscious expression of our disowned half can usually be found in our complaints about our partners. Our complaints are indications of how we are not taking care of ourselves effectively. And not taking care of ourselves in specific ways allows the acting out of that aspect of our experience for which we are not yet ready to take conscious responsibility. Our resentment about not enough connection, our focus on what's missing, is actually the disguised expression of our separateness. It's the way we justify withholding ourselves from relationship, because we are not owning this part of ourselves consciously. Our blame about not being given the space we want, about endless demands, is actually the disguised expression of our connection. We justify our dependency by claiming it's being done to us, thus excusing us from owning this part of ourselves consciously.

Those of us who have done personal work—in therapy or as part of our spiritual path—often have a strong hope or belief that we've left the pain and suffering of codependent relationship dynamics behind. However, many of us find that even after this work, there's still an aspect of our experience with our partners that is indeed codependent. It feels gluey or sticky; there's still some complaint; we find we're still withholding ourselves from full engagement. If we find this inquiry disturbing, that probably means there's something to look at. That's a good thing. If codependency is there, it's there. If it's not, it's not. If it's still operating, it's good to become aware of it, because then we can work with it. In that way, any disturbance about codependency—or about anything, for that matter—can be understood as indicating exactly what we need to work with. It's a red flag, a signal that there's something unresolved that needs to be seen and experienced consciously. ◾

If it's a good (codependent) fit, both my partner and I will be concurrently blaming each other for our disturbance and our pain. A common theme in relationship is this fantasy: if only our partner would be who we want them to be, then everything would be okay. But the codependent dynamic requires that neither person effectively confront this dynamic. Both of us have to unconsciously be willing to receive the other person's blame, without setting appropriate boundaries. It's an unconscious agreement: "I'll blame you, and you'll blame me, and both of us will sort of complain about it." But we won't do what's necessary in order to dissolve the pattern—which would be to take care of *ourselves*.

That's the deal in codependency; we don't set the kind of boundaries that would interrupt the cycle of blame. We don't say, "I'm sorry, but this isn't really working for me. So I'm going to take some time to cool off, and I'll come back when I feel like I can relate to you as the adult I am." Because of this, codependency works, just like neurosis works, and it continues because it creates a sense of illusory safety and security. But as I've mentioned, there's a high price tag attached. Just as neurotic organization leaves us feeling divided from ourselves, codependent dynamics leave a couple feeling divided from each other. Just as personal neurosis can have incredibly damaging effects on one's sense of self and confidence in the world, so codependency can slowly kill the love between two people. The more each of us blames and feels blamed, without taking care of ourselves, the more damage is caused. It's like we keep putting tiny knives into each other; over time, it's going to have a cumulative effect. So while codependency appears to get us what we want in the short run, it actually leads to deterioration in the quality of the relationship over time.

Bradley and Craig had just this kind of deterioration going on. Having met in grad school, they'd experienced an initial year and a half of wonder and even bliss together. But around the two-year mark, they'd started experiencing increasing conflict. They weren't sure whether the relationship was viable. Craig seemed to be considering ending the relationship; Bradley was dissatisfied, but had more confidence that they could save the relationship. He thought they should hang in there and had initiated the idea of therapy.

As we got into the couple's specific complaints, I learned that Bradley felt he was doing most of the work to keep the relationship going. If they had a fight, he was the one who ended up apologizing and trying to get them talking again. If they felt distant, he was the one who initiated talking about their feelings. In the meantime, he felt Craig was becoming increasingly private and disengaged. While he appreciated the fact that Craig had the more successful job and contributed more money to the relationship, he wanted more emotional involvement.

Craig, on the other hand, felt that Bradley was becoming increasingly dependent on him for all of his emotional needs. He complained that Bradley hadn't maintained his network of friends from school and that he wasn't bringing in much money. He appreciated the fact that Bradley liked to cook and keep the house clean, but overall it seemed he just wanted Craig to take care of him.

ON NONTRADITIONAL PARTNERSHIPS

Craig and Bradley had a story that is very typical of what I hear in my office every day. The same neurotic, codependent dynamics seem to occur whether a couple is heterosexual, gay, or lesbian. Usually, the more relative the level of experiencing, the more we will deal with our differences—with how we are unique. As we investigate deeper levels of experiencing, I find that we're all dealing with the same basic human issues and vulnerabilities. In general, one partner is the voice of separateness in the relationship—in this case, Craig—and one partner is the voice of connection, which here would be Bradley. ▪

I started with Bradley and Craig like I start with most couples: by talking about personal responsibility. I introduced the possibility that the reason each had a complaint about the other was actually because neither seemed to be doing a very good job of taking care of himself. When we're taking good care of ourselves—paying attention to our own needs and not expecting our partners to do it for us—we are still affected by our mates, but their behavior doesn't occur as a survival-level threat.

I asked Bradley and Craig to try on the view that each of them could do such a good job taking care of himself that he would have no complaint, blame, or resentment toward the other. This is a practice, of course, not a sudden achievement. In the process, they might even start to recover the sense of their hearts being open to their partners. At the moment, both of them were in the process of starting to close their hearts. To me, this seemed to be serving a boundary function: they needed boundaries in the relationship, but neither was very skillful in setting those boundaries. So instead, they were starting to close their hearts as an unconscious way of expressing the fact that they were emotionally separate, as well as connected, persons.

Taking care of ourselves includes setting boundaries and communicating them to our partner. To illustrate this, I asked Bradley for one of his favorite complaints. "I really, really hate it when Craig blows up and yells at me," he said.

I asked if he'd ever requested that Craig not blow up at him—had he set that boundary? The answer was no, that he hadn't specifically made that request. I suggested he try doing it right at that moment, there in my office. This was a first step toward taking good care of himself: naming a boundary, and then asking his partner for that behavior. Making the request is no guarantee it will happen, of course. But the outcome is not the most important point. The point is to begin asserting personal responsibility in the relationship, which in turn leads to feeling less victimized by one's partner.

I coached Bradley through making the request, which went something like, "Craig, I have a request. Would you be willing to not yell at me or raise your voice? Would you be willing to use 'I' statements rather than 'you' statements?"

Of course, Craig may agree to the request or he may not. He may remember not to raise his voice or he may forget. But it doesn't really matter: It's not his responsibility to deal with Bradley's disturbance. It's Bradley's responsibility to deal with his own disturbance, and he was not yet doing a very good job of this. But he was on his way.

After making the boundary request, I introduced another very basic practice. If Craig did at some point raise his voice, I suggested Bradley might simply remove himself from the situation. "I couldn't do that!" he said. When I asked why, he said, "I don't want to hurt Craig's feelings." At this point I find it's helpful to name the priority that's being held in the situation. We all want to have everything—Bradley didn't want to be yelled at, but he didn't want Craig to feel abandoned, either. Yet of course our human existence is characterized by loss and limitation. So I will frequently invite people to put into words what they are actually prioritizing—to say it out loud—so they are aware of the choices they're making.

"How would it be," I asked Bradley, "to say out loud, 'Apparently, not hurting Craig's feelings is a higher priority than my own integrity.'" Bradley found it uncomfortable, but he managed to say it. I went on to ask him to consider what it might be like to treat Craig like an adult, allowing him to take responsibility for his own experience. I tend to invite my clients to consider behaving in a new way and to welcome any feelings that get triggered at the thought. I do this not to try to convince them to behave differently but to increase their willingness to feel their own disturbing emotions—since it's a new relationship with our disturbance that offers the potential for transformative change.

Like Bradley and Craig, most of us have not yet decided to take responsibility for our vulnerabilities, our disturbances, and our uncertainty in how to live. For this reason, many couples allow their codependency to progress to the point where it has caused significant damage to the relationship. That's the point at which most couples come into therapy. Sometimes it is, for practical reasons, too late. The couple has let it get to the point where the love between them has basically been killed. Fortunately, many couples get there while there's still a ground of appreciation. They have the sense that they're torturing each other unnecessarily, and they're ready to change. They just can't figure out what to do about it—which, as it turns out, is the subject of the next chapter. We'll continue the discussion about relationships, beginning with a short discussion about four basic stages in our personal and relationship evolution. Then we'll talk about some specific views and practices that I introduce to the couples I work with that can help increase the understanding and skill that's so important in working with the inherently provocative and never-resolvable experience of intimate relationships.

LOOSENING OUR IDENTIFICATION WITH OUR RELATIONSHIP STYLE

Does it make sense that you probably come into adult relationships consciously preferring to feel like either a connecting person or a separate person? If so, then it may be helpful to explore your experience of the style you're not so comfortable with. Increasing your capacity to participate in the full range of your feelings challenges the central driver of codependent dynamics. Here are two practices to get you started.

Clarify your preferred style. If it's not obvious, look at the roles you've played in your history of relationships, ask friends for their feedback, see which style provokes more anxiety. Then, for a week or two, practice inviting the felt sense of being the other style. If you like to connect, invite feeling fundamentally alone, look for evidence of your aloneness in your life, imagine never being in relationship again. As we've discussed, stay embodied, with no interpretations or story; see if there's actually any problem. As another step, look for opportunities to behave (in small ways) as a separate person. If someone asks you to do something, decline. Express your differences with friends.

If you like to feel separate, look for all of the ways in which you are, in fact, dependent on others. Imagine dedicating your life to the service of others and always putting their needs first. Stay embodied. If you care to, actually behave (in small ways) as if you're so grateful to be here that you look for ways to express your appreciation to others. When the clerk at the grocery store asks if you'd like help with your bags, accept.

The point isn't to change your style but to learn to tolerate more emotional complexity. Just see what it's like. ▪

If you're in relationship and there's enough playfulness available, clarify your usual styles and then alternate the roles every day for a week or two. On odd days, one of you connects, and the other separates. On even days, you switch. Stay embodied; no interpretations. Just see how it feels to not always do it in your familiar way. ▪

7

RELATIONSHIP
AS AN EVOLVING PATH

WHEN WE HAVE THE INSPIRATION to improve our lives, to grow, and to wake up—and if you're reading this book, it's likely you have that inspiration—I find it's helpful to clarify our intentions. Our efforts, to be most effective, should be in alignment with our highest priorities. Walking a progressive path is an expression of such an intention, and I find it helpful to talk about the sequential stages we are likely to encounter as we set out on this path. This idea of a sequence of stages is central to Western psychotherapy, to evolutionary theory, certainly to Buddhism, and, I think, to most spiritual paths. In both my own Buddhist practice and my clinical work with relationships, I find that the work we do at one stage lays the foundation for the work we do at the next stage. If we try to jump ahead of our actual current capacities and prematurely work at a later or "higher" stage—because it may be more emotionally or spiritually attractive—we will probably find that our progress is not sustainable and may even appear to stop. Part of bringing our efforts into alignment with our intentions is to be very honest with ourselves about what we're actually willing and able to do at any moment.

There are, of course, a lot of different theoretical frameworks one could take on the journey of personal evolution. There are theories with three stages and nine stages and twelve stages and seven stages. Here, I'm going to present a simple, four-stage path of working with ourselves through relationship. Over the course of time, I have found this particular theory to be consistent with my clients' experiences. In fact, I developed it directly out of my clinical work with couples. I have also found this view to be resonant with the Buddhist understanding of path as progressing through three *yanas,* or vehicles.

The four stages I want to discuss could be called the **prepersonal,** the **personal,** the **interpersonal** and the **nonpersonal.** Each stage can be understood as representing a different attitude toward our already-existing basic nature of open awareness and freedom. Each stage is a description of our capacity and our willingness to be fully present and fully embodied, to integrate open awareness into our daily lives. Or, to say it in a different way, each stage is a description of how we *defend against* open mind—how we generate chronic states of self-absorption to avoid the experience of groundlessness, of no objectively existing reality to stand on. From this point of view, each stage is not really about some past wound or historic conditioning. Nor is it about some future ability that we want to have. It's really about our choice, in each moment, to at least practice being fully present and open—or not—and the variety of ways in which we pretend we don't have a choice at all.

A BUDDHIST PARADOX

From the Vajrayana Buddhist viewpoint, progressive, evolutionary work feels paradoxical. This view is that we are already free, so none of this work is actually necessary. In the same way, we can say that we are already fully intimate with ourselves, our partners, and life. As Dōgen, the Zen patriarch, said: "The awakened mind is that mind intimate with all things." This means that it is possible to consciously participate in what's already true; we are always fully and inescapably in relationship with life. It's not an option to *not* be fully engaged. But relationship *is* the disturbing simultaneity of other and self, of connection and separation. *Fully intimate* means feeling fully connected and feeling fully separate. This experience of "not two, not one" invites a direct sense of reality as nondivided.

But because we are invested in the dramas of life—the certainty that there is some problem—it's very helpful, for practical reasons, to progress through these stages. Over time, we can gradually increase our tolerance for open awareness, embodied immediacy, and always-present intimacy in our daily life and in our relationships, in our moment-by-moment experiencing. As this occurs, we develop the ability to hold a complex experiential state in which we see that, in a more absolute way, none of this work is or was necessary and, in a more relative way, it is and was completely necessary. We learn to hold both views simultaneously, with no need to take sides, no need to resolve these apparent contradictions. ◾

THE PREPERSONAL

The prepersonal stage is the arena of codependent dynamics, which we discussed at some length in chapter 6. It's characterized by a claim that we are unable to change the familiar, historically conditioned ways in which we engage with ourselves and with life. Either we can't do it because there's too much fear or we don't know how or we can't change because our partner is not being who we want her to be. Whatever the circumstances, we take the position that there's some obstacle blocking our ability to make evolutionary change.

This position is like that of a child—we relate to intense experience as if we were incapable of handling it. This was true when we were young. As adults, it's no longer true, but most of us have not yet given up our historic survival strategies. Within this stage, there is still a strong dissociative split; there's a tendency to leave our immediate, embodied experiencing out of a sense that it's just too much to tolerate. As with neurotic organization, our unconscious investment is in *not* solving our apparent problems. The drama that we are a problematic person—or that our relationship is problematic—is serving a protective function. As children, our self-aggression was very healthy, necessary, and intelligent. It was how we prevented ourselves from being aware of feeling overwhelmed and flooded by intense experience over which we had no control. But now, as adequately functional adults, this organization is no longer necessary. Most of us can, in fact, train ourselves to have a conscious relationship with very intense experience. We simply choose not to do so.

To be clear, the choice isn't to have a sudden ability to stay fully present and embodied with intensity. The choice is to *practice* staying present, to increase our capacity. But instead, at this prepersonal stage of relationship, we rely on our partners to support our sense of being stuck or unable to be present. We use them as a decoy, avoiding the truth that we're unwilling to stay present, with the claim that they are making it impossible for us to do so. When working with couples at this stage, I hear endless versions of the claim, "I would show up more in my vulnerability if only my partner would be who I want him to be first." But of course, our partners are always going to be who they are and never who we want them to be. So we can always find justification to keep some distance, keep our guard up, collapse in self-absorption—basically, to not be fully engaged and present. If it's a good fit, our partner is using us in a similar way. In that way, we both are maintaining an unconscious agreement to provide each other with justification for not being more present, openhearted, and intimate. As discussed earlier, this cooperation arises from the reality that we all learn how to have relationships from the position of being a dependent, powerless child relating to all-powerful adults. It is impossible as a young child to learn how to relate with personal power and mutuality, however kind our parents may have been. We all begin our experiments with adult intimacy as if we were one child relating to another child.

The basic story at the prepersonal stage is that our partner *could* give us what we need and want but is not willing to do so. We manufacture an endless series of complaints and frustrations about our partners and the relationship, and they do the same. This atmosphere of conflict and hurt generates experiential evidence, over and over again, justifying why we cannot be open. Who wants to be open in a war zone? It's just not smart. So the prepersonal stage guarantees chronic self-absorption—an intermittent but continuing focus on our self-created dramas—which of course takes our attention away from our always already-present environment of open awareness and choice.

Sometimes when I'm teaching, I'll do a little enactment in the classroom to illustrate how our internal dramas operate. I invite the students to relax their awareness, let their sense of attention fill the whole room, and see if they can maintain this experience. As everyone is practicing this expansive awareness, I'll have a student engage me in a prearranged conflict of some sort. Perhaps they'll claim they don't like the way I'm talking or complain about the content of the exercise. The more heated this apparent conflict becomes, the more everyone's attention contracts and focuses on the conflict. I've done this exercise a number of times, and I don't think I've yet had anyone report that their attention remained expansive during the argument. What this illustrates is how engaging conflict is for us. Any sense of a problem is so fascinating—and perhaps feels so threatening—that it magnetizes our attention on a very basic, biological level. Even when there's no actual harm happening, any sense of conflict attracts our attention away from the open, expansive awareness that's already there. This operates at both individual and relationship levels. At the prepersonal level, we are still trying to take care of ourselves using young, out-of-date survival strategies. Our refusal to experience disowned energies results in the chronic conflict of trying to feel whole while trying to not participate in all of our experiencing, which tends to perpetuate our sense of being a powerless child in an overwhelming world and distracts us from the open awareness that would free us from taking these dramas seriously.

THE PERSONAL

Over the course of our lives, many of us eventually cultivate a strong enough sense of ourselves that we can stand alone—we don't need to involve other people in our unresolved difficult emotions. I call this the personal stage of relationship. Whether through a gradual maturation process or through deliberate personal work, at this stage we become willing to at least *practice* not seeing others as the cause of, or the solution to, our difficult experiences. I think of this practice of personal responsibility as the antidote to codependent dynamics. It's this stage at which the majority of my work with couples is done. First, we challenge the codependent dynamics. Then we use ongoing daily life experiences to practice strengthening the attitude of personal responsibility.

Let's go back to the example of Bradley and Craig from chapter 6. After Bradley was willing to take personal responsibility for his conflicts with Craig—by asserting his boundaries, making requests, and removing himself from situations that didn't work for him—he was poised to enter the personal stage. He became progressively more willing to feel the disturbing emotions that arose when he stood up for himself, and he stopped holding himself responsible for Craig's emotional well-being. At this point, like many but not all people doing this work, he became interested in exploring the origins of his style of relating—which for most of us stem from our childhood experiences. In his case, we uncovered the fact that he'd had an angry, rigidly independent mother. He'd been the one responsible for initiating connection with her, all the while living in fear of triggering her. We might speculate that, as part of his neurotic survival strategy, he had found it wise to disconnect from his own energies of anger and independence in order to have the greatest sense of safety and connection possible.

As part of taking back personal responsibility—we might also call it his personal power—I asked him what it would be like to recover his sense of being an emotionally separate person, even while relating to an important partner. What if he could experience his fundamental aloneness as life giving, and not as some big problem? What would it be like to be ready at any moment to have a satisfying life alone? I suggested asking himself each day when he woke up, "How would I have a satisfying life today if Craig and I weren't together? If I were on my own, what would I do?"

This practice is essentially strengthening our commitment to not abandon ourselves. The more we stay grounded in our own embodied experience—the more intimate we are willing to be with ourselves—the safer it is to be intimate with another person. It's actually very difficult to be more intimate with our partner than we are willing and able to be intimate with ourselves. Our relating with someone who's important to us is guaranteed to force into the open any unresolved issues we have about relationship. If we are unwilling to experience certain types of disturbing feelings, we will make sure that we maintain an adequate distance from these feelings by maintaining an adequate distance from the person who will trigger these feelings. If we see another as the location of our well-being—whether in a positive or negative way—that person becomes inappropriately important to us. If we give a friend a dollar, we don't worry too much about what he'll do with it. If we give a friend our life savings, we'll probably become hypervigilant about his lifestyle, any vacations he takes, and so forth.

In relationship, when we've projected our disowned vulnerabilities onto our partners, we create the feeling that our well-being is in their hands, and any little thing they say or do can take on exaggerated significance. As we practice taking responsibility for our difficult feelings, however, it becomes emotionally safer for us to be close to another person. We gradually cultivate the confidence that feeling disturbed is not synonymous with being harmed. Feeling unsafe does not mean we are unsafe. Just as feeling safe doesn't mean we are safe. We discover for ourselves whether our situation is workable. On the other hand, when we're blaming others—subtly or not so subtly—we have nothing to work with, because we think *they're* the ones who need to change. It's beyond our control. So at some point, we must be willing to swallow that bitter pill of "no more complaints" and actually take ownership of what we have to work with.

This is the stage at which we are willing to have a relationship with the "other" as an equal, because we're willing to commit to valuing and protecting our relationship with our "self." We're willing to experience connection, because we're willing to experience separateness. That "other" may be our partner, our friends, or our coworkers; it's also the "other" of our disowned unconscious experiencing. As we develop a more and more conscious relationship with our fears, we find that pretty much everything we experience is workable. It doesn't mean we'll do a perfect job, but we do become confident that we will stay present and engaged and give it our best shot. This increasing confidence gradually dissolves the dissociative split we've been living with for so long. We no longer need to defend against those emotions and energies that we had to defend against as children, because we know we'll work with them when they arise. As our awareness relaxes and expands, we actually dissolve our subtle but chronic anxiety and paranoia. We start to be less guarded. As we relax our attention, we begin to have more and more moments of being aware of an already-existing context, or environment, of freedom.

THE INTERPERSONAL

The next stage could be called the interpersonal stage. Our confidence and our capacity to take care of ourselves has increased to the point at which we can risk revealing our authentic experience—even to somebody who's incredibly important to us, like our partner. Our self-absorption has decreased to the point at which we actually become more interested in others and in the world than we are in our own identity dramas. We take such good care of ourselves that we no longer live driven by a sense of need; instead, we become interested in what *others* need. We are now willing and able to not only relate to others but also to be *kind* to what is perceived as that other outside of ourselves or our own internal "other." As we are able to have a more embodied, kind, conscious relationship with our vulnerability, we organically and spontaneously become more empathic to others' vulnerability. So even though we may never really understand our partner, we increasingly have the sense that we're in the same boat. We all have difficult, vulnerable experience. It's not a problem, actually. It's not easy, but it's not a problem. As our sense of greater expansiveness, empathy, and kindness grows, we have an increasing sense of immediacy, openheartedness, and curiosity. Not knowing who we are or how to have an intimate relationship actually becomes pleasurable. Uncertainty becomes a source of creativity and not a problem to be solved. This is the stage of mutuality. We experience relationship as both separate and connected, but without an unconscious effort to cover over or get rid of the never-resolvable energy or tension of there always being both self and other. We have more frequent moments of what Martin Buber described as an "I and Thou" experience—a direct appreciation of relationship without agenda.

THE NONPERSONAL

The last stage could be called the nonpersonal stage. Here, our experience consistently arises in the environment of open awareness or freedom. Not knowing who we are has become much more interesting than maintaining a familiar personal identity. Not knowing who our partner is becomes much more interesting than our familiar stories about him or her. We show up fully in each moment, because that's the only moment in which we will ever be living. We stop pretending not to be present. We could describe our experience as that of engaged spontaneity. We deal with our life, with our relationship, not knowing what will happen next but confident that we will work with whatever comes up. We have that confidence about the future because we're already working with the present moment, without withholding ourselves. We know that when the future comes, it will be only experienced as the present, and we find over and over that we are able and willing to be fully engaged with whatever our immediate experiencing may be. Increasingly, there's a sense that there's not really even a "self" relating to a partner or to the world. Actually, it's just life relating to life.

AN EVOLVING PATH

You may have noticed that, as we progress through these four stages, I have less and less to say about each one. That reflects our actual experience. The more we pretend not to be present, the more we refuse to acknowledge the truth of our experience, the more complicated is our state of mind. It's this complication that serves to fascinate and distract us—to contract our attention away from our already-present environment of freedom. The more complicated our sense of self and the more complicated our relationships, the more fascinated we become. This complication is not particularly pleasurable, but as drama, it captures our attention. As we move through these four stages, however, there's less and less of an experience of there being a problem. There will still be life difficulties to work with; they don't go away. But we're not looking at them from a complicated state of mind anymore.

I think it's important to note that these stages are just tools, just ways of thinking. They're not actually a description of reality, so I hope you won't take them too seriously. In fact, all of these stages are present all the time. But our emotional and psychic center of gravity—what we return to over and over, our home base—tends to progress and evolve in a particular direction: from the prepersonal, to the personal, to the interpersonal, to the nonpersonal.

For example, couples who are very invested in the drama of codependency are both living in the prepersonal fantasy *and* are having moments of openness all the time—moments of genuine curiosity and compassion for their partners, their children, and the world. Those of us who have done a lot of personal work—whose emotional centers of gravity are progressing through the stages described above—of course still have codependent dynamics to work with. But to whatever degree we've become willing to give up our fantasy that we, or our partners, are a problem, our awareness relaxes. And in terms of our energetic center of gravity, we more and more frequently experience our lives and our relationships as increasingly alive, interesting, and spontaneous.

As we evolve through these stages of relationship, our basic intention remains the same. We are challenging our central fantasy of being a separate, objectively existing, significant "self" that is living in a world of separate, objectively existing, significant "others." These others include persons, objects, natural processes, and our own inner experiences with which we don't identify. As long as we take both self and other to have independent existence, there will always be a basic biological tension about "who eats whom." And because our "self" is almost infinitely small in relation to a seemingly infinitely large "other," we all tend to experience a subtle but powerful sense of chronic anxiety and even paranoia. We all know that sooner or later, but inevitably, we will die. The self we identify with will apparently end, and the other will apparently continue. Our fear-based response to this sense of ongoing threat seems to be a continuing effort to generate an ongoing experience of self-absorption. The greater our chronic anxiety, the greater our unconscious investment in self-absorption as an attempt to distract our awareness from the reality of our experiencing.

From a spiritual path point of view, the vivid appearance of a separate self who is relating to separate others is only that—an appearance, empty of essential nature. The experience of self and other are found to be cocreated, each dependent on the other and on many complex conditions. No independently existing self. No independently existing other. Both experiences can be seen as expressions of the larger nature of reality. The disturbing tension between self and other does not go away, but because self and other are not in fundamental conflict, this tension does not *need* to go away.

These stages of relationship, then, can be understood as a progressive challenge to our chronic but inaccurate anxiety and to the various strategies of self-absorption we bring to our relationships and to our lives. Each stage arises from a different attitude we take between self and other. In the prepersonal, we relate to other as both threat and savior, as parent. In the personal, we relate to other as adult partner; as equal. In the interpersonal, we relate to other as never-fully-understood friend and as an opportunity to practice compassion. And in the nonpersonal, other becomes another manifestation of life and mystery, just as we are ourselves.

In the rest of this chapter, I describe some of the specific interventions and practices that I have found most useful for each specific stage. As a reminder, practices make sense as expressions of particular views. Our intentions and our ways of understanding imply the relevant practices. Because there are many ways of understanding relationships, there are many ways of working—there is no one correct way.

PREPERSONAL: CHALLENGING CODEPENDENT DYNAMICS

Most couples come to therapy with a sense of dilemma. They've gone through what is often called the "honeymoon stage," where most of us have the wonderful conviction that we've found a partner with whom we will be happy the rest of our lives. There's no evidence of any deep problems; we enjoy each other. Conflicts are handled very smoothly and quickly. A lot of times, there's sexual passion, and we want to spend as much time as possible with the other person.

But generally speaking, at some point—perhaps it's six months, or a year, or two years down the road—the honeymoon ends. We discover that this stage of only positive experience has, strangely enough, been supported by a lack of deep intimacy. We didn't even know this person yet. Our need for separateness was being met by not yet sharing a full, complex life over time—not living together, not having kids, not sharing a mortgage, and so forth. In the early months, for a year or two, it's very easy to continue wanting to be closer and more connected, because our needs for separateness have been taken care of by our life circumstances.

However, after some period, a couple almost inevitably will become intimate enough that any unresolved relationship issues will start to be triggered. Usually this is experienced as a type of deep disappointment, and it's when many couples end the relationship. When I take a history of relationships from my clients, it's common for them to report ending a number of relationships around the two- to three-year mark. Conflicts and hurt feelings have become more frequent. Sex has become less frequent. And so on. However, if there's enough appreciation, interest, and perhaps maturity, the couple may decide to continue their relationship despite the disturbance they're experiencing. There's often a sense of dilemma—the feeling of being torn in two directions. On the one hand, there is genuine love, care, and compassion between them; they really do feel connected. At the same time, there's a lot of pain resulting from the dynamics of prepersonal ways of relating. In my experience, this situation brings the majority of couples into therapy. They really care about each other, but they find their current situation so painful that they feel like it's destroying their love. They don't know what to do about it, so they decide to get help.

As I hope I've made clear, I see codependency as a type of intense aggression toward fundamental reality—the reality of our already-existing open nature within which arises the never resolvable disturbance of relative experiencing. For this reason, I have found that the response to codependency has to be aggressive in return. When a therapist is only supportive, kind, and empathic with a couple trying to deal with strong codependent energy, it often doesn't go anywhere. I've worked with a number of couples who have reported that their previous therapist was an insightful and kind person but that nothing changed as a result of their work together. It seems that many therapists don't consider the possibility that sometimes kindness involves healthy aggressive energy, just as being a kind parent involves discipline and conflict with one's children. Healthy aggressive energy does not mean anger. It means engaging from the basic energy of separateness while keeping one's heart open. It's a willingness to manifest as an existentially separate person, with different experiences, views, feelings, and boundaries. As a therapist, it means that I actively challenge what I see as dysfunctional, often take the lead rather than listen and follow, interrupt what doesn't seem helpful, express my opinions, and remain in control of the therapy session. When therapists are willing to relate as emotionally separate persons, express differences, not avoid conflict, they are demonstrating—in the moment—what it might feel like to challenge emotional fusion.

CORE VULNERABILITIES: THE EMOTIONS WE REFUSE TO EXPERIENCE

In my clinical work, I challenge codependent dynamics in a variety of ways. I often present a fair amount of education at first about the dynamics of codependency. I talk especially about the mutuality involved in codependent dynamics, as most partners come into therapy blaming one another for their pain and disappointment. Pointing out the mutuality of their drama seems to help transition the couple toward personal responsibility. I explain the unconscious agreements the couple is perpetuating, including "hiring" one another to be the location of their own difficult and disowned emotions. I often reframe intimacy as inherently disturbing. Provocative, rich, and meaningful, yes, but also painful and irresolvable. I challenge the fantasy that there is such a thing as a life without disturbance. When I present these types of views, I'm not thinking the couple is suddenly going to change their behavior. Instead, I hope to engender an experiential dialogue. Each can watch their impulse to blame their partner, while hopefully recalling our discussion. "Gosh, I remember that Bruce said I might actually be hiring my partner to behave exactly this way." Over time, it starts to invite a little bit of doubt around our familiar explanations.

I will often offer some general explanations for codependent dynamics based on the developmental view. I suggest to clients that, growing up, most of us had very healthy motivations to disconnect from any feelings or experiences that felt unworkably disturbing and unsafe. I suggest that now as adults, most of us continue—without awareness—to devote large parts of our lives to the effort to not feel those feelings. Paradoxically, however, this means we end up putting exactly those feelings at the very center of our psychic organization. And by not bringing these difficult emotions into our daily life, our ability to work with them does not mature. Over time, our initially accurate healthy avoidance becomes an inaccurate phobic avoidance, which has a self-perpetuating quality. We believe that we're refusing to experience these feelings because they're a problem, not realizing that they appear to be a problem because we refuse to experience them.

As adults, these difficult emotions that we refuse to participate in become what we experience as our core vulnerabilities. And in my experience, most couples get together with a very deep resonance between their core vulnerabilities. For example, two people with similar abandonment histories will connect, both living with this sense that they are continually in danger of being left. But actually, they already feel like abandoned persons; this very painful feeling has usually been with them most of their lives. But they're each unconsciously pretending that abandonment is something that might happen in the future. This allows the fantasy that if only I do this or that, if only my partner would do this or that, then I won't have to experience these horrible feelings. But because each person already lives with this particular pain, they really "get" each other. Although they share this deep unconscious resonance, neither is yet willing to have a conscious relationship with this core vulnerability.

As discussed previously, what usually happens is that the partners work with this common issue in opposite or complementary ways. One may have the strategy of, "Well, nobody's going to be there for me, so I guess I have to do all of the work. If I want a relationship, I will have to be the one who connects. I have to keep on trying. I have to pull emotional engagement out of my partner." Their partner, mysteriously, may have the strategy that, "Well, no one's there for me, so I guess I'd better be self-sufficient. It's stupid to extend to other people, because I know I'll be hurt and disappointed. My partner's so needy that I'd better keep my distance." So now you have a couple in which one person has the style of always trying to make connection, and the other the style of being self-sufficient. This allows both to argue endlessly about their stylistic differences. The self-sufficient person can feel like the other is being smothering, inappropriately dependent, or controlling: "Why are you always wanting more? You're never satisfied." The connecting person can feel uncared for, exhausted by being the only one doing the work of the relationship: "Why are you always on the computer instead of spending time with me?" Actually, both are unconsciously agreeing to maintain a sense of problem in the relationship. Each can feel that the other is the problem, and this serves as evidence for why we can't include all of who we are in our intimate relationship. Who's going to show their most vulnerable and sensitive issues when they know that they'll feel criticized or rejected? What I would suggest to this couple is that they are ritualizing their relationship in a way that justifies to each their refusal to go into their own immediate, most disturbing emotions. Unfortunately, by focusing on their complementary styles, they keep their attention at the level of their differences. But it's what they have in common—their very similar core vulnerabilities—that will potentially allow mutual empathy and that could become the basis of a genuine friendship.

If helpful, I might also offer a more Buddhist view of how we cocreate these familiar dynamics. To the extent that we feel unsafe, overwhelmed, not protected as children, we must construct a "sense of self" as protection from an unworkable experience of openness. This is necessary and healthy when we are powerless, dependent young beings; but because this constructed self *does* help us, it tends to become internalized as character structure and carried into adulthood, when it is no longer necessary and helpful. By then, most of us have associated our survival with this familiar sense of self, and as biological beings, most of us will instinctually put survival as a higher priority than quality of life. Because of this association, if we were to challenge our sense of self, we would need to be willing to work with the anxiety and panic that seem to signal that our survival is at risk. Most of us are trying to avoid anxiety, not welcome it.

From the perspective of immediacy, it's not really a question of how our history may have shaped this familiar identity drama but, rather, of how we are able to maintain this drama in the present when there's no longer any real evidence that it's necessary. In relationship, we are invested in experiencing our partner as constantly proving that these survival strategies are necessary and justified. "See! I knew that nothing I do would be good enough, so I'm not going to even try." "See! I knew that you'd never be responsible, so I do need to do all the work for both of us." We perpetuate this constant "case" for our familiar sense of self in several ways. We continually cocreate life circumstances that appear to confirm the accuracy and need for our identity drama. In relationship, this is a powerful factor—first in our choice of partner, and later in our ritualized ways of relating. We also provide evidence with our interpretations of our experience. "My partner agreed to watch the kids, but I know he doesn't really want to." As another strategy, we're constantly making use of selective attention, though usually not consciously. If I'm invested in my drama of self-sufficiency, I will pay attention to ways I can't count on my partner and ignore ways in which my partner supports me.

To free ourselves from our identification with our conditioned history and from our investment in a familiar sense of self, we may need a conscious, embodied relationship with exactly the feelings we've dedicated most of our lives to avoiding. Again, here I'm presenting a view that is incompatible with the codependent idea that our partner is the cause of our pain or should be the solution to it. I challenge any language or patterns of thinking that allow clients to position themselves as victims and their partners as perpetrators. When we're engaged with codependent dynamics, we're invested in the fantasy of being a victim. As I said earlier, this is a very aggressive attitude toward life. Our culture doesn't identify the victim position as one of aggression, yet that's what it is. It usually involves blaming others and making claims that we need their help in order to be okay. At the same time, it requires the victim to frustrate any attempts at actual help. In that way, it's actually quite a sadistic position. I often label it as such with my clients, which, I hope, makes it increasingly unpleasant for them to continue referring to themselves that way. Once again, I am not talking about someone who has actually been victimized and needs our help or protection; rather, I am talking about someone who maintains the identity drama of victim.

INTRODUCING PERSONAL RESPONSIBILITY

Beyond education, I begin to introduce the view of personal responsibility. Most of us at this stage are still quite resistant to this practice, so it's just a beginning, an introduction to the work, which is central to the personal stage of relationship. As a concrete example of personal responsibility, I challenge the tendency people usually have to describe their experience in terms of their partner or the relationship. I frequently invite my clients to use "I" language rather than "we/you/he/she" language. Instead of saying, "You're always interfering when I'm trying to parent," I might suggest, "I don't say no to you effectively because I'm afraid of conflict." When people are involved with codependency, there's a strong temptation to try to understand what's going on from the position of "we" or one's partner. It's an unconscious reflection of the effort to be one emotional unit, rather than tolerate being emotionally separate persons.

Because blame is such an important function in these dynamics, serving to deflect attention from the reality of one's own experience, I present blame as actually a disguised victim drama. When we claim that our partner is responsible for our difficult feelings, we're positioning ourselves as a powerless, and usually resentful, victim. We're saying the other person is the cause of our state of mind, which implies that the other person must be the solution. We're powerless to make the change we want—we've done everything we can. Our partner has to change in order for our state of mind to improve. But we have no power to make our partner change. This insures that we can continue to believe that we want to change but are unable to do so, which is the basic theme of the prepersonal stage. We are perpetuating our experience of relationship learned as children, often desperately wanting things to change but having no power to make this happen. When clients are ready to begin looking into their experience of blame, I often suggest that, as an emotional experiment, they say out loud to their partner, "I love you, but I'm not here on the planet to be who you want me to be or to take care of your feelings for you. And I guess you're not here to be who I want you to be or to take care of my feelings."

As another experiential introduction to personal responsibility, I often invite clients to put into words their actual priorities, as opposed to their fantasized priorities. As I suggested to Bradley in the last chapter, I might ask a connecting-style person how it might feel to say out loud, "Apparently, purchasing security is a higher priority for me than my integrity." For a separate-style person who discounts dependency needs, I might say, "Apparently, riding my bicycle is a higher priority for me than making my marriage work well." These statements are usually uncomfortable, especially when said out loud, but they usually reflect that person's actual behavior. I don't suggest that they are making the wrong choice but that they will probably act more skillfully if they're aware of the choice they're really making.

PRACTICE OUR FAVORITE COMPLAINTS

Most of us have a list of favorite complaints about our partners—or perhaps our parents or siblings. These hurts and irritations are very reliable; we can always pull them out in a conflict or use them to defend ourselves. But maybe these complaints are actually serving an emotional function. It may be helpful to investigate this possibility. This exercise will help you do just that.

Choose a favorite complaint. It could be superficial: "My partner never puts the dishes in the sink to soak." Or deeper: "They make everything a higher priority than our relationship." Then *imagine* that you may have an investment in this problem continuing. Your mind will deny this, but just try it out as an emotional exercise.

Let's use an example: "No matter what I do, it will never be enough; he's never satisfied." First, examine the position this complaint seems to leave you in. "Why try? Obviously, this relationship isn't about my needs getting met. I'll never get the recognition I want. He's not giving me what I want, so I don't have to give him what he wants. I'll go through the motions, but my real satisfaction will be from work or friends or activities." And so on.

You may see that all of these responses have a common theme: they justify your withholding of your full participation in the relationship. They are actually serving as unconscious boundary functions, probably because you have not yet allowed yourself to have overt conflict, to assert your needs effectively, with your partner. And until you are willing to bring healthy aggressive energy into your relationship, you may actually have an investment in this complaint about your partner continuing.

So bring to mind a favorite complaint about someone important to you. Examine your response. What position does your complaint justify? What would you be forced to feel if this problem were solved? What if there were no reason to withhold what feels most vulnerable from this person?

To explore further, reverse the ways in which you prove to yourself that your familiar survival strategies are necessary. For a week or two:

1. *Change behaviors:* Behave as if your partner were your best friend, was on your side, as if you were appreciative of their trying their best.

2. *Change interpretations:* Whenever you realize you're interpreting your experience of your partner as a familiar complaint, practice new ways of understanding that present their behavior as an expression of their health and their good intentions.

3. *Change attention:* Focus on what you appreciate about your partner, on all of the evidence that doesn't support your complaint.

Obviously, this is an emotional practice, a way to challenge what may be an unconscious process. It's not a suggestion that you become naive and ignore actual problems. But you may find that you actually have powerful investments in enabling and continuing exactly the "problems" you like to complain about. ▪

CONSTRUCTIVE CONFLICT SKILLS

Almost by definition, a couple engaged in codependent dynamics is invested in maintaining a sense of irresolvable conflict. For this reason, I spend quite a bit of time addressing constructive conflict skills. What follow are several techniques I have found to be helpful in working constructively with the energy of conflict. Note that the intention of these techniques is to take the heat out of conflict, which is not always attractive in the moment. Many couples have an unexamined attitude that emotional intensity is synonymous with intimacy, so the coolness of this approach seems counterinstinctual. For this reason, these techniques don't work for everyone. But I have found they can be helpful when the couple is willing and interested.

Taking a Break

Perhaps the most fundamental skill in conflict is to learn that we are not obligated to participate in it. We always have a choice. This actually requires an *unlearning* from our young experience in which we were obligated to take part in whatever was happening. This is often the first technique I coach a couple to use. The practice is simple: When either person has the sense that a conflict is becoming hurtful or possibly destructive, it is their right—and even their responsibility to the relationship—to call for a break. The deeper understanding is that: "I need to take a time out when I begin to have difficulty dealing with my own emotional reactivity." This works best as an agreement between both persons, but it remains a personal practice even without the other's cooperation. If our partner is unable or unwilling to disengage, we still have the choice to leave the room (or even the house), end the phone call, or do whatever we must do, even if it's inconvenient.

As an agreement, the break is immediately respected, with no further discussion or processing. I've found that it works best for the person asking for the time-out to be responsible for checking in later and to tell their partner, before they leave, when they will check back in. This helps reassure the partner, who may feel "left," and makes it less likely the break will be used as an avoidant tactic or as punishment. It is usually best to discuss using this technique as an experiment beforehand, when things feel friendly or at least neutral. Trying to negotiate agreements in the middle of an emotionally reactive episode is rarely productive.

Removing the Emotional Energy

If the couple is willing to experiment, I invite them to consider using only behavioral negotiations—problem-solving language—for a period in any and all of their conflictual communications. This means removing all emotional language and, as they are able, emotional energy from their conflicts. Of course, this doesn't mean not talking about feelings with each other; it just means waiting to do so until things are friendly. Sometimes there is no choice but to discuss feelings when things are difficult. In that instance, the practice is to agree on a set (short) period of time in which each person can express feelings with no interruptions, questions, or discussion from the other and without any expectation that this is about solving anything.

When trying to deal with practical issues of immediate daily life—finances, parenting, time together and apart, scheduling, and so on—which often involve conflict and anxiety, most of us unconsciously piggyback these immediate concrete issues onto our long-term emotional vulnerabilities. The current issue is used as a vehicle for expressing our long-standing hurts and resentments. In codependent dynamics, these conflicts are used as an opportunity to ventilate the pressure that has built up from our refusal to relate to our difficult feelings. There is unlikely to be any resolution to these feelings if we're unwilling to be aware of and work with them; therefore, when we join our real practical issues to irresolvable emotional issues, it's rare that the practical issues will be resolved. I've found that it works best to separate our conflicts about concrete life issues from our feelings that are triggered by these issues. This means disciplining ourselves in our conflictual communications to not share how we feel, refer to history, give examples, or explain. We just ask our partners if they would be willing to behave in a particular way. We make a request.

Making Requests

Understanding that it's not our partners' responsibility to be who we want them to be, we ask them to make a specific behavior change. Instead of expressing our frustration in always picking up after our partner, for example, we might simply ask if they would be willing to take five minutes each evening before dinner to put their things away. They'll say yes or no, and we may need to continue negotiating for awhile. But not using this conflict as one more instance of long-term emotional complaint may force us to examine the choices we ourselves are making—and, in turn, perhaps take better care of ourselves—rather than waiting for our partner to do so. In truth, we are asking for our partner's help with *our* issue. They are not doing anything wrong; they're just being themselves. They'll probably continue to be themselves for as long as we know them. They're never going to be who we want them to be. But we can ask for their help in the moment.

If we want our partner's cooperation, it's just intelligent to not talk to them in a way that's going to trigger their defensiveness or their emotional reactivity. It's better to talk in a neutral or even friendly way. That's hard to do when there's a conflict, but that's the practice. And of course, if they're kind enough to give the help we're requesting, it's appropriate to thank them for doing so. It's also appropriate to be prepared to consider any requests our partner makes of us, understanding that equity of effort is an important part of an adult intimate relationship. A simple but sometimes useful technique to keep in mind is that when our partner seems to be speaking to us from an emotionally reactive state, we can ask them: "Do you have a request? Are you asking me if I will do something?"

At this stage of working with a couple, I will often invite them to redo a recent conflict from the viewpoint of negotiating behavioral change. Earlier I described my client Bradley's work in learning to ask his partner Craig to change his behavior when he felt frustrated—to not yell and talk about Bradley's shortcomings, but instead to talk quietly in "I" statements. Bradley found that this worked much better than his ineffectively talking about how hurt he felt when this happened.

However, Craig reported that he continued to feel that he was doing all the work and that his impulse was still to withdraw from Bradley. Working at the behavioral level, we explored what action Craig might ask of his partner that could help him feel that the relationship was more equitable. Money seemed at the heart of Craig's complaint, so we worked on his putting his feelings into the form of a specific request. He was able to ask Bradley to commit to contributing a certain amount of money to the relationship every month. After some negotiating, they both agreed on what seemed like a workable amount. This behavioral work did not, of course, resolve the deeper codependent dynamics at play. But by each learning to advocate for what they wanted without destructive emotional escalation, they were then able to begin looking at their personal emotional issues as emotional issues, without confusing them with current relationship conflicts about practical realities. By negotiating workable behavioral agreements, it becomes harder to maintain the fantasy that one's partner is the location of the problem. In disciplining how he spoke, Craig had an opportunity to investigate his life-long anger about giving more than he received. By committing to help financially, Bradley could look at his childhood fantasy of finally being taken care of.

In working with the prepersonal stage, a strong intervention is usually required. When one is not yet capable of spontaneous inner discipline, the next best thing seems to be external structure. And so, as discussed, in challenging codependent dynamics, there seems to be the need for a lot of simple, even formulaic, interventions and practices, such as agreements to take a break, remove emotional language from conflicts, make requests, and so on. And in my style, there's usually a lot of education as well. The more one learns about codependent dynamics, the harder it seems to be to continue any drama of mutual blame.

THE PERSONAL: PERSONAL RESPONSIBILITY AND DISCIPLINE

A significant shift begins as one or both partners become willing to be the location of structure, discipline, and choice themselves, rather than waiting to have this supplied from the outside. As one or both partners experiment with this work, I find there's an increasing interest in and willingness to practice personal responsibility. At this point, the individual or couple is entering the personal stage. Here, I continue to use a lot of education, a lot of reframing, a lot of discussion of view. Education continues to be helpful because, as I mentioned earlier, many of the practices I invite people to take on at this stage are counterinstinctual—we don't want to do them. These practices involve staying embodied with the very feelings we've spent our lives trying to not feel. So I talk with people a fair amount about why it might be to their own selfish benefit to take responsibility for working with their own difficult experiences.

Because a person at the personal stage is more willing to look inward, it can make sense that another person or event is not *causing* their disturbance, but instead is triggering an already-existing emotional sensitivity. Our emotional reactivity is not really about what our partner has said or done, but about our not wanting to feel the feelings that have been triggered in us. Our reactivity is actually the expression of our refusal to stay present and embodied with some deeper core vulnerability. We're experiencing anger or collapse or anxiety because we're having to feel some emotion we really don't want to feel. The accurate location of the issue is our relationship with our own feelings, not our relationship with our partner. As we gain more clarity that focusing on our partner is a distraction and really a waste of our time and energy, we find that it's to our own benefit to leave our partner out of any explanation about our emotional reactivity. Upon investigation, we're almost always going to find that we've been living with these feelings all of our lives. We had these difficult feelings before we met our partner, and if we ended the relationship tomorrow, we'd still have these difficult feelings. Our partner is not the cause and so will never be the solution.

I sometimes suggest that each partner commit to the practice of never again claiming that the disturbance is caused by, or is even about, their partner. This usually gets a laugh, but it's a real practice. This doesn't mean that we stop negotiating about behaviors; we just practice dropping our fascination with the claim that our partner is responsible for our disturbance, even while we recognize that they will continue to *trigger* our disturbance. And, surprisingly, we begin to find that committing to the initial disappointment of not blaming others gives rise to an increased sense of personal power and dignity.

PERSONAL WORK AND RELATIONAL WORK

At this stage, there's an increased capacity to discriminate between personal work and relational work. "What issues are about me? What issues are about the relationship?" Our personal work has to do with investigating why we're claiming that certain feelings are a big deal. Why are we relating to certain emotions as if our survival were being threatened? We are developing enough confidence in ourselves at this point that we commit to the continuing investigation of deeper and deeper levels of vulnerability. This is the stage at which the practice of embodied immediacy, as explored in chapter 5, is especially valuable. When we're willing to stay at the sensation level of our experience—without interpretation—we discover for ourselves whether feeling abandoned, smothered, controlled, or hurt is actually harmful. If we jump into our interpretations, we'll always be able to find evidence of some problem. But in our immediate embodied experience, we're never going to find any evidence of harm being done. We're not going to discover any evidence about our worth as a person, or find shame or guilt, or any basic flaw. Those aren't sensations; they're already strongly interpretive experiences. They are part of our conditioned history. If we want to begin to step out of our history, the practice of embodied immediacy can be a powerful tool.

When relating with our partner, our personal work invites us to take all disturbance as an opportunity to look within our own experience. Any emotional reactivity—any response obviously out of proportion to the immediate circumstance—is a signal of some unresolved issue we still carry. We understand that it's to our benefit to bring this deeper vulnerability into awareness, so that we can work with it using our adult capacities. We also understand that this work is counterinstinctual, that it will provoke anxiety, and that we can't wait until we're comfortable to do it.

Our relational work is about slowly developing a wide range of skillful means with which to relate to our partner. As discussed, what is skillful will depend on many factors, including our understanding and capacities, our partner's capacities, the immediate situation, timing, our history together, familiarity with our own and our partner's vulnerabilities, and so on. I've found it most helpful to relate with a variety of connection skills when things feel friendly and cooperative, and with a variety of separation skills when things feel conflictual. As we progress through the relational stages, there is a basic shift from an emphasis on how to be skillfully separate, to an increasing interest in how to be skillfully connected, to an ability to hold both simultaneously.

FEELINGS AND BEHAVIOR: NO NECESSARY CONNECTION

Another practice I often introduce is the discrimination between feelings and behavior. In the realm of intimacy, many people believe that if we feel a certain way, then we're entitled to, and even *should*, behave in that way. For instance, if we feel like we've been treated rudely, then we should be able to attack or to withhold relating as punishment. Or if setting a boundary involves the other person having hurt feelings, then our feelings of guilt mean that we've made a mistake and should collapse that boundary. If we really examine our lives, though, we're going to see that's not how the world really works. If we want to keep our job, we get up in the morning and go to work, even if we'd rather stay in bed. If we don't want to go to jail, we pay our taxes, even if we'd rather use that money to take a vacation. If we want a committed, long-term relationship, we're probably not going to be sexual with everyone we feel attracted to. We don't just punch anybody we're angry at. If we want to get good at a skill—at a craft or a musical instrument, for example—we have to discipline ourselves to hang in there, even when we feel frustrated. When we look at what fosters competence and skill in the world, we see it's, in part, the capacity to consciously choose our behavior, rather than letting our behavior be determined by our feelings. In fact, the ability to discriminate between feelings and behavior, to experience a feeling without having to do anything about it, is one of the qualities of emotional adulthood.

DISCIPLINE

For many of us, intimacy is its own private dissociative realm. Even though we're acting as adults in the world, with our partners, we're suddenly acting like young children in our families of origin, behaving in ways that are driven by emotions. We often display primitive, impulsive behavior, which we then rationalize in a variety of ways. At the personal stage, however, we begin experimenting with an attitude of discipline. Discipline is actually necessary for healthy intimacy, but for many of us, this is an alien idea. We think of intimacy as spontaneous and feelings-based—which it was for us as children; so it seems a little strange to practice an attitude of discipline in relating to our partners. But the work of committing to and feeling our emotional disturbance is so counterinstinctual that we aren't just going to stumble into it. We must be willing to experiment with a sense of discipline in order to train ourselves out of codependent dynamics and into personal responsibility. In the personal stage, we discover that discipline is not optional; it's necessary. And to sustain the effort required of these counterinstinctual practices, we must discover that it's to our own benefit to do so.

EFFECTIVE SELFISHNESS

The practice of taking better care of ourselves is something I call *effective selfishness*. Our culture has a lot of negative connotations about selfishness, so this language can be provocative and confusing for people. Most of us think of being selfish as the opposite of being relational. We assume that taking care of our self is incompatible with taking care of our relationship. As we've discussed, this reflects our culture's unexamined idea that intimacy is synonymous with connection and that feelings of separateness are evidence of problems that need to be fixed. The view explored in this book is that intimate relationships—like all of life—require an irresolvable interplay between these two basic life energies. Our very sense of "self" *is* this irresolvable interplay. And because relationship does require both energies, we can understand that being effectively selfish must include our relationship needs as well. If we are in a relationship, it's to our benefit to have a healthy satisfying experience. It's to our benefit to treat our partner kindly.

In addition to our cultural bias, we've also discussed the training in relationship we experience as children, in which we must learn how to compromise our own sense of self in order to fit with our parents' and then society's realities. Regardless of whether our overt, conscious style is that of independence or dependence, underneath, very few of us enter adulthood knowing how to take even adequate care of ourselves in relationship.

"HOW CAN I BE SELFISH IF THERE'S NO SELF?"

The concept of effective selfishness can be especially confusing for those exposed to Buddhism or other philosophies that hold the view of "no self." When I have clients who make this case, I point out all the ways in which they are still acting as if they were a very solid, significant self. If they were actually capable of behaving and experiencing with no self-reference, I would congratulate them, although this hasn't happened yet. A Buddhist slogan is for practice to be informed by a vast view but in accordance with our current understanding and capacities. We might have been exposed to the theory that there's no self, but in our actual experience, there seems to be a very real self that we want to protect and improve. With that in mind, at this stage, we work with

> the appearance of self—not yet really addressing the
> idea of no self. After all, as long as we're living with an
> experience of self, doesn't it make sense to do a good job
> of it? ▪

The real question is how to be *effectively* selfish. Most of us in relationships are actually being quite ineffectively selfish—meaning
that, even as adults, we're still trying to take care of ourselves
as if we were children in our families of origin. Our strategy is
several decades out of date. It's not wrong; it's just not working
very well. Here I start talking with people about how they can
take such good care of themselves that they stop accumulating
any complaint about their partners. What would they need to
do in order to have no resentment, no blame? Or, in more positive language, how can they actually keep their hearts open to
their partners—even when things are difficult?

If we were taking really good care of ourselves, we would not
have complaints. We would still be affected by our partners, of
course, but it wouldn't be a big deal. We'd be taking such good
care of ourselves that we wouldn't need our partners to be any
different than they already are. At this point, I often suggest that
whatever complaint they have about the other person is actually an indication that somehow they have not taken effective
responsibility for their own well-being. Perhaps they have com-
promised when they should not have, avoided conflict and not
asserted their needs, or acted like a caretaker and then not felt
supported. Perhaps they have put all of their time and energy
into work and now face a divorce and don't know their children.

The evidence should be pretty clear by now that our partners are not here on the planet to take care of us. So rather
than perpetuating any drama of complaint, deficit, problem, or
disappointment, we become ready to take such good care of

ourselves that we can keep our hearts open. We no longer need to wait for our partners to become who we want them to be in order for us to have a satisfying life. This is the foundation of effective selfishness. We are willing to treat ourselves so well—to have such effective boundaries, to protect our integrity, to advocate for what we want, to have conflict when necessary—that, strangely enough, we can keep our hearts open to our partners without requiring them to change.

Effective selfishness—keeping our hearts open—is not a guarantee that we will stay together. Perhaps the ritualized distance of codependent dynamics is what has allowed us to maintain a dysfunctional relationship. Dissolving complaints and giving up our "if onlys" may clarify what's really available to us. Maybe we just grow apart over time. However, when a couple is seriously considering ending a relationship, I often suggest that they give themselves some time—maybe six months—during which they practice effective selfishness. Perhaps it's time to move on. But rather than end out of blame and failure, why not use this rich situation to practice taking such good care of ourselves that there is no complaint about our partner? Why not do our best to have whatever decision we make arise from an open heart, from a sense of well-being and workability?

In my experience, when we do not take good care of ourselves in relationship, we almost always contract into a state of self-absorption. We try to take care of ourselves in some compensatory way. Maybe we rehearse what we should've said; maybe we go off and exercise or meditate instead of relating to our partner. Yet paradoxically, the more we trust that we'll take good care of ourselves in relationship, the safer it is to be very, very intimate with our partners. We start to challenge our unconscious assumptions that too much vulnerability with our partner is going to work to our disadvantage. We become committed to effective selfishness. At this point, the natural, organic rhythm of intimacy—that is, alternating between feeling close and feeling separate—starts to lose its sense of being a problem at all.

In fact, as a couple moves in this direction, a lot of forward and backward movement can be expected. Personally, I see the backward movement not as a problem but as a type of unconscious reassurance. The couple is reassuring themselves that they don't have to step into too much vulnerability yet. They can always go back and have a fight and feel pissed off at each other if things are starting to feel too open. As a couple learns that feeling separate is just as valid and necessary as feeling close, they no longer need "problems" as a way of getting relief from inaccurate closeness. Healthy separateness paradoxically opens the way to a greater capacity to practice being kind to one's partner.

THE INTERPERSONAL: PRACTICING KINDNESS IN RELATIONSHIP

As a couple moves in the direction of dissolving complaints and blame, both people begin taking such good care of themselves that it becomes possible to keep their hearts open, even when things are difficult. At this point, our experience starts to enter the stage of the interpersonal. Here it's possible to practice kindness. Kindness is a practice, because often we're not going to feel like being kind. So we discipline ourselves to apply unconditional kindness in our behavior—and, even more difficultly, in our thinking—toward everything we experience, without exception. This means that we are willing to treat our partners kindly, regardless of how we feel toward them. We don't do this out of some moral obligation or because we think we "should" be kind. Such efforts usually don't last very long, nor do they go very deep. Instead, we are kind for practical reasons. We have experiential knowledge that it is to our benefit to treat others kindly, in the same way that it's to our benefit to treat ourselves kindly.

This kindness practice requires us to have cultivated the capacity to discriminate between feelings and behavior, to relax our fascination with complaint, and to find out for ourselves, "Is it true that when I treat my partner kindly it works out better than when I blame him for my difficult feelings?" That last piece sounds a little silly, of course. Doesn't it just seem logical that if we treat our partners kindly, they're more likely to treat us kindly in return? There's no guarantee, but it's more likely. If I am choosing to be in this relationship, why wouldn't I want us to treat each other well and kindly? Yet I've found in my work that few of us have much experience with choosing to practice unconditional kindness.

This choice is a major shift, as it takes us from the personal into the interpersonal stage. Here we begin to experience being in relationship as choice. We've pretty much dissolved our fantasy of being trapped in the relationship—whether by the kids, or by a mortgage, or because we don't want to hurt our partner's feelings, or because we're afraid of being alone. It has become obvious that we're not trapped in any relationship. We always have the option to leave. We might have to deal with very difficult consequences if we do, but we're not trapped. It's not until this stage of our work that we actually start to live with the experience of choosing our relationship, that every day we are once again choosing to be in this relationship. Just as our partner is once again choosing to be with us. Because we're clear that this is a choice, our partner doesn't owe us anything. At this point, it's just common sense to treat our partner well, because we will likely have a better experience of being in the relationship if we do.

In this stage, we may become curious about the practice of being generous to our partners and patient with their various limitations. At first it may make sense to call our generosity to our partner's attention, to get credit for it. That's actually part of being effectively selfish. But at a certain point, we stop keeping score and wanting acknowledgment or credit. We just experiment with being kind, generous, and patient with our partners in so many ways that are possible every day—without any fantasy of recognition. Again, we don't do this because it's the moral thing to do; we do it because it's actually to our benefit. It gives rise to a better state of mind. I work with some couples who are entering this stage, but not many who are at this stage in a stable way. When a couple is experiencing this degree of kindness, they usually don't want to continue spending their valuable time and money in therapy when they could be spending them in much more interesting ways. As we continue our practices at this stage and cultivate more and more experiential confidence in embodied, openhearted immediacy, we feel increasingly at home with the sense of continuing change. We not only do not rely on formulas for our sense of self and for our relationship, but any such formulas actually feel painful. Because each moment is experienced as fresh, our experience of our partner is fresh. Habitual patterns may not disappear, but they arise as fresh experience. An organic momentum seems to develop, and as we find more and more moments of spontaneous interest and appreciation, we begin to enter the stage of the nonpersonal.

THE NONPERSONAL: LIVING
WITHOUT A SENSE OF PROBLEM

At this point we've pretty much dropped any project of self-improvement or greater intimacy, because we're no longer living with a sense that there is any deficit or problem. Nothing is missing, because we are fully participating in whatever is present. Our experience is mostly arising in the environment of open awareness—freedom. We keep spontaneously and organically returning to that as our home base, and we discover that it's inherently satisfying to be alive and interesting to be in an intimate relationship. It's actually interesting to be provoked. It gives us some interesting things to work with, to look at. We find that we feel hurt about something or sad, or that irritation and judgment arise. We see these feelings arising out of our conditioned history and our current circumstances. But because their insubstantial nature is clear, we have a choice about how to relate: Do we act in this way or that way? Do we investigate our deeper vulnerability? Do we just watch our reactivity come and go? We've pretty much dissolved the fantasy of being a problematic person and therefore needing a problematic relationship. It doesn't mean that our relationship is always passionate and fun and without difficulties, of course. We still have our human lives to live. We still have bills to pay; we might have health problems. Our partner might still trigger disturbing feelings. It's just that none of this is a problem anymore—it's simply what it is.

At this point, we might look back and feel very appreciative of our codependency, our struggles with personal responsibility, and our difficulty in being kind. We see that all of that was exactly what we needed to work on to free ourselves of our fascination with chronic self-absorption and identity drama. So we don't have the sense that we've wasted any time. My partner has helped me force out into the open exactly what I have had to work on. I haven't always enjoyed it, maybe, but it's been incredibly generous of her to help me. I probably wouldn't have brought these issues out into the open all on my own. We start to see that there's a certain sense of path in relationship and that there's a reason to do certain practices to help us move in a direction we might want to move in.

It's all an experiment, of course, and there are no guarantees. But it seems to me that, in our culture, an intimate relationship is often the most powerful vehicle that most of us have for waking up. Our culture doesn't have many viable spiritual disciplines. Luckily, intimacy is going to give us exactly what we need to work on in order to relax our refusal to be fully present—to relax into expansive awareness and openheartedness. I'm very grateful for my own relationship and for the opportunity to work with couples. I haven't found many other paths that are more powerful for helping us have a good state of mind, regardless of circumstance—which is the subject of the next and final chapter.

8

A GOOD STATE OF MIND,
REGARDLESS OF CIRCUMSTANCE

WHY AM I WRITING THIS BOOK? Why are you reading it? It seems that we all want to experience our lives in the most satisfying way possible. But the whole thing is so complicated. There are so many theories about how to be happy but none that have proven to be "the correct one." It seems to be true that having good health, money, a good relationship, a safe environment, and so on are part of having a good life. But at the same time, we sense that we can't really count on these circumstances to be permanent. And we find that even having these things doesn't prevent our emotional suffering or provide a sense of deeper meaning. Is it possible to learn to cultivate a good state of mind that is not dependent on any of these realities? This is what we will explore in this last chapter.

WHERE WE BEGIN: GROUND

All of us want to have as much positive experience as possible and to avoid as much negative experience as possible. This is very human—probably biological. It's also an incredibly powerful motivating energy for all of us. We all tend to understand and approve of others' efforts to create a positive experience for themselves and those around them. We don't understand, and often even try to prevent, actions that will result in a negative experience for ourselves or for others. When we are experiencing life as adequately positive, we take it as evidence that we are successful—perhaps that we are a "good person." When we are experiencing negativity, on the other hand, we take it as evidence that we have failed in some way—that we are, in some sense, problematic.

There is an almost infinite variety of ways in which we try to have a positive experience of our life. Almost all philosophical and religious traditions have their own assertions about how to have the most satisfying life possible. For thousands of years, there have been ongoing debates about how to balance immediate benefit with long-term benefit; about whether physical, emotional, intellectual, or spiritual experiences will prove most satisfying.

In this book, we have been exploring two basic strategies for having the most positive experience of our lives. The first approach is to try to generate as many positive conditions as we can: stay healthy, be attractive to others and have a good relationship, eat tasty food, have enough money, protect our children, travel, try to have upbeat emotions and ways to understand life, work on self-improvement, and so on. These are all very intelligent efforts, and, when successful, these positive conditions will usually result in positive experiences. This approach, of course, is the basic position taken by our culture. Psychotherapy, as an expression of our culture, tends to be aligned with this effort. It helps us challenge negative experience and strengthen a positive sense of ourselves and of life.

The second strategy we've explored for having a more positive life experience is to cultivate an open attitude toward all conditions, without exception, whether those conditions are positive or negative. From this point of view, all conscious experiencing happens through our state of mind. Our experiences of our bodies, our emotions, our relationships, our social and physical world—all are mediated by our state of mind. We can be healthy and depressed or dying and joyful. We can have money but never feel there's enough or have few resources and feel deep appreciation. From this point of view, our state of mind is a more powerful influence on our quality of experiencing than the specific content of the experience.

From this view, and for completely practical reasons, it makes sense to learn how to cultivate a good state of mind at all times—to focus more on *how* we relate to any and all conditions, rather than on *what* those conditions might be. It may appear paradoxical that being open to negative experience is an effective way to have a positive experience of life, but this is the Buddhist, or fruitional, position. The view explored in this book is that although improving our sense of self and our life circumstances is valuable, this ongoing effort to have more that's positive and less that's negative will never result in the experience of freedom. And experiencing one's life as an expression of freedom is seen as the most positive and satisfying way to participate in this precious human adventure.

Perhaps we finally go on that vacation we've been looking forward to. If a good life is one of positive experiences, the success of this vacation carries a heavy burden. Transportation problems, a bad meal, or disappointing weather are not only difficulties in themselves; they also carry a deeper emotional meaning. This vacation was to be our reward—our compensation for a stressful job or a chance to have more affection with our partner. Even if we're lucky and everything goes well, things will probably get complicated when we're back in our daily life. Then the contrast of our vacation with our everyday job or our day-to-day relationship might leave us feeling like there's some problem with our life.

From a more fruitional view, however, we have an ongoing discipline of engaging as fully as possible in every moment, whether we like it or not. We may find that saying "yes" to all experience gives rise to a generalized sense that all experience is worth participating in. We become clear that, at any moment, what we're experiencing is actually the only thing we *can* relate to. We may not have any control over the weather or our partner's mood, but we have a lot of potential control over how we relate to these circumstances. When our vacation is not a reward that is "compensating" for a daily life of "problems," we're more likely to deal with whatever arises in an immediate practical way—without complaint and possibly with appreciation.

A GOOD STATE OF MIND

So if a good state of mind is not the same as having positive experiences, then what is a good state of mind? Although impossible to really pin down, it could be understood as a mind trained into an attitude of unconditional appreciation. Some qualities of this attitude include embodied presence, spontaneity, openheartedness, alertness, humor, courage, clarity, resilience, equanimity, confidence. These are all ways in which we engage with our experience—they are not experiences in themselves. It's having an almost neutral attitude, one that's ready and interested in whatever may come in the next moment. One that's ready to taste and feel and be affected, as deeply as we are able. We are prepared to experience and engage with anything that may arise in the stream of our experiencing. If it's some vulnerability, we participate fully in that. If we are avoiding some vulnerability, we participate fully in our experience of our avoidance. It doesn't mean we'll do a great job of it or that others will approve. It doesn't mean that we won't get cancer and die or that we won't feel fear. It just means that we're willing to enter each moment of our life with no formula, no reassurance, and to fully participate in whatever we find.

This appreciation is supported by our various practices of immediacy. By returning over and over to what's most true in this moment—to our embodied experiencing with no interpretations and to openheartedness toward whatever we find—we discover for ourselves whether it's workable to be present and engaged. We begin to understand that a workable mind is even more reliable and important than workable circumstances. We may discover that the most satisfying life is one that is fully lived, rather than one in which we've accumulated the most positive experiences.

HOW WE PROGRESS: PATH

From a fruitional view, path is understood as the work we do that will enable us to *consciously participate in what is already true but currently out of our awareness.* The activity of pretending to not be aware of what is already true is the activity of *ignoring*. Of course, we must be aware of something to selectively ignore it, so ignoring is not a mistake or stupidity. Rather, it's an ongoing activity of intelligence, not to be confused with wisdom. For instance, if someone is angry, it's now a common idea that perhaps under that anger that person is feeling hurt or scared. He is using the anger as a way of "pretending" to not be aware of the deeper vulnerability. But he has to really be aware of these deeper feelings to have the impulse to defend against them. He is consciously "not aware" while unconsciously "aware." He is actively ignoring what he is actually aware of feeling. As another example, a parent who claims she was not aware of her child being abused was almost certainly aware of *something* being hidden. In this case, the ignoring is not about knowing specifics but about a refusal to acknowledge and investigate a sensed problem.

Of the three forms of fundamental aggression toward reality—attachment, anger, and ignorance—Vajrayana Buddhism focuses on ignoring as the most basic cause of unnecessary suffering. The capacity to ignore seems to be an inherent ability we have as humans. Just as we have an innate ability to learn to use language, think about the future, and have empathy, we seem to have an innate ability to ignore that which is disturbing. And, like most abilities, our ignoring capacity will have both sane and neurotic expressions. It's very helpful to be able to ignore what could be a distraction when we're focused on some task, to not be constantly overwhelmed by the suffering in this world, and to be able to choose what aspect of our experiencing to pay attention to. But it's not so helpful when we ignore important realities of our practical and emotional lives just because they make us uncomfortable.

The accomplishment of neurotic organization as a child is really the capacity for a stabilized ignoring function, which is vital to the child's ability to not be continually overwhelmed by too much intensity. But as we've discussed throughout the book, such a stabilized process becomes, over time, what we think of as neurotic structure. When this structured ignoring—which was completely necessary and healthy when young—gets carried into adulthood, it comes with a very significant price tag: the experience of feeling divided against oneself. The resulting layers of dissociation, confusion, and struggle generate a chronic state of hypervigilance and self-absorption.

Our path of cultivating a good state of mind can be understood as the process of dissolving our continually maintained states of self-absorption. Both psychotherapy and Buddhist practices share the intention of gradually dissolving this experience of self-absorption. Because therapy takes the self as real and existent, however, the most basic sense of split is rarely addressed. Usually the result of a successful therapeutic process is an improved experience of self-absorption. This is very valuable, as it reduces unnecessary suffering and should not be trivialized, but it will never give rise to unconditional freedom. In therapy, we work to bring into conscious awareness and ownership exactly what we had to disown as powerless, dependent children. We stop pretending that we don't feel anger or grief or powerlessness. By bringing our sense of self into alignment with our current adult realities and capacities, we relax our anxiety-driven need for self-absorption.

In fruitional practices, we work to bring conscious participation into our always-existing open awareness. We stop pretending that our most basic experiencing is not already that of open awareness. We discover that this basic awareness provides no support for a personal self, and we may realize that our self-absorption has actually served as a no-longer-needed defense against open experiencing.

As we dissolve the vivid appearance of self-absorption, what we experience gradually becomes less about "me" and more about the experience itself. The weather becomes about the weather, not about how it affects "me." Our partner's behavior becomes about our partner, not about how "I" am affected. In general, our engagement with life becomes more practical and less emotionally reactive. As we develop an attitude of nonbias, we are increasingly able to see life as it is, rather than through our self-referential, and thus distorted, filters. Our good state of mind becomes resilient and reliable as we shift from *what* we experience—which is always changing—to *how we relate* to everything we experience. And how we relate from open awareness is to be unconditionally engaged, appreciative, embodied, and present.

A view is being asserted here: It is possible to have a good state of mind while we simultaneously feel very disturbed. It's possible to feel grief or rage or anxiety and to have these difficult experiences arise within a type of well-being that is not dependent on positive thoughts or emotions. This view is unfamiliar in our culture, so it must be investigated, not taken as an unquestioned belief. As discussed, this investigation requires discipline, because it usually requires our full participation in exactly what we don't want to feel, what we've been organizing our lives around avoiding. We must do the counterinstinctual work of remaining embodied with our fears in order to develop the confidence that these intense energies are not problematic in themselves, will not harm us, and in fact do not even have an independent, ongoing existence.

Discovering that what we have been afraid to feel is, in fact, workable supports our practice of relating to all experience without bias. In turn, relating to all experience with a sense of open confidence supports our investigation into our disowned energies. For example, if I use anger to ignore my fear, it will be very helpful to bring nonjudgmental awareness and kindness to this anger, to not make myself wrong for having this feeling, to discover that it's workable to feel angry. In turn, finding the confidence that owning my anger is workable may then help me investigate the possibility of deeper vulnerabilities. This positive cycle strengthens my willingness to practice including all experiences, however positive or negative, as equally valid expressions of a good state of mind.

The path of dissolving self-absorption can be discussed in many ways. I remember coming across an interesting summary of this path some time ago, though I regret that I can't recall who proposed it. We can understand our work to evolve through four stages: absorption in content, awareness of content, awareness of awareness, and absorption in awareness.

Absorption in Content

At this basic stage, our attention is so captured and identified with what we are experiencing that there is little likelihood that we will examine or be curious about whether there's more to the story than what's right in front of us. All children and many adults live in this stage, relating to what arises with an unexamined assumption that there's only one reality, which is what we're experiencing right now. It's like watching a movie and being fully captured by the display. It doesn't even occur to us to think that it is a display. Because there's no conscious sense of self-reflection, there's little conscious sense of hesitation or self-doubt. And so this type of experiencing can have a very fresh, alive, and even charismatic quality. Because there's little self-reflection, however, there will be a strong tendency for one's life to be run by a continuing reenactment of habitual patterns, of what's familiar.

Awareness of Content

Out of the normal process of maturing, of education, of having to relate to other people's realities, many of us become aware that there are other realities than that which is arising for us in this moment. We notice that what we are experiencing is not the same as the self who is experiencing it. At this stage, we are beginning the process of disidentifying with our experiencing—we begin to *have* our experience rather than *be* our experience. This may be like going to the movie knowing that we'll be captured but confident that we won't confuse what's on the screen with reality. We may even have moments when we recognize that we're just watching a vivid display. At this stage, we can become fascinated with examining our experience, and we may try to make everything into something to be investigated. Taken to an extreme, we can generate a lot of confusion and actually feel paralyzed by the attempt to turn ourselves into an object to be understood, to find our "true self."

As we gain confidence that what we are feeling or thinking is not the same as our self, we are willing to explore difficult aspects of our experiencing and recover conscious awareness of energies we've historically disowned. Because there is awareness of the content of our experience, there is choice about how to relate to that content. At this stage we can challenge our identification with our habitual conditioning. This is the stage of most work in psychotherapy.

Awareness of Awareness

If we continue exploring what is most true about our experiencing, we may have more and more moments in which we realize that, regardless of the ever-changing content of our experience, there is *always* awareness of this content. At any moment, we may remember to ask: "What is it that is aware of what I'm experiencing? What is the actual nature of this awareness?" The process of disidentification continues but now includes the sense of self—the apparent "experiencer." I *have* a sense of self, but I may not *be* a self. This increasingly conscious participation in awareness seems to progress along a continuum of wakefulness and is the stage in which spiritual path work is most useful. There is still a subtle dissociative split with an effort to explore or attain or increase our experience of awareness, as if this were somehow different from our relative experiencing. At this stage, we may experience a shift in our experiential center of gravity, with an organic spontaneous return over and over to awareness as our home base. This is the point at which our sense of "a good state of mind regardless of circumstance" becomes an ongoing experience, rather than a practice.

Absorption in Awareness

The idea of being absorbed in awareness seems to be a way of referring to the experience of enlightenment. The activity of ignoring has been fully dissolved, with no remnant of a dissociative split, no sense that self and other have separate essential natures. Awareness is inseparable from display, and awareness is "self-aware." This nondivided awareness is said to be completely ordinary and natural—what's always present and most basic in all of our experiencing—not some transcendent or esoteric state. But from our usual unquestioned sense of being an essentially separate self, we tend to imagine this experience as nonordinary; therefore, we look for it outside of our immediate experiencing. At this stage, a good state of mind becomes a nonissue. With any sense of division dissolved, every moment is experienced as always fresh and workable. We engage spontaneously and fully because it's impossible to do otherwise, and we work with whatever arises as the expression of mystery, with an inherently deep and unconditional appreciation.

Progressing along this path is essentially an ever-increasing conscious participation in awareness. We discover that awareness is what is most basic, always present, in every moment of our conscious experiencing. We don't find anything beneath awareness. It's not a secondary composite expression of something more fundamental. While all relative experience is constructed, awareness is unconstructed. As such, it's the most reliable aspect of our experiencing. Happy or sad, healthy or sick, clear or confused—there's always awareness. It's described as unconditional freedom, open knowing, mirrorlike, without bias, pregnant with unformed potential, without ascribable qualities. This can sound very mystical. But awareness is so basic and ever-present that it is also described as "ordinary mind." The real mystery is how we are able to be so unaware of awareness. The path of waking up is the experiential investigation of this question: how can we stop pretending to not be aware of what is already true, of what is always present in every moment?

This view of path is one of an evolution of experiencing, characterized by a gradual dissolving of self-absorption and a gradual shift from *what* we experience, to *how we relate* to what we experience, to *awareness* of both what we experience and how we relate to it. This interaction of awareness and self-absorption unfolds sequentially. First, awareness interrupts self-absorption; it then calls self-absorption into question. Gradually, awareness becomes as real as self-absorption. It next surrounds, and then pervades, self-absorption. Finally, self-absorption becomes unsustainable.

There are so many different and valuable approaches to this path, but in this book, we have focused on both a developmental/therapeutic view and a fruitional/Buddhist view. Each chapter can be understood as an attempt to work with these basic themes as applied to specific issues that are commonly worked with in psychotherapy.

In chapter 1, we addressed the developmental view as not really about our past, but rather about how—with great effort—we maintain a familiar sense of ourselves in the present. Especially when feeling anxious or vulnerable, we experience ourselves as if we were still dependent, powerless children living in a world in which feelings can both harm us and save us. Our history serves as the simplistic template into which we try to fit our current, incredibly complex reality. Our strategy of self-absorption is most reliably justified by investing in the sense of being a problematic self, living in a problematic world. Therapy challenges this position by helping to bring our experiencing into alignment with current adult realities and capacities. As we engage with our lives more effectively and with more kindness to self and others, we begin to not need our young survival strategies, and we can relax our self-absorption to a certain extent. This work can support our spiritual path, as it seems that it is usually easier to practice letting go of our sense of solid self from a ground of sanity than it is from a ground of neurosis.

Chapter 2 introduced the potentially faster path of bringing ourselves into direct engagement with immediate, noninterpretive experiencing. Rather than improving our sense of self, we investigate the ways in which we maintain it. We find out whether this project is really necessary, now that we're adults. In each moment, we are free to find out for ourselves if there is actually any problem, anything missing. These moments of open experiencing call into question our investment in self-absorption but do not, in themselves, shift our sense of self out of our habitual patterns.

In chapter 3, we discussed the benefits of alternating between the developmental and fruitional views. Buddhist teachings have almost nothing to say about the profound influence of our young experiences, and psychotherapy has, until recently, had little access to noninterpretive awareness practices. By cultivating our capacity to consciously participate in each fresh moment of experiencing, free of interpretations, we introduce an experiential dialogue between the powerful momentum of our conditioned history—what *used* to be true—and our immediate experiencing—what is *actually* true in this moment. We begin to free ourselves of our conditioned history—not by making it go away, but by no longer being captured by it. In Buddhist language, we can think of this experiential interaction as "mixing mind/form with space." In therapeutic language, we can talk about it as metabolizing the experience of open awareness and integrating this with our more familiar sense of self.

In chapter 4, anxiety was presented as both a signal that our survival is at risk (from an evolutionary, biological view) and an approximation of open mind (from a spiritual path view). If we want to take advantage of the luxury of living more than biological lives, it is important to learn how to hold both experiences. We can learn to participate in our survival panic without having to escape from it, and we can then investigate this panic as a signal that we are being brought into relationship with basic openness. The avoidance of anxiety is central to the impulse to maintain the primitive survival strategy of self-absorption, which is basically like putting one's head in the sand. Committing to the experience of anxiety is central to the practices necessary to dissolve self-absorption. Deconstructing stabilized struggle is often an accessible place to begin.

Chapter 5 explored embodied awareness as a direct and powerful challenge to neurotic organization. Neurosis, as the habitual refusal to consciously participate in certain difficult experiences, is the most familiar way in which we perpetuate our claim to be problematic persons. Finding no problems—only difficult energies—in our immediate, noninterpretive, sensation-level experience, we cultivate a deep personal confidence in the workability of our selves and our lives. As we practice embodied immediacy, we find that self-absorption, based on—and perpetuating—the assumption that we and life are problematic, is increasingly difficult to sustain.

Chapters 6 and 7 focused on relationship as one of the most effective and provocative ways in which our familiar states of self-absorption will be challenged and frustrated. We enter relationship partly as relief from the deadness of our own private, self-absorbed worlds, and we then feel continually disturbed when our partners will not be who we want them to be. The view was presented that all relative experiencing is relational and therefore inherently irresolvable and disturbing. Intimate relationships are an especially intense experience of this open energy. The discipline of fully engaging in the disturbance of intimacy, without fighting to resolve it, can serve as a very powerful antidote to our investment in self-absorption.

SOME THEMES THAT MAY ARISE ALONG THE PATH

As we evolve our experiencing in all of these ways, we gradually cultivate a good state of mind. That state of mind is independent of our history, independent of our life circumstances, independent of our current mood, even independent of whether we're living or in the process of dying. Along this path, there are often some recurring themes that may be helpful to briefly discuss. These are basic life issues for which there are no formulaic answers and that may arise as we loosen our identification with our familiar sense of self and with our historic conditioning. Engaging with these issues is another opportunity to have the direct experience of "being the question, not the answer."

Acceptance and Improvement

When I invite a person I'm working with to experiment with an unconditional commitment to some difficult feeling or thought, a frequent response is, "But I don't want to be like that. I want to live to my fullest potential. If I really *accept* these feelings, maybe

I won't be motivated to change." Or in Boulder, where I live, "If I accept these feelings, won't that create the very reality that I'm working to change? Shouldn't I only have positive energy, so that I only magnetize positive experience?" This tension between acceptance and improvement is basic and—once again—not resolvable. This tension is good. It prevents us from ever really being able to comfortably take sides and feel that the issue is settled. The problem comes when we take these two energies, or styles of engagement, as if they each have their own independent existence. "If I believe that one excludes the other, then I can never have both; when I choose one, I don't get the other. If I accept, I don't get to improve; I'm giving up and surrendering to less than my life could be. If I work to improve, I have to postpone acceptance—wait until various conditions are achieved before I can let myself be fully present and at peace." More accurately, however, these two energies are co-arising, or cocreative; they are inescapably relational. And so a neurotic expression of either will occur when we do not maintain an experiential connection with both. It's not either/or; more accurately, it's both/and. For practical reasons, however, when we act, we lead with one style and allow the other to remain in the background. "At this moment, I am accepting this situation, even while I know that I'm free to shift my stance and work to improve it at any time." Or, "Right now, I'm working to challenge a habitual pattern, even while I know that an equally valid practice would be to accept this pattern as undeniably a part of my life."

In a way that is perhaps becoming familiar, we are shifting from a self-referential position to a practical position. Given our priorities, our intentions, what will work best right now? In general, it seems most useful to lead with the style of improvement when we are dealing with more relative concrete issues. It's very intelligent to try to improve our health, our finances, our relationship skills, our livelihood opportunities, and so on—anything in which efforts in the present might improve the quality of life for ourselves and others in the future. When we are dealing with the most fundamental aspects of our human experience, however, it seems most useful to lead with the style of acceptance. Coming into relationship with whatever we are actually feeling in the moment—existential aloneness, aging, the truth of limitations, the experiences of pain/anxiety/grief/anger, or the experiences of unconditional kindness and of freedom. It seems most intelligent, when dealing with these realities, to accept in the immediate moment our experience of what are probably nonnegotiable aspects of the human condition.

Leading with one style does not rule out the other; it's just a question of which comes first. In doing the work of therapy and in spiritual path work, I have found it usually most helpful to approach this issue as a two-step sequence. I usually begin with acceptance, as my clinical work is usually addressing the more basic issues beneath the presenting problems. Also, because we are only living in each present moment, it's helpful to learn how to engage in and be committed to our immediate experiencing, rather than waiting for our preferred version of reality to arise before engaging fully. After identifying what experience clients may be already having but trying to escape from, I'll invite them in a variety of ways to stay embodied with that energy, to imagine living with it off and on for the rest of their lives, to commit to this difficult feeling as a valid part of their life, to practice bringing unconditional kindness to it, and so on. After this initial step, we then might explore what it would mean to try to improve this experience from the already-explored ground of acceptance. What would it mean to deal with this situation in a completely practical way, without needing to resolve or heal or fix the disturbance?

For instance, perhaps I have accepted the painful reality that my history has left me with the identity drama of feeling like a disappointment to others. I can stay in my body and feel this disturbance; it's not harming me, and I can even be kind to it. I may have this issue triggered off and on the rest of my life. So what? I'll work with it. Now that I don't have to heal or fix this experience, I may still want to have it activated less frequently. It's out of date; I don't need it anymore. At this point, I may choose to investigate my relation with anger. How would it feel to be disappointed in others? To not collapse when there's conflict as if I'm the one who's automatically wrong? I can do this work to improve my experience of relationship and not because there's something wrong with me.

Approaching improvement in this way can remove the burden of change being a necessary condition for acceptance, which of course tends to always put acceptance into the future. Sometimes it's also helpful to point out that acceptance of reality must include accepting our efforts to improve. Wanting to have a more positive experience of life is a necessary—probably evolutionary—part of life itself. And improvement, which is oriented to the future, must include acceptance of immediate reality as the ground from which our efforts begin.

Contrast

The experience of *contrast* confounds our fantasy of a reality that we can know, control, and be at home in. If this is true *and* that is true, but they are not the same, then we will be unable to count on either as the whole story. If life is both wonderful and horrible, what position can we take? Our experiencing self is left somewhere in the middle, with no ground to stand on. As we have discussed in a variety of ways, our usual response to the anxiety this generates is to take sides and do our best to ignore, or at least discount, what does not support whatever we have identified with. But this open, anxious ground is exactly the experience we must train ourselves to continually return to. As long as we invest in the sense of being a separate, significant self, we will usually experience open awareness as some type of disturbance. Because avoiding this anxiety is avoiding open mind, it is important to discipline ourselves to look deeply into the actual experience of contrast. This means going beyond the content of what's contrasted and into that meeting point where both are true and neither is true. What is our actual experience of holding both the wonder of life and the tragedy of life at the same time, with no resolution? Of wanting to be close to one's partner and not wanting to be close at all, with no resolution? This open ground, initially difficult to rest in, is exactly what holds the full range of our experiencing, without bias and with appreciation. It's contrast that forces us to acknowledge this experience, as most of us will not voluntarily look for this groundless anxiety. Because of this function, contrast seems to be a necessary quality in any path of waking up.

As one example of this view, in Tibetan Buddhism, our various states of mind are sometimes described as being like six realms, each having distinct qualities, through which we are continually moving and with which we are identifying. The nature of these realms ranges from god-like bliss to hell-like torture, but it is thought that the only realm that allows for freeing oneself from unnecessary suffering and confusion is the human state of contrasting experience. All of the other realms, however pleasant or painful, are uniform in their nature. There is no contrast, nothing to help free one from taking one's experience as if it were the only reality. The human realm experience, however, is constantly alternating between pleasure and pain, birth and death, confusion and clarity. It is this never-ending contrast of experiencing that provides the necessary opening—the questioning of the drama of one's experience—which, when investigated in a persistent and disciplined way, gradually trains one to rest continually in open mind. We find that it is only open mind, open awareness, that can hold the full range of our often contradictory and intense human experiencing.

Not Knowing and Living with Confidence

As we train ourselves to return, over and over, to this open energy, we find that it is more fundamental than any theory or description of reality. We find that it is more true to say that we don't really know anything with certainty than to say that we do. Even science has placed uncertainty at the heart of its methodology and focuses on describing the activity of matter and energy, rather than making claims about the nature of reality. Especially in the arenas of therapy and spiritual path work, we tend to be most certain about what's most trivial and least certain about what's most important. We know where we live, what we usually like to eat, what language we speak. We don't know who we are, what happens when we die, the meaning of life, how to have the best relationship or be the best parents possible. No one has ever been able to prove just what it means to live the best life possible or how to do so. Basically, we're all just falling through space, making it up as we go. Frequently in my work, clients will claim that they are feeling confused or conflicted about some life circumstance. Maybe they'll say, "I've just begun a new relationship, and I don't know when I should begin introducing my new partner to my children." That is actually what's true: They *don't* know, and there's no way of having certainty about this important decision. But rather than accepting and experiencing this uncertainty, they generate a fantasy of struggle or confusion that keeps alive the hope that there is some correct answer. I may invite these clients to participate fully in what's most true in their experience—that they don't know the answer and perhaps they never will. Often there is relief in finding out that it's not going to damage them to not have an answer, even to important questions.

As we become familiar with the disturbance associated with this basically open experiencing, we find that our anxiety is not an accurate signal of some imminent harm and that our confidence actually increases as we engage with each moment from the "ground" of not knowing. In our culture, confidence is usually based on a sense of knowing how to deal with a situation, feeling in control, having worked with similar problems, getting good feedback from others. However, unconditional confidence arises out of a willingness to not know why a situation has occurred, how to best handle it, or what the outcome will be—and to fully engage anyway, without requiring certain conditions to first be met.

The more we engage with our lives without requiring reassurance, the more we realize that this is already the case at all times. We can never have objective confirmation that we are making the right choice. We never get a do-over and so can never know if another choice might have been better. We will never know the final, long-term consequences of our choices, because there is never a point of final assessment—only an ongoing process of unfolding, with one situation evolving into the next without end. And we can never *not* act. Every second, we engage with our lives. Even when it looks like we're doing nothing, our doing nothing is an engagement, with its own consequences. Realizing that we are always acting and that we will never have confirmation that we're making the best choice, we do have the choice about our attitude of engagement. We can choose to act and live with a confidence that has no objective justification, or we can choose to act and live with hesitation and self-doubt—which, as it turns out, also has no objective justification. It's actually a choice. As a completely practical issue, we might want to try both and see which we prefer—which one seems to support a more positive experiencing for ourselves and for others? We may find that, as we practice showing up without apology, a deeper confidence is cultivated—an attitude that arises out of not knowing but that manifests as a fully embodied presence. We know that we're just winging it, that we will continually make mistakes, but we learn that this will be true regardless of whether we do so with confidence or with self-doubt. We learn that we really only have our own unique version of being human to offer to the world.

Authenticity

Like any important concept, authenticity has different meanings at different levels of understanding. When we first become aware of aspects of ourselves that we have historically disowned, we usually sense the potential for a greater authenticity. As we recover the ability to consciously participate in our previously prohibited feelings, we begin to feel more integrated. If we grow up needing to never be angry, we will feel more authentic as we allow ourselves to feel our rage, assert needs, have boundaries in relationships, and stop avoiding conflict. We begin to take ownership of a more complex sense of self. As we continue to recover disowned aspects of ourselves, we will almost certainly find deeper vulnerabilities, such as feelings of powerlessness, grief, fear of being wrong, and so on. As we are able to cultivate a conscious and kind experience of these difficult feelings, we will probably feel less internally conflicted and therefore less reactive and more able to engage with others with a greater sense of really being ourselves, of authenticity. Often, the experience of feeling better about ourselves and getting better feedback from others can then activate a genuine interest in further self-exploration.

As we evolve and mature ourselves, the sense of being divided into conflicting parts gradually dissolves. We may then begin to participate in all of our experiencing, however deep or superficial, and move beyond the project of finding our "true self." We understand that authenticity refers not only to the content of our experience, but, even more importantly, to how we relate to this content. We may stop pretending to be divided, problematic people and accept our always-existing wholeness—which, of course, has to include everything, both positive and negative, sane and neurotic. Perhaps nothing is missing, nothing left unresolved in our past, no wounds to heal before we can be fully present. It's true, though, that we're messy humans with no access to some objective reality, so we continue to work with our conditioned experience—not because it's wrong or inauthentic, but so that we might cause less harm to ourselves and to others and so that we may even be of some benefit. We realize that we are always fully and authentically ourselves; that it's impossible to be otherwise. And so we commit to a more and more skillful and compassionate expression of who we already are.

Not Self-Acceptance, but an Accepting Self

Self-acceptance is a project of the divided self. It's really like a dog chasing its tail, trying to catch itself. The only way we can maintain this drama is by pretending that the self to be accepted is somehow different from the self that is accepting. As discussed, this sense of being divided against oneself is probably an unavoidable developmental stage to be experienced and worked through, but it is probably helpful to not take it too seriously.

And as long as we try to make ourselves into an object to be either accepted or rejected, better to accept it. Better to have a positive self-as-object than a negative self-as-object. This is the arena of most of the work we do in psychotherapy. We understand the historic origins of our negative sense of self, bring into awareness the underlying vulnerabilities that continue to be converted into negativity, reframe our understanding into more accurate adult ideas, learn to soothe ourselves when anxious, and learn to behave as dignified and considerate persons in order to get better feedback from the world. As we gradually cultivate a more positive sense of self, it, of course, becomes easier to accept that self.

However, until this deeper experience of pretending to be divided against ourselves is adequately dissolved, we will maintain what is a fundamentally paranoid drama. If the *self* to be accepted is essentially different from the *I* that tries to accept it, then the *I* will always be vulnerable to a self that has its own survival to worry about, not the *I's*. This *self* might act out in primitive ways that are hurtful, and the *I* is powerless to really do anything about it. At the biological level, our immune systems are designed to identify and attack anything that is non-self. Maintaining the drama of being a divided self can be understood as analogous to an autoimmune disease. By relating to this *self* as if it were essentially different from the *I* who is trying to accept it, we guarantee a deeply conflicted experience. Even if this *self* is positive, it's still alien and a potential threat. We could think of this "positive self-as-object" as like an autoimmune disease that's in remission, waiting to be reactivated by some stress or life crisis.

The deeper work to be done has been discussed in a variety of ways. In this discussion, we can understand it as gradually giving up the project of self-acceptance and instead cultivating the experience of an accepting self. We practice an attitude of openhearted, embodied, alert engagement at all times, without regard to what may be arising in each moment. We have a "yes" in place before we even know what will come next. We soften our stance rather than brace for what may happen. We train our attention to relax, over and over, into expansive awareness, instead of centralizing it in a constant monitoring about what we think and feel. Our commitment to fully engage and work with our experience is unconditional, not dependent on whether it fits our preferred sense of self.

As we practice this experience of being an accepting self, we find ourselves naturally living with greater appreciation and confidence in each moment. As our participation in immediacy increases, we find that what we have called a self is not a *thing* to accept; rather, it is an ever-evolving process, always changing in unpredictable ways, to participate in but never to really know. Because every moment is fresh, accepting must be renewed in each moment. Accepting is seen to be a never-ending practice, never an accomplishment. As this practice dissolves the sense of being somehow divided against oneself, we may find—once again—that what is always present is awareness: awareness of *I,* awareness of *self,* awareness of *other.* Even though these experiences continue to appear to be distinct and separate, the pervasiveness of awareness becomes the more compelling reality, erasing any sense of *essential* difference. Self-acceptance has become a nonissue.

THE FRUITION: A GOOD STATE OF MIND, REGARDLESS OF CIRCUMSTANCE

As we experiment with these practices, think about these views, and try them out in our daily life, how can we tell if movement is happening or progress is being made? An early indication will be a lessening of complaint, struggle, self-doubt, defensiveness, and emotional reactivity. We are captured by our usual dramas less often, don't take them quite so seriously, and recover from them faster. In a very straightforward way, as we begin to cultivate a good state of mind at all times, the factors that give rise to unnecessary negativity begin to be unsupportable and to fall away. A generalized sense of confidence may be noticed, with more frequent moments of clarity, embodied presence, and kindness to whatever may arise. We may find that we are more curious about and feel more of an empathic commonality with others. We will probably experience an increased alignment between what we believe to really be our highest priorities and our actual behavior, thinking, emotional processing, and awareness practices. We act more in accord with our intentions and with less inner struggle. We may find ourselves pausing at random moments with the sense of deep appreciation and gratitude, for no specific reason. A generalized sense of well-being and contentment may become a familiar presence. And we may find an increasing frequency of moments in which whatever is being experienced is arising in an environment of freedom and open awareness. It's likely that these indicators will sometimes be more present, sometimes appear to be lost for awhile; but over time, we may see clear evidence that an evolution in our experiencing is taking place.

If in fact this is our experience, we will probably gain more confidence that taking on certain practices actually does make a difference, and we will probably find a more organic motivation arising. As we continue, we're likely to go through several different types of understanding of this path that we're increasingly committed to. At first, most of us will understandably try to create this good state of mind as an achievement. Our cultural training is to work hard, over time, and accomplish a goal that we can then enjoy. We gradually learn, though, that a good state of mind is a *way of relating* to each fresh moment, never knowing what we'll do next, with no formula, confident that we'll work with anything, including not experiencing a good state of mind. At this stage, we understand a good state of mind as a practice, never an accomplishment; but it is a practice that can become reliable and resilient. At some point, we may discover that even the attitude of practice subtly generates a sense that our present moment should still be improved upon. With this understanding, we drop the sense of project as we realize that we're already only living in each present moment, spontaneously engaged, making it all up—even the formula of a practice. This is when language becomes somewhat paradoxical: effortless effort, a stateless state. Our "practice" is now to return, over and over, to a conscious participation in what's already always our immediate experiencing. There's a very light touch, which is more about remembering to redirect our attention than trying to reach some better state of mind. An unconditional confidence develops: whether we remember to be consciously present or not, we're still always present anyway. It's simply a practical issue to work with if we want more conscious participation, not an issue of any special significance. It's similar to the confidence most of have that we will be breathing whether or not we attend to it. If, for some reason, we want to improve our habitual style of breathing, we direct our attention to it, participate consciously in some practice or discipline, then return to other interests without monitoring or worrying about whether we will successfully breathe or not.

The more that we trust in ourselves and dissolve our self-absorption, the more we find our experiencing to be most fundamentally the energy of open awareness. As we live with this realization, we find that while we can directly and consciously participate in this basic nature, we can never fully describe or express it. The experience of open awareness is said to be beyond description, without ascribable qualities. This does not have to mean that it is something hard to experience; it's just hard to describe—open means open, without anything defining it. A mother holding her newborn infant, an artist in synch, an athlete in the zone: these are at least temporary experiences of nondivision, of relative freedom. But it's probably impossible to ever really describe what was experienced. Traditionally, words, symbols, and art are used to point toward or suggest this experience, without the expectation that it will ever be captured or represented adequately. Sometimes negative language is used to make this point: "It's not this; it's not that." When words are used, they often are terms like *basic nature, spirit, mystery.* In this book, we have used *open awareness* and *freedom* most frequently to point in this direction. Hopefully, none of these terms will be taken as representing something that actually exists as an objective reality, with its own essential nature.

Unlike our cultural tendency to see moments of freedom as unique and somehow qualitatively different from our usual experiencing, the fruitional view asserts that all limited, relative experiencing is inherently the expression of freedom. All relative experience is seen as constructed, as arising out of an incredibly complex web of conditions, as present for a moment in vivid appearance and then dissolving as it's replaced by the next moment's appearance. This includes the continually constructed appearance of the "experiencer" of this display. Because all of our relative experiencing is equally without objective existence, it is all an equally valid expression of the same never-resolvable reality. This display is always present, and awareness of this display is always present. The two are inseparable. In Buddhist terms, relative reality and absolute reality are inseparable. Because all of our experiencing is without essential nature, without permanence, it is actually impossible to be trapped or limited by it. It's only when we "freeze" our experience—with great effort—that we can have the fantasy of being limited selves in a world of limitation. Our very nature is that of an open, never-resolvable stream of experiencing and the always-present awareness of this display. Our very nature is that of freedom. Precisely because there's never any ground, there's never any entrapment. Trungpa Rinpoche said, "The bad news is you're falling through the air, nothing to hang on to, no parachute. The good news is there's no ground."

As our path clarifies our confusion and our confusion is revealed to be only a distorted way of relating to what we are already experiencing, we wake up to the unconditional confidence and appreciation that comes from realizing that all of our experiencing is the expression of freedom. This experiential confidence invites a reengagement with the full range of our human experiencing. Rather than trying to escape into some fantasy of a life without limitations, we engage fully, spontaneously, and in embodied vulnerability, choosing what to work with and what not to work with. We discover that a good state of mind, regardless of circumstance, is the relative expression, in form and limitation, of the unconditional energy of awareness and freedom.

THE SUN AND THE CLOUDS

Imagine that we live where it's always cloudy. We never see the sun. And we, of course, take our everyday experience as if it's reality—the only reality. The clouds are perhaps a little claustrophobic in some vague way, but they're comfortable and familiar.

One day we meet a visitor who tells us that what we're used to isn't the whole story, that there's something else. Curious, we go with him, and he guides us up a mountain. We climb up and up, through the cloud cover. There, at the top, we step into this incredibly intense experience of sun and expansive sky. It completely changes our sense of what's possible, what's available to us. We return to our daily lives, but we'll never be the same.

We might unconsciously allow that experience to become only a memory—something very valuable that we experienced. But we might also use this memory to remind ourselves that, in each present moment, the sun is still there. Perhaps that one experience on the mountaintop might have been enough for us to feel confident that the sun really exists. Or perhaps we might climb that mountain many times to strengthen our confidence. But increasingly, we may begin to live as if the sun were always there. We start to live with a sense of greater expansiveness. We don't take daily life as if it's the whole story anymore. We don't feel so oppressed by the experience of limitation. We begin to realize that, in fact, the sun, the clouds, and our daily life all exist together and are one piece, that the clouds are just as valid as the sun. We may recognize a fantasy of how nice it would be to only live in the sun. We realize, though, that we always have that choice; we can go live on top of the mountain if we want. But we can also choose to live in our daily life, because it's all the same reality. What makes it the same reality is our awareness. We're aware of the clouds; we're aware of the sun. It's always the same awareness, and that open knowing has no preference itself. We're free to choose, and whatever choice we make is an expression of that freedom. Because what's always there is awareness and freedom, we may be willing to relax into the actual experience of *being awareness* as our most fundamental sense of self, the experience of *being freedom*.

If you'll recall, at the start of this book I shared the story of how I ended up doing what I do. How I had begun training as a psychotherapist but had found it very difficult to continue in the typical Western view. How my connection with Buddhism and with my teacher Chögyam Trungpa Rinpoche helped me find a way to return to therapy, informed by a Buddhist understanding of mind. It's been more than forty years of practice and study and more than thirty-five years of clinical work since then, and I still feel so grateful to my teacher, Trungpa Rinpoche. There were so many gifts that came from being his student, listening to his teachings, and being in his presence. I think one of the greatest gifts was experiencing his energy of outrageous confidence. He was completely engaged with being human. I never witnessed him as unwilling to experience and work with anything that came up. This is one reason why Vajrayana Buddhism is sometimes understood as a "fast path"—nothing is discarded. Everything is used—however disturbing, however joyful. If I could pass on one of these gifts, it would be this encouragement: Discard nothing, appreciate everything. Look for wakefulness, look for compassion, and look for freedom in every moment of your life. Look for these energies in every moment, whether you're experiencing anger, hunger, depression, or joy. If you look for what's already there, you are likely to find it. And I feel confident in saying that the experience of freedom is, in fact, already there.

ACKNOWLEDGMENTS

I AM ESPECIALLY APPRECIATIVE of my wife, Reva, for all of her unconditional support and love, her hugs and check-ins, and her tolerance of my hours in front of the computer. Like my other great teachers, I more and more understand all that she's given me as my heart continues to open. Diane Israel has continually supported me in this project, with her genuine appreciation, engagement, and feedback. I probably would not have begun this book without her encouragement. Tami Simon has very generously given both her friendship and the resources of Sounds True to transform these ideas into an offering to a larger audience. The staff at Sounds True has been always friendly and professional. I've been very fortunate to have Kelly Notaras as my editor. She's done a great job editing and, even more important, has really understood the material and given great insights about how to express difficult ideas. Thank you all so much.

I am also so grateful to the countless teachers and therapists who continually do their best for the benefit of us all. And to all of us who, as students and clients, support these efforts and then take what we learn to share with others. And to the overwhelming majority of people on this planet who are doing their best to live with dignity and kindness. Thank you all so much.

ABOUT THE AUTHOR

BRUCE TIFT, MA, LMFT, has been in private practice since 1979, taught at Naropa University for twenty-five years, worked in a psychiatric ward and as a family therapist with social services, and has given presentations in the United States, Mexico, and Japan. In his twenties he traveled for two years by motorcycle in Europe, North Africa, and overland to India and Nepal. He has worked as a laborer, clerk, postal worker, longshoreman, painter, school bus driver, paper mill worker, miner, and truck driver. He and his wife, Reva, are now empty-nesters living in Boulder, Colorado. A practitioner of Vajrayana Buddhism for more than forty years, he had the good fortune to be a student of Chögyam Trungpa, Rinpoche, and to meet a number of realized teachers.

ABOUT SOUNDS TRUE

SOUNDS TRUE is a multimedia publisher whose mission is to inspire and support personal transformation and spiritual awakening. Founded in 1985 and located in Boulder, Colorado, we work with many of the leading spiritual teachers, thinkers, healers, and visionary artists of our time. We strive with every title to preserve the essential "living wisdom" of the author or artist. It is our goal to create products that not only provide information to a reader or listener, but that also embody the quality of a wisdom transmission.

For those seeking genuine transformation, Sounds True is your trusted partner. At SoundsTrue.com you will find a wealth of free resources to support your journey, including exclusive weekly audio interviews, free downloads, interactive learning tools, and other special savings on all our titles.

To learn more, please visit SoundsTrue.com/freegifts or call us toll-free at 800-333-9185.